Cyber Fortress: Building Robust Defenses for Digital Realms

Table of Content

Chapter 1: Foundations of Defense

1.1 Introduction to Cybersecurity

- Defining Cybersecurity and its Importance
- Historical Perspectives on Cyber Threats

1.2 Core Principles of Cybersecurity

- Encryption Techniques and Protocols
- Authentication Methods for Secure Access
- Intrusion Detection and Prevention Systems

1.3 Understanding the Threat Landscape

- Common Types of Cyber Threats (Malware, Phishing, etc.)
- Profiling Adversaries: From Script Kiddies to Nation-States
- The Dynamic Nature of Cyber Threats

1.4 Customizing Defense Strategies

- Tailoring Cybersecurity to Specific Environments
- Proactive vs. Reactive Approaches
- The Role of Risk Assessment in Cybersecurity Planning

Chapter 2: Guardians of the Gateways: Understanding Network Security

2.1 Network Fundamentals

- OSI Model and Networking Protocols
- Types of Networks: LAN, WAN, and Beyond

2.2 Threats to Network Security

- Network-Based Attacks: DDoS, Man-in-the-Middle, etc.
- Vulnerabilities in Network Infrastructure

2.3 Firewalls and Intrusion Detection Systems

- Role of Firewalls in Network Security
- Implementing Effective Intrusion Detection and Prevention

2.4 Secure Network Design

- Principles of Secure Network Architecture
- Best Practices for Securing Network Gateways

Chapter 3: The Human Firewall: Cyber Hygiene and User Awareness

3.1 Importance of Human Factor in Cybersecurity

- Recognizing Humans as a Security Asset
- Common Human-Related Security Risks

3.2 Cyber Hygiene Best Practices

- Password Management and Complexity
- Software Updates and Patch Management

3.3 User Awareness Training

- Educating Users on Social Engineering Tactics
- Promoting a Security-Conscious Culture

3.4 Building a Resilient Human Firewall

- Integrating Security into Employee Onboarding
- Monitoring and Measuring User Awareness Programs

Chapter 4: Code Bastions: Fortifying Software and Applications

4.1 Software Security Fundamentals

- Understanding Software Vulnerabilities
- Importance of Secure Coding Practices

4.2 Threats to Software Security

- Exploitation of Software Vulnerabilities
- Common Attacks on Applications

4.3 Secure Software Development Life Cycle (SDLC)

- Integrating Security into Development Processes
- Code Review and Security Testing

4.4 Best Practices for Application Security

- Implementing Web Application Firewalls
- Securing APIs and Microservices

Chapter 5: Cloud Citadel: Ensuring Security in the Virtual Sky

5.1 The Rise of Cloud Computing

- Understanding Cloud Service Models (IaaS, PaaS, SaaS)
- Cloud Deployment Models (Public, Private, Hybrid)

5.2 Security Challenges in the Cloud

- Shared Responsibility Model
- Data Privacy and Compliance Concerns

5.3 Cloud Security Best Practices

- Identity and Access Management in the Cloud
- Encryption and Key Management

5.4 Continuous Monitoring and Compliance

- Tools and Strategies for Cloud Security Monitoring
- Ensuring Compliance in Cloud Environments

Chapter 6: Biometric Bastions: The Future of Identity Authentication

6.1 Evolution of Identity Authentication

- Traditional Authentication Methods and Their Limitations
- Introduction to Biometric Authentication

6.2 Types of Biometric Authentication

- Fingerprint Recognition, Facial Recognition, Iris Scanning, etc.
- Advantages and Challenges of Biometric Technologies

6.3 Implementing Biometric Authentication

- Integration with Devices and Applications
- Addressing Privacy and Ethical Considerations

6.4 Multi-Factor Authentication (MFA)

- Combining Biometrics with Other Authentication Factors
- Enhancing Security Through MFA

Chapter 7: Insider Threats: Defending Against the Enemy Within

7.1 Understanding Insider Threats

- Differentiating Between Malicious and Non-Malicious Insiders
- Insider Threat Indicators and Warning Signs

7.2 Insider Threat Mitigation Strategies

- Role-Based Access Control
- User Activity Monitoring and Analysis

7.3 Building a Culture of Trust and Security

- Balancing Security Measures with Employee Trust
- Educating Employees on Insider Threat Risks

7.4 Case Studies and Lessons Learned

- Real-world Examples of Insider Threats
- Extracting Key Lessons for Insider Threat Prevention

Chapter 8: Blockchain Armor: Safeguarding the Decentralized Frontiers

8.1 Introduction to Blockchain Technology

- Decentralization and Distributed Ledger Concepts
- Blockchain in Cybersecurity: A Paradigm Shift

8.2 Securing Transactions with Blockchain

- Cryptographic Techniques in Blockchain
- Smart Contracts and Their Security Implications

8.3 Decentralized Identity Management

- Eliminating Single Points of Failure in Identity Systems
- Privacy and Security Considerations in Decentralized Identity

8.4 Challenges and Future Trends

- Scalability and Performance Challenges
- Emerging Innovations in Blockchain Security

Introduction

In the ever-evolving landscape of the digital age, where technology permeates every aspect of our lives and interconnectedness is the norm, the significance of establishing a formidable "Cyber Fortress" has reached unprecedented heights. This concept transcends the mere notion of cybersecurity; it embodies a strategic imperative to safeguard our digital realms against an ever-growing array of cyber threats. As we witness an increasing entanglement of our personal and professional lives within the intricate webs of digital networks, the imperative to fortify our virtual strongholds becomes not just a recommendation but a paramount necessity.

"Cyber Fortress: Building Robust Defenses for Digital Realms" transcends the conventional boundaries of a book; it stands as a comprehensive guide, a beacon illuminating the complex terrain of cybersecurity. At its core, this guide is a testament to the need for empowerment in the face of digital vulnerabilities. It seeks to arm individuals and organizations alike with the knowledge and tools required to navigate the intricate labyrinth of cyber threats with confidence.

The journey commences with an exploration of the foundations of defense, recognizing that to build an impregnable fortress, one must first comprehend the fundamental principles of cybersecurity. Encryption, authentication, and intrusion detection systems become the building blocks, laying a solid groundwork for the subsequent chapters. In this interconnected realm, understanding the dynamic and diverse threat landscape becomes imperative. From commonplace malware to sophisticated cyber-attacks orchestrated by nation-states, the adversaries are numerous and diverse, necessitating a nuanced and adaptive approach to defense.

As the narrative unfolds, the guide delves into the guardianship of gateways, elucidating the intricacies of network security. Networks, the lifeblood of the digital realm, require vigilant protection against threats such as DDoS attacks and vulnerabilities within the network infrastructure. Firewalls and intrusion detection systems emerge as stalwart guardians, reinforcing the gateways against malevolent forces. Secure network design becomes a focal point, emphasizing the principles that underpin resilient network architecture.

The exploration extends to the human element, recognizing individuals as the frontline defenders in this digital warfare. The concept of the "Human Firewall" takes center stage, highlighting the importance of cyber hygiene and user awareness. Best practices in password management, software updates, and the cultivation of a security-conscious culture become pivotal in fortifying this human defense line.

Moving deeper into the digital bastions, the guide navigates through the intricacies of fortifying software and applications. Understanding software vulnerabilities, threats to application security, and implementing secure software development life cycles become critical in this chapter. The code bastions erected here contribute to the overall strength of the Cyber Fortress, ensuring that the very applications we rely on are resilient to malicious intent.

The virtual sky becomes the next battleground as the guide ascends to the Cloud Citadel. Cloud computing, while transformative, introduces its own set of security challenges. The shared responsibility model, data privacy concerns, and best practices for securing the cloud environment are meticulously explored. Identity and access management, encryption, and continuous monitoring emerge as the pillars supporting the security infrastructure in the virtual domain.

The journey takes an intriguing turn towards biometric bastions, revealing the future of identity authentication. Traditional methods prove inadequate in the face of evolving threats, necessitating a paradigm shift towards biometric technologies. Fingerprint recognition, facial recognition, and multi-factor authentication become integral components of this advanced defense mechanism. The chapter not only explores the technicalities but also addresses the ethical considerations surrounding biometric authentication.

As the narrative unfolds, the guide turns its gaze inward, examining the often-overlooked threat posed by insiders. Insider threats, whether intentional or unintentional, can compromise the integrity of the Cyber Fortress. Mitigation strategies, user activity monitoring, and the cultivation of a culture of trust and security form the crux of this chapter. Real-world case studies illuminate the potential risks, offering valuable insights into effective prevention strategies.

The exploration culminates in the final chapter, where the guide embraces the decentralized frontiers guarded by blockchain armor. Blockchain technology, with its decentralized and transparent nature, emerges as a potential game-changer in cybersecurity. Securing transactions, decentralized identity management, and addressing the challenges and future trends in blockchain security become the concluding notes in the symphony of building a resilient Cyber Fortress.

In essence, "Cyber Fortress: Building Robust Defenses for Digital Realms" transcends the realms of a traditional book, emerging as a comprehensive manifesto for the digital age. It beckons individuals and organizations to not only understand the intricacies of cybersecurity but to actively engage in fortifying their digital strongholds. In this collective endeavor, the guide stands as a beacon of empowerment, illuminating the path toward a future where the Cyber Fortress stands unwavering against the tides of cyber threats.

Chapter 1: Foundations of Defense

1. Introduction to Cybersecurity

In the vast expanse of the digital landscape, the Introduction to Cybersecurity serves as a gateway to a realm where the convergence of technology and interconnectedness unveils both unprecedented possibilities and inherent vulnerabilities. Cybersecurity, at its core, is the collective response to the relentless and ever-evolving onslaught of cyber threats that permeate every facet of our digitally entwined lives. This introductory exploration is an invitation to comprehend the critical role that cybersecurity plays in mitigating the risks and protecting the integrity of our digital realms.

As we traverse the historical trajectory of technological evolution, from the nascent stages of the internet to the sophisticated interconnected systems of today, the imperative for cybersecurity becomes glaringly apparent. The digital revolution has bestowed upon us unparalleled convenience, innovation, and efficiency, but it has also unearthed a complex labyrinth of vulnerabilities that demand diligent guardianship. The introduction thus becomes a chronicle, tracing the evolution of cybersecurity from its embryonic stages to the present, where the stakes have never been higher.

In dissecting the anatomy of cybersecurity, a fundamental understanding of its essence comes to light. It is not merely a set of tools or protocols; rather, it embodies a holistic and strategic approach to fortifying our digital strongholds. The term "cybersecurity" transcends the simplistic notion of safeguarding against external threats;

it encapsulates a proactive and dynamic stance, where defenders anticipate, adapt, and counteract the myriad tactics employed by cyber adversaries. The introduction seeks to imbue the reader with this nuanced perspective, laying the groundwork for a comprehensive exploration of the multifaceted dimensions of cybersecurity.

Central to this exploration is the concept of encryption, a cornerstone in the edifice of cybersecurity. The introduction unravels the mysteries of encryption, elucidating its role as the cryptographic guardian that renders sensitive information impervious to prying eyes. Authentication, the process of verifying the legitimacy of entities seeking access to digital domains, emerges as another vital pillar. The reader is guided through the intricate dance of cryptographic keys and digital signatures, understanding how authentication forms an integral part of the defense mechanisms that characterize cybersecurity.

Yet, the narrative doesn't confine itself to the technicalities alone. The human element, often the linchpin in the cybersecurity equation, is brought into focus. Cybersecurity is not a distant and abstract concept; it is a discipline that implicates individuals at every level. The introduction delves into the concept of cyber hygiene, emphasizing the significance of cultivating habits that mitigate risks—ranging from robust password management to vigilant software updates. Here, the human becomes both the defender and the potential weak link, underscoring the importance of user awareness and education in fortifying the human firewall.

As the introduction unfolds, it casts a discerning eye on the diverse and dynamic threat landscape that defines the cybersecurity battleground. The adversaries are not monolithic; they range from opportunistic hackers seeking vulnerabilities to state-sponsored actors orchestrating sophisticated cyber-espionage campaigns. Understanding this dynamic ecosystem is paramount to formulating effective defense strategies, and the introduction sets the stage for this exploration, preparing the reader to confront the diverse cast of characters in the cyber threat narrative.

In essence, the Introduction to Cybersecurity transcends the perfunctory gestures of defining terms; it immerses the reader in the ethos of cybersecurity as a proactive and adaptive discipline. It is an overture to a symphony where encryption, authentication, and cyber hygiene harmonize to create a resilient defense against the ever-shifting tides of digital threats. It beckons the reader to embark on a journey—an exploration of a realm where the guardianship of digital strongholds is not just a necessity but a shared responsibility in the intricate tapestry of the digital age.

Defining Cybersecurity and its Importance

Defining Cybersecurity is an intricate endeavor that delves into the very fabric of our digital existence, unraveling the complexities inherent in safeguarding the vast and interconnected realms of the cyber domain. At its essence, Cybersecurity constitutes a multidimensional discipline, encompassing a myriad of practices, technologies, and strategies designed to shield digital systems, networks, and data from malicious threats. It is not a static or rigid concept but rather a dynamic and adaptive framework, continuously evolving in response to the ever-changing landscape of cyber threats. In its most fundamental form, Cybersecurity represents a commitment to preserving the confidentiality, integrity, and availability of digital assets, acknowledging that the digital infrastructure underpins the fabric of modern society.

The importance of Cybersecurity cannot be overstated in an era where the ubiquity of technology and interconnectivity defines our daily lives. As we immerse ourselves deeper into the digital age, relying on digital platforms for communication, commerce, education, and virtually every facet of our existence, the vulnerabilities multiply exponentially. Cybersecurity emerges as the proverbial shield, the frontline defense against a spectrum of threats that range from opportunistic cybercriminals to state-sponsored actors wielding sophisticated tools of espionage and disruption. The interconnected nature of our digital ecosystems amplifies the potential impact of cyber threats, making the protection of sensitive information, critical infrastructure, and personal data a matter of paramount concern.

In delineating the importance of Cybersecurity, it is crucial to recognize its role as a linchpin in preserving trust. Trust forms the bedrock of digital interactions, whether it be in online transactions, communication platforms, or the seamless flow of information across networks. Cybersecurity functions as the custodian of this trust, assuring individuals, organizations, and governments that their digital interactions are secure and free from compromise. The erosion of this trust, as witnessed in high-profile data breaches and cyber-attacks, reverberates not only through the digital realm but permeates societal and economic landscapes, sowing seeds of doubt and apprehension.

Moreover, Cybersecurity assumes a central role in safeguarding privacy—a cornerstone of democratic societies. As our lives become increasingly digitized, a vast trove of personal information finds itself traversing digital channels. The protection of this information, from financial details to intimate communication, is intrinsically linked to the efficacy of Cybersecurity measures. Breaches in this digital fortress have far-reaching consequences, not only compromising individual privacy but potentially leading to identity theft, financial fraud, and other forms of malicious exploitation.

In the business landscape, the importance of Cybersecurity extends beyond individual privacy to encompass the resilience and continuity of operations. Organizations, irrespective of size or industry, are custodians of sensitive data and proprietary information. The compromise of such assets can lead to financial losses, reputational damage, and even existential threats. Cybersecurity, therefore, becomes a business imperative, safeguarding intellectual property, trade secrets, and the trust that customers and partners place in an organization.

The interplay between Cybersecurity and national security is equally profound. In an era where geopolitical conflicts extend into the digital domain, nation-states grapple with the challenges of protecting critical infrastructure, military capabilities, and sensitive intelligence from cyber-espionage and cyber warfare. The importance of robust Cybersecurity measures is underscored by the recognition that a cyber-attack on critical infrastructure—be it energy grids, communication networks, or financial systems—can have cascading and devastating effects on a nation's security and stability.

In the educational realm, the importance of Cybersecurity becomes evident as institutions increasingly rely on digital platforms for disseminating knowledge and managing administrative functions. The protection of student records, research data, and institutional information is not just a matter of compliance but an ethical obligation to ensure the integrity of academic pursuits and the trust placed in educational institutions.

As technology advances and new frontiers like artificial intelligence, the Internet of Things, and quantum computing emerge, the importance of Cybersecurity takes on new dimensions. These technological advancements bring unprecedented opportunities but also introduce novel risks and attack vectors. Cybersecurity becomes the vanguard in navigating this technological frontier, ensuring that innovation is not undermined by the shadows of cyber threats.

In conclusion, defining Cybersecurity goes beyond a mere articulation of its components; it is an acknowledgment of its pivotal role in the fabric of our digital society. Its importance reverberates through every sector, from individual privacy to national security, from business continuity to the preservation of trust. The digital age, with its vast opportunities and intricate challenges, demands a robust and adaptive approach to Cybersecurity, recognizing it not as a mere technical discipline but as a cornerstone in the foundation of a secure and resilient digital future.

Historical Perspectives on Cyber Threats

Examining Historical Perspectives on Cyber Threats unveils a captivating narrative that spans the evolution of digital technology, illustrating the relentless tug-of-war between innovation and malicious intent. The genesis of cyber threats traces back to the early days of computing, a time when the very notion of a connected digital world was in its infancy. In the 1970s and 1980s, what began as mere pranks and experiments within the nascent hacker community soon escalated into more insidious activities. The era bore witness to the emergence of notable figures like Kevin Mitnick, who gained notoriety for exploiting vulnerabilities and social engineering techniques to access sensitive systems.

The 1990s marked a significant turning point with the advent of the internet as a ubiquitous force. This period witnessed a surge in cybercrime, fueled by the proliferation of personal computers and the increasing connectivity of individuals and businesses. The Morris Worm of 1988, though more an inadvertent experiment than a malicious attack, foreshadowed the potential havoc that could be wreaked through digital channels. The infamous "ILOVEYOU" worm in 2000 capitalized on social engineering, infecting millions of computers worldwide by enticing users to open a seemingly innocent email attachment.

As the new millennium unfolded, the landscape of cyber threats underwent a profound transformation. The motivations behind cyber-attacks expanded beyond mischief and curiosity to encompass financial gain, political espionage, and ideological warfare. The emergence of sophisticated malware, exemplified by the likes of Stuxnet in 2010, signaled a paradigm shift. Stuxnet, believed to be a joint creation of nation-states, demonstrated the potential for cyber-attacks to target critical infrastructure, in this case, Iran's nuclear facilities.

This marked the dawn of cyber weapons with the capability to cause physical damage in the real world.

The rise of hacktivism, where politically motivated actors deploy cyber-attacks to promote their causes, added a layer of complexity to the threat landscape. Groups like Anonymous became synonymous with leveraging digital means to protest, disrupt, or expose perceived injustices. The distributed denial-of-service (DDoS) attacks orchestrated by hacktivist groups underscored the power of cyber threats as tools of activism.

Simultaneously, cyber threats evolved into lucrative enterprises for organized crime. The dark web became a breeding ground for cybercriminal activities, offering a marketplace for stolen data, malware, and hacking services. The business model shifted from individual hackers seeking notoriety to sophisticated criminal syndicates driven by financial incentives. Ransomware emerged as a particularly pernicious form of cyber threat, encrypting user data and demanding payment for its release.

The latter half of the 2010s witnessed a surge in state-sponsored cyber-espionage and cyber warfare. Nation-states, recognizing the potential impact of cyber capabilities, invested heavily in offensive cyber operations. The SolarWinds supply chain attack in 2020 exemplified the extent to which sophisticated adversaries could compromise trusted software to infiltrate high-profile targets. Alleged state-sponsored attacks on critical infrastructure, election interference, and large-scale data breaches underscored the geopolitical dimensions of cyber threats.

As we approach the present day, the cyber threat landscape continues to evolve at a relentless pace. The weaponization of artificial intelligence, the growing menace of ransomware-as-a-service, and the increasing sophistication of phishing attacks are emblematic of the persistent ingenuity displayed by cyber adversaries. The geopolitical tensions in the digital realm have not subsided; instead, they have become more pronounced as nation-states engage in a perpetual game of one-upmanship in cyberspace.

Historical perspectives on cyber threats, therefore, offer more than a chronological account of events; they provide invaluable insights into the motivations, methodologies, and consequences of a digital arms race that defines the contemporary era. From the playful exploits of early hackers to the sophisticated operations of nation-states and criminal enterprises, the historical trajectory underscores the gravity of the challenge we face in securing the digital future. As we navigate this complex and ever-changing landscape, the lessons of the past become guideposts, reminding us that the evolution of technology demands a corresponding evolution in our approach to cybersecurity.

1.2 Core Principles of Cybersecurity

Unveiling the Core Principles of Cybersecurity is akin to dissecting the very DNA that fortifies the digital realms against the relentless onslaught of cyber threats. At its core, Cybersecurity is not a monolithic entity but a dynamic discipline that draws strength from a set of foundational principles, each contributing to the resilience and adaptability of the digital defense ecosystem. Encryption emerges as a bedrock principle, a cryptographic shield that cloaks sensitive information in a veil of indecipherability. By encoding data in such a way that only authorized entities possess the keys to unlock it, encryption safeguards the confidentiality of information in transit and at rest, forming an indispensable layer of the Cybersecurity fortress.

Authentication stands as a stalwart companion to encryption, embodying the principle of verifying the legitimacy of entities seeking access to digital domains. In a world where identity is both a key and a vulnerability, robust authentication mechanisms become imperative. Whether through the use of passwords, biometrics, or multi-factor authentication, the process of authentication ensures that only authorized individuals or systems navigate the corridors of digital strongholds. It is the sentry at the gate, discerning friend from foe in the expansive landscape of interconnected networks.

Intrusion Detection and Prevention Systems (IDPS) embody another core principle, representing the vigilant guardians that monitor digital environments for signs of malevolent activity. These systems, equipped with sophisticated algorithms and heuristics, act as digital sentinels, scanning the digital horizon for anomalies, patterns indicative of cyber threats, or deviations from the norm. By swiftly detecting and, in some cases, preventing unauthorized access or malicious behavior, IDPS adds a proactive layer to Cybersecurity, transforming it from a reactive endeavor to a preemptive defense strategy.

The principle of Least Privilege navigates the delicate balance between accessibility and security. Recognizing that not all users or systems require unfettered access to sensitive resources, the principle advocates for the restriction of privileges to the minimum necessary for legitimate tasks. By limiting access rights, organizations minimize the potential impact of a compromised account or system, mitigating the risk of unauthorized access or malicious actions.

Anchored in the principle of Defense in Depth, Cybersecurity architects its defenses as a multi-layered tapestry rather than a singular impenetrable barrier. This approach acknowledges the inevitability of breaches and seeks to minimize their impact by introducing redundancy and diversity in defense mechanisms. Firewalls, antivirus software, and regular security audits become layers in this intricate defense stratagem, creating a formidable barrier that necessitates a multifaceted attack for successful penetration.

The principle of Patch Management addresses the inherent vulnerabilities that arise in software and systems as they evolve. Regularly updating and patching software is not merely a matter of feature enhancement but a critical facet of Cybersecurity. Software vulnerabilities are often exploited by cyber adversaries, and timely patches serve as virtual repairs, closing doors to potential exploits. This principle reflects the recognition that the digital landscape is dynamic, and proactive maintenance is essential to preemptively plug security holes.

Risk Assessment assumes a pivotal role in the realm of Cybersecurity, compelling organizations to adopt a pragmatic and strategic approach to threat mitigation. By systematically identifying and evaluating potential risks, organizations can allocate resources judiciously, prioritizing their defenses based on the likelihood and potential impact of threats. Risk assessment fosters a holistic understanding of the threat landscape, enabling organizations to tailor their Cybersecurity strategies to the specific vulnerabilities and challenges they face.

Interconnected with these principles is the overarching notion of Adaptability. The digital realm is not a static entity, and Cybersecurity must mirror this dynamism. Adaptable Cybersecurity strategies acknowledge the inevitability of change, whether in the form of evolving threats, emerging technologies, or shifting organizational landscapes. The ability to pivot and recalibrate defenses in response to new challenges is a cornerstone principle, ensuring that Cybersecurity remains a resilient and effective shield in the face of an ever-evolving threat landscape.

Furthermore, the principle of Transparency fosters an environment where the inner workings of Cybersecurity measures are not shrouded in mystery. Open communication about security policies, incidents, and best practices cultivates a culture of awareness and accountability. Transparency extends beyond organizational boundaries, as collaboration and information-sharing within the broader Cybersecurity community become essential in collectively fortifying the digital frontier.

Ethical considerations represent an intrinsic principle that transcends technicalities, emphasizing the importance of responsible and lawful conduct in the pursuit of Cybersecurity. The principle of Ethics underscores the need for Cybersecurity practitioners to operate within legal and ethical frameworks, respecting privacy, civil liberties, and international norms. As stewards of digital trust, adhering to ethical principles ensures that Cybersecurity efforts align with societal values and contribute to the greater good.

In essence, the Core Principles of Cybersecurity form a cohesive and interdependent framework, woven together to create a resilient tapestry of defense. Encryption, authentication, intrusion detection, least privilege, defense in depth, patch management, risk assessment, adaptability, transparency, and ethics collectively propel Cybersecurity beyond a set of technical measures. They embody a philosophy—one that recognizes the intricate nuances of the digital landscape and aligns the pursuit of security with the principles of prudence, adaptability, and ethical responsibility.

Encryption Techniques and Protocols

Delving into the realm of Encryption Techniques and Protocols unveils a multifaceted landscape where the quest for securing digital communication and data transcends mere complexity to become a nuanced dance of mathematical algorithms, cryptographic keys, and evolving standards. At its core, encryption is the art of encoding information in a manner that renders it indecipherable to unauthorized entities, ensuring that even if intercepted, the data remains confidential and secure. The historical evolution of encryption techniques dates back to ancient civilizations, where rudimentary methods involved the substitution of characters or the transposition of letters to obfuscate messages. However, the contemporary digital era demands more robust and sophisticated approaches, and a plethora of encryption techniques and protocols have emerged to meet this need.

Symmetric key encryption, a fundamental technique, involves the use of a shared key for both the encryption and decryption processes. In this scenario, the challenge lies in securely distributing and managing the shared key, as any compromise could jeopardize the confidentiality of the encrypted data. Advanced Encryption Standard (AES) stands as a prominent example of symmetric key encryption, renowned for its efficiency and security. AES, adopted as a federal standard by the U.S. government, employs a symmetric key of varying lengths to encrypt data blocks, providing a robust foundation for secure communication and data storage.

In contrast, asymmetric key encryption, also known as public-key encryption, introduces a pair of mathematically related keys: a public key used for encryption and a private key for decryption. This paradigm eliminates the need for a shared secret, mitigating the challenges associated with key distribution in symmetric key encryption. The RSA algorithm, named after its inventors Rivest, Shamir, and Adleman, exemplifies asymmetric key encryption. The security of RSA relies on the difficulty of factoring the product of two large prime numbers, a mathematical problem believed to be challenging for classical computers.

Elliptic Curve Cryptography (ECC) represents a modern and efficient variant of asymmetric key encryption, leveraging the mathematical properties of elliptic curves over finite fields. ECC provides equivalent security to traditional asymmetric algorithms with shorter key lengths, making it particularly appealing for resource-constrained environments, such as mobile devices and Internet of Things (IoT) devices. Its efficiency in terms of computational requirements and bandwidth utilization has positioned ECC as a favored choice in contemporary cryptographic applications.

Hash functions, while not encryption per se, play a pivotal role in cryptographic protocols by generating fixed-size outputs, known as hash values, from variable-size inputs. The one-way nature of hash functions ensures that it is computationally infeasible to reverse the process and derive the original input from the hash value. Hash functions find application in various security protocols, including digital signatures, password storage, and data integrity verification. Commonly used hash functions include the Secure Hash Algorithm (SHA) family, with SHA-256 and SHA-3 standing out as prevalent choices for cryptographic applications.

Digital signatures, an essential component of many cryptographic protocols, combine asymmetric key encryption and hash functions to provide authentication and non-repudiation. In this process, the sender generates a digital signature using their private key, and the recipient verifies the signature using the sender's public key. If the signature is valid, it not only authenticates the sender but also attests that the message has not been altered during transit. Digital signatures play a pivotal role in ensuring the integrity and authenticity of digital communication, forming the cornerstone of secure transactions and electronic document verification.

Transport Layer Security (TLS) and its predecessor, Secure Sockets Layer (SSL), represent protocols designed to secure communication over a network, typically the internet. TLS/SSL employ a combination of asymmetric and symmetric key encryption to establish a secure channel between a client and a server. During the TLS handshake, asymmetric key encryption is used to exchange a shared secret, which subsequently serves as the basis for symmetric key encryption throughout the session. TLS/SSL protocols underpin secure communication in various applications, including web browsing, email, and virtual private networks (VPNs).

In the realm of virtual private networks, IPsec (Internet Protocol Security) stands as a comprehensive suite of protocols designed to secure communication at the network layer. IPsec employs a combination of symmetric and asymmetric key encryption to ensure the confidentiality, integrity, and authenticity of data transmitted between network nodes. IPsec is widely employed in the implementation of VPNs, offering a robust framework for securing data exchanges over the internet and other networks.

Homomorphic encryption represents an avant-garde frontier where the traditional delineation between encryption and computation is blurred. This innovative technique allows computations to be performed directly on encrypted data without decrypting it, a feat previously deemed implausible. Homomorphic encryption holds immense promise for preserving privacy in scenarios where data must remain encrypted during processing, such as in cloud computing environments. While currently computationally intensive, ongoing research aims to enhance the efficiency and practicality of homomorphic encryption for broader adoption.

Post-Quantum Cryptography arises as a response to the potential threat posed by quantum computers to existing cryptographic algorithms, particularly those based on the difficulty of factoring large numbers or solving discrete logarithm problems. Post-Quantum Cryptography explores alternative mathematical problems that are believed to resist quantum algorithms. Candidates in this domain include lattice-based cryptography, hash-based cryptography, and code-based cryptography, each offering unique approaches to securing information in a quantum computing landscape.

In conclusion, Encryption Techniques and Protocols constitute a dynamic and multifaceted domain within the broader landscape of cybersecurity. From symmetric and asymmetric key encryption to hash functions, digital signatures, and innovative approaches like homomorphic encryption, the toolkit available to cybersecurity practitioners is diverse and continually evolving. The selection of encryption techniques and protocols depends on factors such as the specific use case, performance requirements, and the threat landscape. As the digital frontier advances and new challenges emerge, the field of encryption will undoubtedly witness further innovation, ensuring that the delicate dance between security and accessibility continues to evolve in tandem with the dynamic nature of the digital landscape.

Authentication Methods for Secure Access

Navigating the intricate landscape of Authentication Methods for Secure Access unveils a diverse array of techniques and technologies designed to verify the identity of users, devices, or entities seeking entry into digital strongholds. Authentication, a cornerstone of cybersecurity, serves as the digital gatekeeper, ensuring that access is granted only to those with the legitimate credentials. The evolution of authentication methods has been propelled by the imperative to strike a delicate balance between security and usability, recognizing that robust access controls are essential without impeding the seamless flow of legitimate users. This exploration encompasses a spectrum of authentication methods, from traditional knowledge-based approaches to cutting-edge biometrics, adaptive authentication, and multifactor authentication (MFA).

At the foundational level, Knowledge-Based Authentication (KBA) represents a classical method wherein users prove their identity by presenting information that only they should know. This typically involves the use of passwords, Personal Identification Numbers (PINs), or responses to predefined security questions. While passwords have been a ubiquitous and cost-effective means of authentication, they are not without vulnerabilities. The prevalence of password-related breaches, the challenge of users maintaining strong and unique passwords, and the susceptibility to various attacks, such as phishing and brute force attacks, have prompted a reevaluation of the reliance on passwords as a sole authentication method.

In response to the shortcomings of knowledge-based methods, Multi-Factor Authentication (MFA) has emerged as a robust paradigm, requiring users to present multiple forms of identification to access a system or resource. MFA acknowledges that a single authentication factor may not provide sufficient security, and combining different factors enhances the overall robustness of access controls. The three primary authentication factors are typically categorized as something the user knows (knowledge-based), something the user has (possession-based), and something the user is (biometric-based). MFA is instrumental in mitigating the risks associated with compromised passwords and unauthorized access, significantly bolstering the security posture of systems and applications.

Possession-based authentication methods introduce an additional layer of security by requiring users to possess a physical token or device to authenticate their identity. One prevalent form is the use of One-Time Passwords (OTP), where a temporary code is generated and delivered to a user's registered device. Hardware tokens, smart cards, or mobile applications can serve as the possession-based element, ensuring that even if a user's password is compromised, unauthorized access is thwarted without the physical token. Time-based OTPs add an extra layer of security by making the generated codes valid only for a short duration, reducing the window of opportunity for malicious actors.

Biometric Authentication, often hailed as a futuristic and intuitive approach, leverages unique physical or behavioral characteristics to verify identity. Biometric identifiers include fingerprints, facial recognition, iris scans, voiceprints, and even behavioral traits like typing patterns or gait. Biometrics offer the advantage of being inherently tied to the individual, eliminating the need for memorized credentials. However, the deployment of biometric authentication comes with its set of challenges, including concerns about privacy, the potential for biometric data theft, and the need for specialized hardware or sensors.

Facial Recognition, a subset of biometric authentication, has gained prominence in recent years due to its convenience and the ubiquity of cameras in modern devices. This method maps and analyzes unique facial features to authenticate users. However, facial recognition systems have faced scrutiny over issues such as accuracy, bias, and the potential for misuse. Ongoing advancements in the technology aim to address these concerns while extending its applications in various domains, from mobile devices to surveillance and access control systems.

Voice Biometrics, another biometric authentication method, relies on the unique characteristics of an individual's voice for identification. Vocal pitch, tone, cadence, and other factors contribute to creating a distinctive voiceprint. Voice biometrics find applications in call centers, voice-activated devices, and authentication for remote access. While voice recognition adds a layer of convenience, challenges exist in mitigating environmental noise, ensuring accuracy, and addressing concerns related to voice recording and playback attacks.

Fingerprint Recognition, one of the oldest and most widely adopted biometric authentication methods, relies on mapping the unique patterns of ridges and valleys on an individual's fingertips. Mobile devices, laptops, and physical access control systems frequently employ fingerprint recognition for secure access. The widespread use of fingerprint recognition has contributed to its acceptance as a reliable and convenient biometric authentication method.

The notion of Adaptive Authentication introduces a dynamic and context-aware dimension to the authentication process. Adaptive authentication systems evaluate multiple factors, including user behavior, location, time, and the device used, to assess the risk level associated with a login attempt. This contextual analysis enables adaptive systems to dynamically adjust the authentication requirements. For example, a login attempt from a recognized device during regular business hours may require fewer authentication factors than an attempt from an unfamiliar device at an unusual time. Adaptive authentication enhances security by tailoring access controls to the specific context, offering a balance between security and user experience.

Risk-Based Authentication extends the principles of adaptive authentication by incorporating risk assessments into the decision-making process. These systems assign a risk score to each login attempt based on a range of factors, such as the user's historical behavior, geographic location, and the presence of anomalies. High-risk events may trigger additional authentication measures, while low-risk events may experience streamlined access. Risk-based authentication is instrumental in identifying and mitigating potential threats, offering a proactive approach to security.

Mobile Authentication leverages the ubiquity of smartphones to enhance access controls. Mobile devices can serve as possession-based factors, generating OTPs or acting as a second authentication channel. Additionally, mobile authentication methods may involve the use of biometrics, such as fingerprint or facial recognition, native to the mobile device. Mobile-based authentication aligns with the modern user's expectation of convenience and portability, making it an increasingly prevalent method for securing access to various services.

Single Sign-On (SSO) represents a convenience-driven approach to authentication, allowing users to access multiple systems or applications with a single set of credentials. While SSO simplifies the user experience, it introduces challenges related to the potential impact of a compromised credential on multiple accounts. Federated Authentication extends the concept of SSO by enabling users to authenticate across multiple domains or organizations using a single set of credentials. Standards like Security Assertion Markup Language (SAML) facilitate the secure exchange of authentication and authorization data between disparate systems.

The emergence of Passwordless Authentication seeks to address the inherent vulnerabilities and user burdens associated with traditional password-based methods. Passwordless authentication methods leverage possession-based factors, such as mobile devices or security keys, and biometric factors, eliminating the need for users to remember passwords. This approach aligns with the growing recognition of the limitations and risks posed by passwords, particularly in the face of evolving cyber threats.

Continuous Authentication, an evolving paradigm, challenges the traditional notion of a one-time authentication event by introducing ongoing and dynamic verification throughout a user's session. This method continuously evaluates user behavior, biometric factors, or other contextual signals to ensure that the authenticated user remains the same throughout the interaction. Continuous authentication addresses scenarios where a session may be compromised after the initial authentication, offering an added layer of security.

In conclusion, Authentication Methods for Secure Access constitute a dynamic and evolving arsenal within the realm of cybersecurity. The landscape spans traditional knowledge-based methods to cutting-edge biometrics, adaptive authentication, and multifactor authentication. The selection of authentication methods depends on factors such as the desired balance between security and user experience, the nature of the protected assets, and the specific threat landscape. As the digital ecosystem advances and threat vectors evolve, the field of authentication will undoubtedly witness continued innovation, ensuring that the delicate equilibrium between accessibility and security remains resilient in the face of an ever-changing cybersecurity landscape.

Intrusion Detection and Prevention Systems

Embarking on an exploration of Intrusion Detection and Prevention Systems (IDPS) unveils a critical dimension within the intricate tapestry of cybersecurity—an ecosystem where vigilant guardians stand watch, poised to detect and thwart potential threats in the vast expanses of digital landscapes. At its essence, an IDPS represents a comprehensive and proactive defense mechanism designed to safeguard networks, systems, and data by identifying and responding to malicious activities or security incidents. The evolution of IDPS reflects the perpetual cat-and-mouse game between cyber adversaries and defenders, each iteration of technology and strategy seeking to outpace the other in this dynamic cyber battleground.

The foundation of an IDPS lies in its ability to analyze network and system activities in real-time, scrutinizing the digital footprints left by users, devices, and applications. This continuous surveillance is underpinned by a multifaceted approach, combining signature-based detection, anomaly-based detection, and behavioral analysis. Signature-based detection operates on the premise of recognizing patterns or signatures associated with known threats, akin to identifying a familiar face in a crowd. This method is effective against well-established and documented threats but falls short in the face of novel or polymorphic malware that can dynamically alter its signature to evade detection.

Anomaly-based detection introduces a dynamic dimension by establishing a baseline of normal behavior within a network or system. Deviations from this baseline are flagged as potential anomalies, signaling the presence of unauthorized or malicious activities. While powerful in identifying previously unknown threats, anomaly-based detection must contend with the challenge of distinguishing between benign anomalies and genuine security incidents. Calibration and tuning are crucial to ensure that the system does not inundate operators with false positives, preserving the efficacy of the intrusion detection process.

Behavioral Analysis, a more advanced facet of IDPS, scrutinizes the behavior of entities within the network, seeking patterns indicative of malicious intent. This approach moves beyond static signatures and predefined baselines, embracing the dynamic and context-specific nature of cyber threats. Behavioral analysis may encompass the study of user behavior, network traffic patterns, or application interactions, offering a nuanced understanding of the normal and abnormal within the digital environment. However, the sophistication of behavioral analysis demands robust computational resources and advanced algorithms to discern subtle anomalies indicative of evolving threats.

Intrusion Detection Systems (IDS) and Intrusion Prevention Systems (IPS) represent two primary categories within the IDPS domain, each serving distinct yet interrelated purposes. An IDS, the vigilant observer, focuses on detection and alerting, providing security personnel with insights into potential security incidents. The IDS analyzes network traffic, system logs, and other data sources, raising alarms when suspicious activities align with known threat signatures or deviate from established baselines. The strength of an IDS lies in its ability to promptly detect and notify security teams, enabling rapid response to potential threats.

Conversely, an IPS takes on a more assertive role by not only detecting but also actively preventing malicious activities. Building on the foundations of an IDS, an IPS intervenes in real-time to block or mitigate identified threats, acting as a digital gatekeeper against unauthorized access, exploits, or other malicious behaviors. The IPS operates at the network layer, employing a range of preventive measures such as packet filtering, access control lists, and protocol validation to neutralize threats before they can manifest. This proactive stance positions an IPS as a frontline defender, offering an immediate and automated response to potential security incidents.

The deployment of IDPS within an organizational infrastructure is not a one-size-fits-all endeavor. Network-based IDPS monitors and analyzes network traffic, making it well-suited for identifying threats traversing the network. Host-based IDPS, on the other hand, focuses on the activities occurring on individual devices or servers, offering a more granular perspective. The selection between network-based and host-based solutions hinges on factors such as the organization's architecture, the nature of assets being protected, and the desired depth of visibility into potential threats.

Signature-based detection, a cornerstone of IDPS, relies on a database of predefined signatures or patterns associated with known threats. This approach is akin to recognizing the unique fingerprints of malicious activities within the vast sea of digital transactions. The effectiveness of signature-based detection, however, is contingent on the timeliness and comprehensiveness of the signature database. Regular updates are imperative to ensure that the IDPS remains equipped to recognize emerging threats and variants.

Complementing signature-based detection, heuristic or anomaly-based detection introduces an element of adaptability by identifying deviations from established norms. Heuristic approaches leverage general rules or behavioral models to flag activities that exhibit characteristics commonly associated with malicious behavior. Anomaly-based detection, as discussed earlier, establishes a baseline of normal behavior and raises alerts when deviations from this baseline are detected. The synergy between signature-based and anomaly-based detection enhances the overall resilience of IDPS, offering a balanced defense against both known and unknown threats.

The advent of machine learning and artificial intelligence injects a transformative dimension into IDPS, empowering these systems with the capacity to learn and adapt. Machine learning algorithms can analyze vast datasets, identifying patterns and correlations that may elude traditional rule-based approaches. By discerning complex relationships within data, machine learning-equipped IDPS can enhance the accuracy of threat detection and reduce false positives. Moreover, these systems can evolve over time, adapting to the shifting tactics employed by cyber adversaries.

Beyond the confines of traditional network perimeters, the proliferation of cloud computing and virtualized environments introduces new challenges and opportunities for IDPS. Cloud-based IDPS extends its protective umbrella to encompass virtualized infrastructure, securing data and applications hosted in the cloud. The dynamic and scalable nature of cloud environments necessitates IDPS solutions that can seamlessly integrate with these architectures, offering continuous protection without impeding the agility and flexibility inherent in cloud deployments.

The symbiotic relationship between IDPS and Security Information and Event Management (SIEM) systems amplifies the effectiveness of both. While IDPS is adept at detecting and preventing security incidents, SIEM serves as the central nervous system, aggregating and correlating information from diverse sources, including IDPS alerts. SIEM enhances the visibility and context surrounding security events, enabling security personnel to make informed decisions and respond to incidents in a timely manner. The integration of IDPS with SIEM exemplifies the holistic approach necessary for effective cybersecurity orchestration.

Challenges persist within the realm of IDPS, reflecting the dynamic and evolving nature of cyber threats. False positives, instances where legitimate activities are mistakenly flagged as security incidents, pose an ongoing challenge. Striking a delicate balance between sensitivity and specificity is paramount to mitigate the impact of false positives on operational efficiency. Moreover, the need for rapid and automated responses to threats introduces the risk of false negatives—instances where genuine security incidents go undetected. This dichotomy underscores the perpetual challenge faced by security practitioners in fine-tuning IDPS to align with the unique characteristics of their organizational environment.

In conclusion, Intrusion Detection and Prevention Systems stand as stalwart guardians in the ceaseless battle against cyber threats, embodying a fusion of technological prowess, adaptive intelligence, and proactive defense. From signature-based detection to heuristic and anomaly-based approaches, the multifaceted capabilities of IDPS underscore its pivotal role in safeguarding digital assets. The evolution of these systems, augmented by machine learning and tailored for cloud environments, reflects a dynamic response to the ever-changing threat landscape. As organizations navigate the complexities of cybersecurity, the integration of IDPS with complementary technologies and a commitment to continuous improvement remain essential pillars in fortifying the digital defenses that protect the integrity and resilience of modern digital ecosystems.

1.3 Understanding the Threat Landscape
Common Types of Cyber Threats (Malware, Phishing, etc.)

Embarking on an exploration of the Common Types of Cyber Threats reveals a vast and dynamic landscape where malevolent actors deploy a myriad of tactics to exploit vulnerabilities, compromise systems, and gain unauthorized access to sensitive information. At the forefront of this digital battleground is Malware, a pervasive category encompassing a multitude of malicious software designed to inflict harm. Viruses, one of the oldest and most notorious forms of malware, attach themselves to legitimate programs and replicate when those programs run, often causing data corruption and system disruptions. Worms, a more independent variant, exploit network vulnerabilities to self-replicate and propagate, spreading across interconnected systems. Trojans disguise themselves as benign applications but harbor malicious intent, often providing backdoor access for attackers to exfiltrate data or execute unauthorized commands. Ransomware, a particularly insidious subtype, encrypts user data, rendering it inaccessible until a ransom is paid, exemplifying the intersection of cyber threats and extortion.

Phishing, a social engineering technique, stands as a deceptive and manipulative method employed by cyber adversaries to trick individuals into divulging sensitive information. Phishing emails masquerade as legitimate communication from trusted entities, prompting recipients to click on malicious links or provide confidential data such as passwords or financial information. Spear Phishing targets specific individuals or organizations, tailoring the deceptive communication to exploit personalized details, making it even more challenging to discern from authentic correspondence. Beyond emails, phishing techniques extend to other communication channels, including SMS, voice calls, and social media platforms, reflecting the adaptability and persistence of cybercriminals in their quest to exploit human vulnerabilities.

Distributed Denial of Service (DDoS) attacks constitute another menacing category of cyber threats designed to disrupt the normal functioning of networks, websites, or online services. DDoS attacks flood the target with an overwhelming volume of traffic, rendering it unavailable to legitimate users. Amplified DDoS attacks leverage vulnerable servers to magnify the volume of attack traffic, exacerbating the impact on the target. These attacks often involve the use of botnets—networks of compromised devices under the control of a malicious actor—illustrating the scale and coordination achievable by cyber adversaries seeking to cripple online resources.

Man-in-the-Middle (MitM) attacks exploit the vulnerability inherent in communication channels, allowing attackers to intercept and manipulate the exchange of information between two parties. In a typical MitM scenario, the attacker positions themselves between the communication flow, intercepting data transmitted between the parties without their knowledge. This technique facilitates eavesdropping, data tampering, and the potential extraction of sensitive information such as login credentials or financial details. Wi-Fi eavesdropping, session hijacking, and SSL-stripping are common variants of MitM attacks, emphasizing the need for robust encryption and secure communication protocols to mitigate these threats.

Bringing economic motivations to the forefront, Financial Cyber Threats target individuals, organizations, and financial institutions with the goal of unauthorized financial gain. Banking Trojans infiltrate systems to steal login credentials for online banking or payment platforms, facilitating fraudulent transactions. ATM skimming involves the installation of devices on automated teller machines to capture card information, enabling criminals to clone cards and withdraw funds. Business Email Compromise (BEC) schemes manipulate email communication to trick individuals into transferring funds or revealing sensitive financial information, often exploiting compromised or spoofed email accounts of executives or vendors.

Advanced Persistent Threats (APTs) represent a sophisticated and targeted form of cyber threat orchestrated by well-funded and organized adversaries, often nation-states or cybercriminal groups with specific objectives. APTs involve a prolonged and stealthy campaign, with attackers employing a combination of malware, social engineering, and advanced tactics to gain persistent access to target networks. The primary goal of APTs is to exfiltrate sensitive information, conduct espionage, or disrupt critical infrastructure, showcasing the strategic and patient nature of these cyber threats.

Zero-Day Exploits, a particularly potent category of cyber threats, leverage vulnerabilities in software or hardware that are unknown to the vendor and, consequently, lack available patches or fixes. Cybercriminals exploit these zero-day vulnerabilities to launch targeted attacks before the affected entity becomes aware of the flaw. The clandestine nature of zero-day exploits amplifies their impact, as they can be employed against unsuspecting targets until the vulnerability is identified and mitigated, underscoring the importance of proactive security measures and rapid response capabilities.

Insider Threats introduce a unique challenge, as individuals within an organization exploit their access and privileges for malicious purposes. Insider threats may arise from disgruntled employees seeking revenge, unwitting personnel falling victim to social engineering, or individuals coerced by external actors. The consequences of insider threats range from the theft of sensitive data to sabotage of systems or networks. Organizations must implement robust access controls, monitor user activities, and cultivate a culture of cybersecurity awareness to mitigate the risks posed by insider threats.

Internet of Things (IoT) Vulnerabilities present a growing concern as the proliferation of connected devices introduces an expanding attack surface. Insecure IoT devices, lacking proper security measures, become prime targets for cyber adversaries seeking to exploit vulnerabilities and compromise networks. Botnets like Mirai have demonstrated the potential for large-scale DDoS attacks orchestrated through compromised IoT devices. The integration of IoT security measures, including secure device authentication, encryption, and regular updates, is imperative to curb the risks associated with the burgeoning IoT landscape.

Supply Chain Attacks underscore the interconnected nature of modern digital ecosystems, as cyber adversaries target vulnerabilities within the supply chain to compromise organizations indirectly. Attackers may infiltrate the software supply chain, injecting malicious code into legitimate applications distributed to end-users. Hardware supply chain attacks involve the compromise of hardware components, such as firmware or integrated circuits, with the aim of introducing vulnerabilities or facilitating unauthorized access. The cascading impact of supply chain attacks highlights the need for comprehensive security measures across the entire ecosystem.

Social Engineering, a pervasive and adaptable form of cyber threat, relies on psychological manipulation to deceive individuals or entities into divulging sensitive information or performing actions that compromise security. Beyond phishing, social engineering encompasses a spectrum of tactics, including pretexting (creating false scenarios to obtain information), baiting (luring individuals with promises of gain), and quid pro quo (offering something in exchange for information or access). The human factor remains a potent vulnerability, emphasizing the importance of cybersecurity education and awareness to fortify defenses against social engineering attacks.

The emergence of Fileless Malware introduces a stealthy and evasive dimension to cyber threats, as these malicious programs operate in the volatile memory of compromised systems, leaving little to no trace on disk. Fileless malware exploits legitimate system tools and processes, making detection and attribution challenging. This category includes Memory-based Malware, which resides in RAM to avoid traditional antivirus scans, and Script-based Malware, which leverages scripting languages to execute malicious activities without the need for traditional executable files. The evasion tactics employed by fileless malware underscore the need for advanced detection methods and behavioral analysis within cybersecurity frameworks.

In conclusion, the panorama of Common Types of Cyber Threats reflects a dynamic and evolving landscape where cyber adversaries continually innovate and adapt their tactics to exploit vulnerabilities and bypass defenses. From the traditional threat vectors of malware and phishing to the sophisticated strategies of APTs and zero-day exploits, the diverse nature of cyber threats underscores the imperative for holistic and proactive cybersecurity measures. Organizations must adopt a multi-layered defense strategy, incorporating technological solutions, user education, and robust incident response capabilities to navigate the ever-changing terrain of cyber threats and fortify their digital fortresses against an array of potential risks.

Profiling Adversaries: From Script Kiddies to Nation-States

Profiling adversaries within the realm of cybersecurity spans a vast spectrum, ranging from novice script kiddies to sophisticated nation-states, each posing unique challenges and motivations. At the lower end of this spectrum are script kiddies, often individuals with limited technical expertise who rely on pre-existing tools and exploit codes developed by others. Driven by a desire for notoriety or a misguided sense of rebellion, script kiddies typically lack the strategic objectives that define more advanced adversaries. Moving up the hierarchy, hacktivists emerge as a distinct category, motivated by ideological or political goals, seeking to make a social or political statement through cyber-attacks. While their technical proficiency varies, hacktivists exhibit a higher degree of purpose compared to script kiddies.

Criminal organizations occupy another tier, leveraging cyber capabilities for financial gain. These adversaries employ advanced techniques, including ransomware and financial fraud, demonstrating a more organized and profit-driven approach. As cyber threats escalate in sophistication, the distinction between cybercrime and cyber espionage blurs, leading to the emergence of cyber mercenaries and mercenaries-for-hire who offer their services to the highest bidder, whether criminal or state actors. State-sponsored adversaries, representing the pinnacle of cyber threat sophistication, operate with strategic objectives that align with national interests. These nation-state actors conduct espionage, engage in cyber-espionage, and deploy advanced persistent threats (APTs) to achieve political, economic, or military advantage.

Nation-states often prioritize stealth, persistence, and long-term strategic planning, utilizing cyber capabilities as a force multiplier in geopolitical conflicts. The blurred lines between state and non-state actors in the cyber domain further complicate the attribution process, as false flags and proxy entities are commonly employed to obfuscate the true origin of cyber-attacks. The proliferation of offensive cyber capabilities has led to an arms race in cyberspace, with states investing heavily in both offensive and defensive capabilities. The realm of cyber warfare introduces the concept of hybrid threats, where conventional military actions are complemented by cyber-attacks, creating a multifaceted threat landscape.

Understanding the motivations and tactics of adversaries is crucial for developing effective cybersecurity strategies. For script kiddies and low-level threat actors, preventive measures such as basic security hygiene, education, and awareness can prove effective. As adversaries advance in sophistication, organizations must invest in advanced threat detection, incident response capabilities, and threat intelligence to stay ahead of evolving tactics. Cooperation between the public and private sectors is paramount, as is international collaboration to address threats that transcend national borders. The dynamic nature of cyber threats requires a proactive and adaptive approach, with continuous learning and innovation in cybersecurity practices to mitigate risks posed by adversaries ranging from script kiddies to nation-states. As the digital landscape continues to evolve, the imperative to profile and understand adversaries becomes increasingly vital in safeguarding individuals, organizations, and nations from the pervasive and ever-evolving threat of cyber-attacks.

The Dynamic Nature of Cyber Threats

The dynamic nature of cyber threats represents an ever-evolving landscape characterized by constant innovation, adaptability, and complexity. In this digital age, where technology permeates every facet of our lives, the interconnectedness of systems and the vast expanse of the internet create an environment ripe for exploitation by malicious actors. Cyber threats encompass a wide spectrum, ranging from relatively simplistic attacks conducted by script kiddies to highly sophisticated campaigns orchestrated by nation-states. What makes this landscape particularly challenging is its inherent fluidity; as defenders bolster their security measures and patch vulnerabilities, adversaries concurrently devise new methods to bypass these safeguards. The cat-and-mouse game between defenders and attackers is relentless, fueled by the rapid pace of technological advancements.

One key aspect of the dynamic nature of cyber threats lies in the diverse motives driving malicious actors. While some seek financial gain through cybercrime, others, such as hacktivists, pursue ideological or political objectives. Nation-states leverage cyber capabilities for espionage, influence operations, and even as tools of war, introducing a geopolitical dimension to the digital realm. This range of motivations adds layers of complexity to the threat landscape, as defenders must contend with adversaries operating under different banners and with distinct tactics, techniques, and procedures (TTPs). The amalgamation of profit-driven cybercrime, politically motivated hacktivism, and state-sponsored cyber espionage creates a multifaceted and volatile environment.

The rapid proliferation of technology, including the Internet of Things (IoT), cloud computing, and artificial intelligence, further amplifies the dynamism of cyber threats. The expanded attack surface resulting from the increasing interconnectivity of devices provides adversaries with more entry points and potential targets. Exploiting vulnerabilities in legacy systems, zero-day exploits, and leveraging social engineering techniques, threat actors continuously innovate to circumvent security measures. The advent of ransomware, in particular, showcases the adaptability of cyber threats, as attackers shift strategies from mere data theft to extortion, causing financial and operational havoc for organizations.

Attribution, a perennial challenge in the cybersecurity domain, adds another layer of complexity to the dynamic landscape. Adversaries frequently employ tactics to obfuscate their true identity, utilizing false flags or routing attacks through proxy entities. This deliberate ambiguity not only complicates the response efforts of defenders but also introduces an element of uncertainty in geopolitical relations. The difficulty in definitively attributing cyber-attacks often leads to debates over responsibility and consequences, highlighting the need for international cooperation and norms in cyberspace.

The emergence of advanced persistent threats (APTs) exemplifies the persistent and stealthy nature of certain cyber adversaries. APTs, often associated with nation-states, are characterized by prolonged, targeted campaigns aimed at infiltrating and exfiltrating sensitive information. These adversaries showcase a level of patience and strategic thinking that distinguishes them from more opportunistic attackers. As organizations and governments invest in bolstering their cyber defenses, APTs adapt by refining their techniques, employing zero-day vulnerabilities, and leveraging supply chain attacks to achieve their objectives.

The dynamic nature of cyber threats necessitates a paradigm shift in cybersecurity strategies. Traditional approaches centered on perimeter defense and static rule-based systems are no longer sufficient. Instead, a proactive and adaptive approach is imperative, incorporating threat intelligence, behavioral analytics, and continuous monitoring. Organizations must adopt a mindset that acknowledges the inevitability of breaches and focuses on rapid detection and response. Threat hunting, a proactive search for signs of malicious activity, has become a critical component of modern cybersecurity, reflecting the understanding that adversaries may already be within the network.

Collaboration between the public and private sectors is vital to effectively combat the dynamic nature of cyber threats. Information sharing, both within industries and across borders, enables a collective defense approach, where insights gained from one incident can enhance the resilience of others. International cooperation becomes increasingly crucial as cyber threats transcend geographical boundaries. Establishing norms and rules of engagement in cyberspace, akin to those in traditional warfare, can help mitigate the risk of escalating cyber conflicts and foster a more secure digital environment.

In conclusion, the dynamic nature of cyber threats is an inherent characteristic of the digital age, fueled by technological advancements, diverse motivations of malicious actors, and the expanding attack surface. Organizations and nations must embrace a proactive and adaptive cybersecurity stance, incorporating innovative technologies and collaboration to stay ahead of evolving threats. The landscape's complexity requires continuous learning, information sharing, and international cooperation to effectively navigate the intricate web of cyber threats and safeguard the integrity of digital systems in an ever-changing environment.

1.4 Customizing Defense Strategies
Tailoring Cybersecurity to Specific Environments

Tailoring cybersecurity to specific environments involves the nuanced adaptation of security measures to align with the unique characteristics, risks, and requirements of distinct operating contexts. As organizations increasingly digitize and integrate technology into their operations, the diversity of environments, from critical infrastructure to healthcare systems and financial institutions, necessitates a tailored approach to address specific challenges. One fundamental aspect of this customization involves recognizing that a one-size-fits-all cybersecurity strategy is inadequate in the face of evolving threats and dynamic landscapes.

Critical infrastructure, comprising sectors such as energy, transportation, and water supply, stands as a prime example of an environment demanding tailored cybersecurity solutions. The interconnected and often aging systems within these sectors pose unique challenges, as disruptions can have cascading effects on national security and public safety. Tailoring cybersecurity for critical infrastructure involves not only securing individual components but also comprehensively assessing the interdependencies among systems. The implementation of robust incident response plans, regular vulnerability assessments, and the incorporation of resilience measures are crucial components of safeguarding critical infrastructure.

Healthcare environments present a distinct set of challenges due to the sensitive nature of patient data and the increasing reliance on interconnected medical devices. Tailored cybersecurity measures for healthcare institutions must prioritize the protection of patient privacy, the integrity of medical records, and the reliability of medical equipment. As healthcare systems embrace digital transformation, strategies encompassing data encryption, access controls, and regular security audits become imperative. The integration of artificial intelligence (AI) and machine learning (ML) in healthcare also introduces new considerations, demanding tailored approaches to address potential vulnerabilities in these advanced technologies.

Financial institutions, given their role as custodians of sensitive financial data, face a constant barrage of cyber threats ranging from financial fraud to ransomware attacks. Tailoring cybersecurity for the financial sector requires a multi-faceted approach, including robust encryption protocols, real-time transaction monitoring, and continuous threat intelligence integration. Regulatory compliance, such as the Payment Card Industry Data Security Standard (PCI DSS) and Basel III, further shapes the cybersecurity landscape for financial institutions, mandating tailored controls to ensure adherence to industry-specific standards.

Government agencies, entrusted with sensitive information and critical national functions, demand cybersecurity strategies that align with their unique roles and responsibilities. The complexity of governmental environments, often characterized by a mix of legacy and modern systems, necessitates a comprehensive approach. Tailored cybersecurity measures for government agencies involve not only safeguarding classified information but also addressing the broader spectrum of threats, including espionage, cyber warfare, and insider threats. Collaboration between government entities, information sharing, and the adoption of advanced technologies are integral components of an effective cybersecurity strategy in this context.

In the context of small and medium-sized enterprises (SMEs), which constitute a significant portion of the global business landscape, tailored cybersecurity solutions must be pragmatic, considering resource limitations. These organizations often lack the extensive budgets and dedicated cybersecurity teams found in larger enterprises. Therefore, solutions tailored to SMEs should focus on cost-effective measures, employee training, and the adoption of security frameworks tailored to smaller-scale operations. Cloud services and managed security solutions can provide viable options for SMEs looking to enhance their cybersecurity posture without overburdening limited resources.

The education sector, encompassing schools, colleges, and universities, faces unique challenges as it increasingly relies on digital platforms for teaching, learning, and administrative functions. Tailoring cybersecurity for educational environments requires a delicate balance between providing open access to information and protecting sensitive student and faculty data. User awareness programs, network segmentation, and the deployment of content filtering systems become crucial in mitigating cybersecurity risks in educational settings. As these institutions become targets for ransomware attacks and data breaches, tailored strategies should prioritize resilience, recovery, and continuous monitoring.

Manufacturing environments, where industrial control systems (ICS) play a pivotal role in production processes, require specialized cybersecurity measures. The convergence of information technology (IT) and operational technology (OT) introduces unique challenges, as attacks on ICS can have severe physical consequences. Tailoring cybersecurity for manufacturing involves implementing measures such as network segmentation, regular ICS security assessments, and the adoption of industry-specific standards like the Manufacturing Execution System (MES). Additionally, employee training on the potential impact of cyber-physical attacks is essential to fortify the human element in manufacturing cybersecurity.

The Internet of Things (IoT) landscape represents yet another environment demanding tailored cybersecurity solutions. The proliferation of connected devices, ranging from smart home gadgets to industrial sensors, introduces diverse entry points for cyber threats. Tailoring cybersecurity for IoT involves robust device authentication, encryption, and continuous monitoring of device behaviors. Standardization efforts, such as the development of security frameworks for IoT devices, contribute to creating a more secure ecosystem. As the IoT landscape expands, considerations for privacy, data integrity, and the potential consequences of compromised devices become paramount in tailoring effective cybersecurity measures.

In conclusion, tailoring cybersecurity to specific environments is an imperative response to the diverse and evolving nature of cyber threats across various sectors. Recognizing the unique challenges, risks, and compliance requirements within critical infrastructure, healthcare, finance, government, SMEs, education, manufacturing, and IoT environments allows for the development of strategies that are not only effective but also contextually relevant. The dynamic nature of the cybersecurity landscape requires continuous adaptation, collaboration, and innovation to safeguard the integrity, confidentiality, and availability of systems and data in an ever-changing digital world.

Proactive vs. Reactive Approaches

The distinction between proactive and reactive approaches forms the crux of strategic thinking across various domains, and in the realm of cybersecurity, this differentiation is fundamental to shaping the resilience and effectiveness of defense mechanisms. A proactive approach to cybersecurity involves anticipating and mitigating potential threats before they materialize, focusing on preventive measures and strategic planning to fortify systems against a broad spectrum of attacks. It encompasses a mindset that seeks to stay ahead of evolving threats, emphasizing continuous improvement, and learning from past incidents to enhance overall security posture. By implementing robust security measures, conducting regular risk assessments, and staying informed about emerging threats, organizations can create a proactive cybersecurity stance that acts as a deterrent and reduces the likelihood of successful cyber-attacks.

In contrast, a reactive approach to cybersecurity involves responding to incidents after they have occurred, often triggered by the detection of a threat or the realization of a security breach. Reactive strategies center on incident response, damage control, and the restoration of systems and services following an attack. While reactive measures are essential for managing the aftermath of a security incident, relying solely on a reactive approach leaves organizations vulnerable to potential harm and might result in prolonged downtimes, data loss, or reputational damage. Reactive measures typically involve analyzing the root cause of an incident, isolating affected systems, and implementing remediation efforts to prevent a recurrence.

Proactive cybersecurity strategies are characterized by their emphasis on prevention, early detection, and continual improvement. This approach involves implementing a robust set of security controls, such as firewalls, intrusion detection systems, and regular security training for personnel. By staying abreast of the evolving threat landscape, organizations employing proactive measures can anticipate potential vulnerabilities, apply patches and updates promptly, and implement security best practices to thwart potential attacks. Proactive cybersecurity extends beyond technology, incorporating elements of risk management, policy development, and a culture of security awareness within the organization.

The proactive approach is not solely confined to technical aspects; it encompasses a holistic understanding of cybersecurity that integrates technology, people, and processes. Threat intelligence plays a pivotal role in proactive cybersecurity, providing organizations with real-time information about emerging threats, tactics, and vulnerabilities. By leveraging threat intelligence, organizations can proactively adjust their security measures to counteract evolving cyber threats. Regular penetration testing and vulnerability assessments are also integral components of a proactive approach, enabling organizations to identify and remediate weaknesses before malicious actors can exploit them.

The reactive approach, on the other hand, is characterized by its response-driven nature. Organizations adopting a reactive cybersecurity stance focus on containing and mitigating the impact of security incidents as they unfold. Incident response plans, which outline the steps to be taken in the event of a security breach, are critical components of a reactive strategy. These plans typically involve coordination between IT and security teams, communication protocols, and steps for analyzing the incident to prevent future occurrences. While reactive measures are essential for addressing incidents, they are inherently less effective at preventing breaches compared to proactive strategies.

The reactive approach often relies on tools and technologies such as Security Information and Event Management (SIEM) systems, which analyze and correlate security event data to identify potential threats. Incident response teams play a crucial role in reacting to and mitigating the impact of security incidents. These teams are responsible for investigating the nature of the incident, isolating affected systems, and implementing corrective actions to restore normal operations. Post-incident analysis, including a detailed examination of the attack vector and lessons learned, contributes to refining and enhancing reactive strategies over time.

One of the challenges with a purely reactive approach is the potential for delayed response times. Discovering a security incident after it has already caused damage can result in extended periods of system compromise and data exfiltration. Moreover, reactive measures may be less effective against sophisticated and stealthy attacks, such as advanced persistent threats (APTs), which can go undetected for extended periods. The reactive model, while essential for incident containment and recovery, underscores the need for organizations to supplement their cybersecurity posture with proactive measures to address vulnerabilities before they can be exploited.

In practice, organizations often adopt a combination of proactive and reactive strategies, recognizing the complementary nature of these approaches. A balanced cybersecurity strategy involves proactively implementing preventive measures, continually assessing and improving security controls, and fostering a culture of security awareness within the organization. Simultaneously, organizations must maintain robust incident response capabilities, conducting regular drills and exercises to ensure readiness in the face of a security incident. This hybrid approach acknowledges the inevitability of incidents while striving to minimize their impact through proactive risk management and response preparedness.

In conclusion, the proactive versus reactive cybersecurity debate underscores the importance of a holistic and adaptive approach to safeguarding digital assets. A purely proactive strategy, while essential for preventing many potential threats, may not account for the dynamic and persistent nature of cyber threats. Conversely, relying solely on reactive measures leaves organizations vulnerable to significant damage before effective response efforts can be initiated. The ideal cybersecurity posture involves a strategic combination of proactive and reactive elements, ensuring a comprehensive defense against a diverse and evolving threat landscape. Continuous learning, adaptation, and integration of both approaches form the foundation for a resilient cybersecurity stance in an increasingly complex and dynamic digital environment.

The Role of Risk Assessment in Cybersecurity Planning

The role of risk assessment in cybersecurity planning is pivotal, serving as the cornerstone of a comprehensive and effective strategy to safeguard digital assets. Risk assessment in the cybersecurity context involves the systematic evaluation of potential threats, vulnerabilities, and the impact of potential incidents on an organization's information systems. This process is fundamental to identifying, prioritizing, and managing risks in a way that aligns with the organization's business objectives and tolerance for risk. By conducting a thorough risk assessment, organizations gain insights into the complex interplay of factors that could compromise the confidentiality, integrity, or availability of their data and systems.

At the heart of risk assessment is the identification of assets and their values within the organization. This encompasses not only tangible assets like hardware and software but also intangible assets such as sensitive data, intellectual property, and the organization's reputation. Understanding the value of these assets is crucial in prioritizing efforts and resources toward protecting what matters most. Risk assessment also involves identifying potential threats, which can range from external cyber-attacks and insider threats to natural disasters and other operational disruptions. By comprehensively cataloging potential threats, organizations can tailor their cybersecurity measures to address specific risks in a targeted manner.

Vulnerability identification constitutes another integral component of risk assessment. This involves scrutinizing the organization's systems, networks, and processes to pinpoint weaknesses that could be exploited by malicious actors. These vulnerabilities may stem from outdated software, misconfigurations, or gaps in security controls. Through a meticulous examination of these weaknesses, organizations can proactively address and remediate vulnerabilities, reducing the likelihood of exploitation. The interplay between threats and vulnerabilities forms the basis for understanding the risk landscape, where the likelihood and potential impact of various risk scenarios are assessed.

Quantifying and qualifying risks are essential steps in risk assessment, providing a basis for informed decision-making. The likelihood of a risk event occurring and the potential impact it may have on the organization are analyzed, often using risk matrices or other frameworks. This quantitative and qualitative analysis allows organizations to prioritize risks based on their significance and allocate resources efficiently. Risks deemed high in likelihood and impact may require immediate attention, while those with lower risk profiles may be addressed through ongoing monitoring and periodic reassessment.

Risk assessment is not a one-time activity but rather an iterative process that adapts to the evolving threat landscape and changes within the organization. As technology advances and new cyber threats emerge, organizations must continuously reassess their risk posture to ensure their cybersecurity measures remain effective. Additionally, changes in business processes, acquisitions, or expansions can introduce new risks that must be evaluated and managed. Regular risk assessments enable organizations to stay proactive in adapting their cybersecurity strategies to the dynamic nature of the digital environment.

One significant outcome of risk assessment is the formulation of a risk management strategy. This strategy guides decision-making on how to treat, transfer, accept, or mitigate identified risks. Risk treatment options may involve implementing additional security controls, transferring certain risks through insurance, or accepting residual risks based on the organization's risk appetite. The risk management strategy becomes an integral part of the broader cybersecurity planning process, providing a roadmap for aligning security measures with the organization's overall risk tolerance and business goals.

Regulatory compliance adds another layer to the role of risk assessment in cybersecurity planning. Many industries and jurisdictions mandate specific cybersecurity requirements to protect sensitive information and ensure the continuity of critical services. Through risk assessment, organizations can identify the gaps between their current cybersecurity posture and regulatory requirements. This insight enables them to implement measures to achieve compliance, avoiding potential legal consequences and reputational damage. Moreover, aligning cybersecurity efforts with regulatory frameworks enhances overall risk management practices, fostering a more resilient and legally compliant organization.

Risk assessment is also integral to incident response planning. By understanding potential risks and their impacts, organizations can develop incident response plans tailored to specific scenarios. These plans outline the steps to be taken in the event of a security incident, facilitating a swift and coordinated response to mitigate damages. Regularly updated incident response plans, informed by ongoing risk assessments, contribute to organizational readiness and the ability to minimize the impact of cyber incidents.

Furthermore, risk assessment plays a crucial role in budgetary decision-making for cybersecurity initiatives. By identifying and prioritizing risks, organizations can allocate resources effectively, ensuring that investments in cybersecurity align with the most significant threats and vulnerabilities. This strategic allocation of resources maximizes the return on investment and optimizes the organization's ability to mitigate the most critical risks.

A holistic risk assessment process also recognizes the human element in cybersecurity. Employee awareness and training are essential components of risk assessment, as human error and malicious insider threats can significantly impact an organization's security posture. Educating employees about potential risks, phishing attacks, and security best practices contributes to a more resilient cybersecurity culture, reducing the likelihood of security incidents caused by human factors.

In conclusion, the role of risk assessment in cybersecurity planning is multifaceted and integral to the development of a robust and adaptive cybersecurity strategy. By systematically identifying assets, evaluating threats and vulnerabilities, and quantifying and qualifying risks, organizations gain a comprehensive understanding of their risk landscape. This knowledge informs decision-making processes, guides the formulation of risk management strategies, supports regulatory compliance efforts, and enhances incident response planning. A continuous and iterative risk assessment process enables organizations to adapt to the evolving cybersecurity landscape, allocate resources effectively, and foster a proactive cybersecurity stance that aligns with business objectives and risk tolerance. Ultimately, risk assessment is a cornerstone in building resilience against the dynamic and persistent threats in the digital age.

Chapter 2: Guardians of the Gateways: Understanding Network Security

2.1 Network Fundamentals

Network fundamentals form the foundational elements that underpin the vast and intricate world of computer networking. At its core, a network is an interconnected system of devices that communicate with each other, facilitating the exchange of data and information. The significance of network fundamentals is evident in their role as the building blocks upon which complex communication infrastructures, both local and global, are constructed. At a fundamental level, networks enable the sharing of resources, the transmission of data, and the seamless connectivity of devices, contributing to the functionality and efficiency of modern digital ecosystems.

The cornerstone of network fundamentals lies in understanding the various types of networks that exist. Local Area Networks (LANs) represent a common starting point, encompassing a limited geographic area such as a single building or a campus. LANs facilitate the efficient sharing of resources among connected devices, allowing for the seamless exchange of information. On a broader scale, Wide Area Networks (WANs) connect geographically dispersed LANs, spanning cities, countries, or even continents. WANs utilize various technologies, including private and public communication infrastructures, to establish connectivity between distant locations. The dichotomy between LANs and WANs illustrates the fundamental concept of scalability, wherein network architectures are tailored to meet specific geographical and operational requirements.

Protocols form the bedrock of network communication, defining the rules and conventions that govern how devices communicate and exchange data. Transmission Control Protocol/Internet Protocol (TCP/IP) is the predominant suite of protocols that underlies the functioning of the Internet and most modern networks. TCP/IP provides a standardized framework for data transmission, encompassing protocols such as Transmission Control Protocol (TCP) for reliable, connection-oriented communication and Internet Protocol (IP) for addressing and routing packets across networks. Understanding the intricacies of TCP/IP is essential in comprehending the seamless communication that occurs across diverse devices and platforms.

The concept of addressing is fundamental in networking, where each device on a network is assigned a unique identifier to enable proper communication. Internet Protocol (IP) addresses, both IPv4 and the more recent IPv6, serve this critical function. IPv4, with its familiar dotted-decimal notation, assigns 32-bit addresses to devices, while IPv6, designed to accommodate the expanding number of connected devices, utilizes a 128-bit addressing scheme. Subnetting, a key aspect of addressing, involves dividing an IP network into smaller, more manageable sub-networks, enhancing the efficiency of address utilization and contributing to effective network management.

Network devices, ranging from computers and servers to routers and switches, play distinctive roles in facilitating communication. Routers operate at the network layer and are responsible for forwarding data between different networks, determining the optimal path for data transmission. Switches, operating at the data link layer, enable efficient communication within a single network by forwarding data based on Media Access Control (MAC) addresses. Hubs, another network device, operate at the physical layer, connecting multiple devices within a network but lacking the intelligence of switches in managing data traffic. Understanding the functionality of these devices is crucial in designing and maintaining efficient network architectures.

The concept of the OSI (Open Systems Interconnection) model further contributes to the understanding of network fundamentals by delineating the various layers involved in network communication. Comprising seven layers, from the physical layer dealing with hardware aspects to the application layer handling user interfaces, the OSI model provides a conceptual framework for comprehending the intricacies of network protocols and interactions. Each layer serves a specific purpose, and the model facilitates a systematic approach to troubleshooting and designing networks, emphasizing the importance of modular and interoperable solutions.

Network topologies, the physical or logical layout of interconnected devices, represent another fundamental aspect of networking. Common topologies include the star topology, where devices connect to a central hub or switch, and the bus topology, where devices share a single communication line. Ring, mesh, and tree topologies are additional variations, each offering unique advantages and trade-offs based on factors like scalability, fault tolerance, and ease of management. Network architects must consider these topological structures when designing networks to ensure they align with the specific requirements and constraints of the intended environment.

Network security stands as an inseparable component of network fundamentals, acknowledging the imperative to protect data and communication from unauthorized access and malicious activities. Encryption, firewalls, and Virtual Private Networks (VPNs) are essential tools in securing networks. Encryption safeguards data by encoding it in a manner that is only decipherable with the appropriate key. Firewalls, acting as barriers between a private network and external threats, filter incoming and outgoing traffic based on predefined security rules. VPNs extend secure communication over public networks, enabling users to access resources remotely while maintaining confidentiality and integrity.

Wireless networking represents a transformative dimension of network fundamentals, liberating devices from physical constraints and enhancing mobility. Wi-Fi, based on IEEE 802.11 standards, enables wireless communication, allowing devices to connect to networks without physical cables. The proliferation of wireless technologies has revolutionized how individuals access information and communicate, shaping the evolution of the modern digital landscape. However, wireless networking introduces unique security considerations, emphasizing the importance of robust authentication mechanisms, encryption protocols, and vigilant monitoring to mitigate potential risks.

Quality of Service (QoS) is a critical consideration in network fundamentals, particularly in environments where the timely and reliable delivery of data is paramount. QoS mechanisms prioritize certain types of traffic, ensuring that real-time applications such as voice and video receive the necessary bandwidth and low latency for optimal performance. This becomes particularly relevant in scenarios where networks carry a mix of data types, and efficient QoS implementations contribute to a seamless user experience.

The evolution of networking technologies, from traditional wired infrastructures to the advent of cloud computing and Software-Defined Networking (SDN), underscores the dynamic nature of network fundamentals. Cloud computing introduces the concept of virtualization, enabling the flexible allocation of resources and services across a network. SDN centralizes network control, providing a programmable and dynamic approach to network management. Both cloud computing and SDN exemplify the ongoing innovation in networking, necessitating a continual commitment to learning and adaptation to stay abreast of emerging technologies.

In conclusion, network fundamentals constitute the bedrock of computer networking, encompassing principles that facilitate the seamless communication and connectivity of devices. From the foundational understanding of network types, protocols, and addressing to the role of devices, topologies, and security mechanisms, the fundamentals provide a comprehensive framework for designing, implementing, and maintaining robust networks. As technology continues to evolve, the continued relevance of network fundamentals underscores their enduring importance in shaping the interconnected and dynamic digital world. The journey through network fundamentals is a continuous exploration, reflecting the perpetual quest for efficient, secure, and scalable networking solutions in an ever-evolving technological landscape.

OSI Model and Networking Protocols

The OSI (Open Systems Interconnection) model, a conceptual framework developed by the International Organization for Standardization (ISO), serves as a comprehensive guide for understanding the intricacies of network communication. Comprising seven layers, each designated to specific functions, the OSI model facilitates a systematic approach to comprehending the complexities of networking protocols and their interactions. At the foundational level is the Physical Layer, responsible for transmitting raw binary data over the physical medium, defining characteristics such as voltage levels, cable types, and data rates. This layer establishes the fundamental connection between devices but does not address concerns related to data formatting or error correction.

Above the Physical Layer lies the Data Link Layer, responsible for framing data into frames and providing mechanisms for error detection and correction within the frames. The Data Link Layer is further divided into the Logical Link Control (LLC) sub-layer, managing flow control and error checking, and the Media Access Control (MAC) sub-layer, responsible for addressing devices on the network using unique identifiers known as MAC addresses. Ethernet, a widely used protocol for local area networks (LANs), operates within the Data Link Layer, defining the framing and addressing standards for data transmission.

The Network Layer, the third layer of the OSI model, introduces the concept of logical addressing, assigning unique IP addresses to devices for identification and routing purposes. Internet Protocol (IP), a core networking protocol, operates within this layer, enabling the routing of data packets between devices across different networks. The Network Layer establishes the fundamental framework for interconnecting disparate networks, playing a pivotal role in enabling global communication.

Sitting atop the Network Layer is the Transport Layer, responsible for end-to-end communication, error recovery, and flow control. Transmission Control Protocol (TCP) and User Datagram Protocol (UDP) are two prominent protocols operating within this layer. TCP ensures reliable, connection-oriented communication by establishing and maintaining a connection between communicating devices, while UDP offers a connectionless, lightweight alternative suitable for real-time applications where speed takes precedence over reliability.

Moving further up the OSI model brings us to the Session Layer, which manages sessions or connections between applications on different devices. This layer facilitates dialog control, allowing devices to establish, maintain, and terminate communication sessions. NetBIOS (Network Basic Input/Output System) is an example of a session layer protocol commonly used in Windows environments, facilitating the communication between applications on different devices.

The Presentation Layer addresses the format and syntax of data exchanged between applications, ensuring that information sent from one system can be properly interpreted by the receiving system. This layer handles tasks such as data compression, encryption, and character set conversions. The Secure Sockets Layer (SSL) and its successor, Transport Layer Security (TLS), operate within the Presentation Layer, providing encryption and secure communication for web-based applications.

At the top of the OSI model is the Application Layer, which directly interacts with end-user applications and provides network services to those applications. Protocols such as Hypertext Transfer Protocol (HTTP), File Transfer Protocol (FTP), and Simple Mail Transfer Protocol (SMTP) operate within the Application Layer, defining the rules for communication between software applications and facilitating tasks like web browsing, file transfers, and email communication.

Understanding the OSI model is essential for grasping the layered architecture that governs network communication. Each layer serves a distinct purpose, and protocols within each layer contribute to the seamless functionality of interconnected devices in a network. The modular design of the OSI model enables the development of interoperable and standardized network protocols, fostering a structured approach to networking that transcends specific hardware or software implementations.

Networking protocols, integral to the OSI model, embody the rules and conventions that govern communication between devices on a network. TCP/IP, despite not aligning precisely with the OSI model, stands as the preeminent suite of networking protocols shaping the functioning of the modern internet. TCP/IP includes protocols such as IP, TCP, UDP, and Internet Control Message Protocol (ICMP), collectively providing the foundation for global communication. IP, in particular, plays a central role in addressing and routing data packets across networks, enabling the reliable and scalable exchange of information.

Dynamic Host Configuration Protocol (DHCP) and Domain Name System (DNS) are essential protocols within the TCP/IP suite. DHCP automates the assignment of IP addresses to devices on a network, streamlining network administration by eliminating the need for manual IP address configuration. DNS, on the other hand, translates human-readable domain names into IP addresses, facilitating the user-friendly access to websites and resources on the internet.

Another crucial component of the TCP/IP suite is the Border Gateway Protocol (BGP), operating at the Network Layer. BGP is instrumental in determining the most efficient path for data to traverse the internet, playing a pivotal role in global routing and ensuring the reliable exchange of data across diverse networks.

Transmission Control Protocol (TCP) and User Datagram Protocol (UDP), both operating within the Transport Layer, represent divergent approaches to data transmission. TCP provides reliable, connection-oriented communication, incorporating mechanisms for error detection, retransmission, and flow control to ensure the accurate and orderly delivery of data. In contrast, UDP offers a connectionless, lightweight alternative suitable for applications where speed is paramount, sacrificing reliability for reduced latency.

Within the Application Layer, the Hypertext Transfer Protocol (HTTP) governs the communication between web browsers and servers, defining the rules for accessing and displaying web content. As the foundation for the World Wide Web, HTTP facilitates the retrieval and presentation of text, images, and multimedia elements, forming the backbone of internet browsing.

The File Transfer Protocol (FTP) is another Application Layer protocol, focusing on the efficient transfer of files between devices on a network. FTP supports both the upload and download of files, providing a standardized method for users to share and exchange data. Secure alternatives, such as FTP Secure (FTPS) and Secure File Transfer Protocol (SFTP), enhance the security of file transfers by incorporating encryption mechanisms.

Simple Mail Transfer Protocol (SMTP), operating within the Application Layer, serves as the protocol for sending emails over a network. SMTP defines the rules for the transmission of email messages, allowing for the seamless exchange of electronic communication across different email servers. Post Office Protocol version 3 (POP3) and Internet Message Access Protocol (IMAP) are complementary protocols that facilitate the retrieval of emails from servers, providing users with different options for managing their email accounts.

As networks evolve, additional protocols and technologies continue to shape the landscape. The emergence of IPv6 addresses the limitations of IPv4, providing an expanded address space to accommodate the growing number of connected devices. The advent of software-defined networking (SDN) introduces programmability and flexibility into network management, enabling centralized control and dynamic adaptation to changing network conditions.

In conclusion, the OSI model and networking protocols together form the bedrock of modern communication infrastructures. The layered architecture of the OSI model provides a conceptual framework for understanding the distinct functions and interactions of networking protocols. The TCP/IP suite, with its foundational protocols such as IP, TCP, and UDP, serves as the linchpin of global communication, underpinning the internet and interconnected networks. As technology advances, the ongoing evolution of networking protocols continues to shape the way devices communicate, fostering innovation, efficiency, and the seamless exchange of information in an interconnected world.

Types of Networks: LAN, WAN, and Beyond

In the vast landscape of computer networking, the classification of networks into distinct types serves as a fundamental framework for understanding their scope, scale, and intended purpose. At the foundational level are Local Area Networks (LANs), cohesive networks typically confined within a limited geographic area such as a single building, a campus, or even a specific floor within an office building. LANs facilitate the seamless communication and resource sharing among connected devices, fostering an environment where computers, printers, servers, and other devices can collaborate efficiently. The proximity of devices within a LAN enables high-speed data transfer, low latency, and simplified administration, making LANs an ideal choice for environments where devices are in close physical proximity.

Expanding beyond the confines of a local area, Wide Area Networks (WANs) interconnect LANs across greater distances, spanning cities, countries, or even continents. WANs leverage various communication technologies, including private leased lines, public internet infrastructure, and satellite links, to establish connectivity between geographically dispersed LANs. The primary goal of WANs is to enable seamless communication and resource sharing across vast distances, overcoming the limitations of physical proximity. This global interconnectivity forms the backbone of modern communication, underpinning the ability to transmit data, access resources, and collaborate on a global scale.

Metropolitan Area Networks (MANs) occupy an intermediate position between LANs and WANs, covering a larger geographical area than a typical LAN but not extending to the vast scale of a WAN. MANs are designed to cater to the connectivity needs of a city or a metropolitan region, providing high-speed data transfer and communication services to entities within the defined geographical boundaries. MANs often utilize technologies such as fiber-optic cables and wireless connections to create a network infrastructure that bridges the gap between local and wide area networks, offering a balance between scalability and efficient data transmission.

In addition to these traditional network types, advancements in technology and the evolving needs of organizations have given rise to specialized networks tailored for specific purposes. Campus Area Networks (CANs) represent networks that interconnect multiple LANs within a university campus, corporate campus, or any large-scale facility where distinct LANs need to communicate. CANs aim to provide seamless connectivity and resource sharing within the defined campus boundaries, optimizing communication and collaboration among different departments or organizational units.

Personal Area Networks (PANs) take a more localized approach, focusing on the connectivity needs of individual users and their personal devices. PANs are often characterized by short-range wireless technologies such as Bluetooth, enabling the establishment of connections between personal devices like smartphones, laptops, and wearable gadgets. The purpose of PANs is to facilitate communication and data transfer within the immediate vicinity of an individual, allowing for the creation of ad-hoc networks that serve the user's specific requirements.

The advent of the Internet of Things (IoT) has given rise to a proliferation of devices connected to the internet, contributing to the formation of specialized networks designed to accommodate the unique demands of IoT deployments. IoT Networks facilitate communication among a multitude of devices, ranging from smart home appliances and industrial sensors to wearable devices and connected vehicles. These networks prioritize scalability, low power consumption, and efficient handling of a massive number of devices, addressing the challenges posed by the interconnected nature of the IoT ecosystem.

In the realm of enterprise networking, Virtual Local Area Networks (VLANs) offer a way to segment a physical LAN into multiple logical networks, providing enhanced security, isolation, and efficient resource utilization. VLANs enable organizations to create distinct broadcast domains within a single physical infrastructure, optimizing network management and addressing the need for segmentation in large-scale networks.

Beyond the conventional categorizations of networks based on geographical scope, there exists a classification based on ownership and access permissions. Public Networks, accessible to the general public, form the foundation of the global internet, providing open access to information, services, and resources. Private Networks, on the other hand, are restricted to specific users or organizations, establishing a closed environment where access is limited to authorized entities. The demarcation between public and private networks is crucial in defining the accessibility, security, and governance of network resources.

The evolution of network types also intersects with the emergence of cloud computing, leading to the development of Cloud Networks. These networks enable seamless connectivity and communication between devices and services hosted in cloud environments. Cloud Networks leverage the underlying infrastructure of cloud service providers to create scalable, flexible, and distributed network architectures that cater to the dynamic requirements of modern computing.

In the context of telecommunications, Cellular Networks represent a specialized category designed to facilitate mobile communication. Cellular networks rely on a grid of base stations to provide wireless coverage over defined geographical areas, allowing mobile devices to connect to the network while moving. Different generations of cellular networks, from 2G to the latest 5G, reflect the ongoing advancements in mobile communication technologies, offering increased data speeds, lower latency, and improved network reliability.

Satellite Networks represent yet another facet of network diversity, leveraging satellite communication technology to establish connectivity over vast and remote areas where traditional terrestrial networks may be impractical. Satellite networks find applications in areas such as global communication, weather monitoring, and remote sensing, extending network coverage to regions beyond the reach of conventional network infrastructures.

As networks continue to evolve, the boundaries between these categories become increasingly fluid, with hybrid and interconnected networks becoming the norm. Hybrid Networks integrate multiple types of networks, combining the strengths of different architectures to create versatile and adaptive communication infrastructures. Interconnected Networks bridge the gaps between disparate network types, fostering seamless communication and resource sharing across diverse environments.

In conclusion, the classification of networks into LANs, WANs, and beyond provides a structured framework for understanding the diverse landscape of computer networking. From the localized efficiency of LANs to the expansive global connectivity enabled by WANs, and the specialized applications of CANs, PANs, IoT Networks, and others, each network type serves a specific purpose tailored to the unique requirements of its intended environment. As technology advances and networking paradigms evolve, the interconnected nature of these network types reflects the dynamic and adaptive character of modern communication infrastructures. The journey from LANs to WANs and beyond exemplifies the continual quest to create versatile, efficient, and interconnected networks that empower the seamless flow of information in an ever-evolving digital world.

2.2 Threats to Network Security
Network-Based Attacks: DDoS, Man-in-the-Middle, etc.

Network-based attacks represent a pervasive and ever-evolving threat landscape in the realm of cybersecurity, encompassing a myriad of tactics employed by malicious actors to compromise the confidentiality, integrity, and availability of networked systems. One prominent form of attack is the Distributed Denial of Service (DDoS) assault, wherein a network or service is overwhelmed by a flood of traffic originating from multiple sources. The sheer volume of incoming requests exhausts the target's resources, rendering it inaccessible to legitimate users. DDoS attacks leverage botnets, networks of compromised devices controlled by a single entity, to orchestrate the barrage of traffic. Mitigation strategies involve deploying specialized DDoS protection services, such as traffic filtering and rate limiting, to absorb or redirect malicious traffic and ensure uninterrupted service availability.

The Man-in-the-Middle (MitM) attack is another insidious tactic, where an unauthorized third party intercepts and potentially alters communication between two parties without their knowledge. This attack vector often involves eavesdropping on sensitive information, such as login credentials or financial transactions. Attackers position themselves between the communicating entities, capturing and analyzing data passing through the compromised connection. Common techniques employed in MitM attacks include ARP spoofing, DNS spoofing, and SSL stripping. To thwart MitM attacks, encryption protocols like Transport Layer Security (TLS) and secure communication channels, combined with robust network monitoring, become imperative.

Phishing attacks, a prevalent form of social engineering, leverage deceptive tactics to manipulate individuals into divulging sensitive information such as login credentials, financial details, or personal information. Phishing often occurs through seemingly legitimate emails, messages, or websites that impersonate trustworthy entities. Once the victim unwittingly provides the requested information, the attacker gains unauthorized access. Network-based phishing defenses include email filtering to detect and quarantine phishing attempts, user awareness training, and multi-factor authentication to add an extra layer of security beyond passwords.

A related threat is Spear Phishing, a more targeted form of phishing wherein attackers tailor their messages to specific individuals or organizations. This approach relies on thorough research to craft convincing and personalized messages that increase the likelihood of success. By exploiting familiarity and trust, spear phishing aims to trick recipients into divulging sensitive information or executing malicious actions. Combating spear phishing necessitates a combination of advanced email filtering, user education, and vigilant monitoring for suspicious activities.

Ransomware attacks have become a pervasive and financially motivated menace, targeting both individuals and organizations. In a typical ransomware attack, malicious software encrypts the victim's files or entire systems, rendering them inaccessible. Attackers then demand a ransom, often payable in cryptocurrency, in exchange for providing the decryption key. Ransomware can spread through networked systems, amplifying its impact. Effective defense strategies involve regular data backups, robust endpoint protection, network segmentation, and user education to prevent inadvertent engagement with malicious content.

Cross-Site Scripting (XSS) attacks exploit vulnerabilities in web applications to inject malicious scripts into web pages viewed by other users. These scripts execute within the context of a user's browser, allowing attackers to steal sensitive information, manipulate web content, or initiate other malicious actions. Stored XSS involves injecting the malicious script into a target website, affecting all users who access the compromised page. Reflected XSS involves tricking users into clicking on a crafted link containing the malicious script. Mitigation strategies involve input validation, output encoding, and secure coding practices to fortify web applications against XSS vulnerabilities.

SQL Injection attacks target the databases underlying web applications by injecting malicious SQL queries through user input fields. Successful SQL injection can lead to unauthorized access, manipulation, or extraction of sensitive data stored in the database. Attackers exploit poorly sanitized user inputs, injecting malicious SQL code that the application unknowingly executes. Mitigation involves using parameterized queries, input validation, and least privilege principles to minimize the attack surface and safeguard against SQL injection vulnerabilities.

Network-based attacks also extend to the exploitation of unpatched vulnerabilities in software or operating systems through techniques such as Zero-Day Exploits. These attacks capitalize on security flaws for which no patches or mitigations are available at the time of discovery. Cybercriminals exploit the window of vulnerability, launching attacks before developers can release and users can apply patches. Robust patch management practices, regular vulnerability assessments, and intrusion detection systems contribute to proactive defense against Zero-Day Exploits.

Infiltrating networks through unauthorized access points is a tactic employed in Wireless Attacks. Attackers exploit weak or misconfigured wireless security protocols to gain unauthorized access to a network. Common wireless attacks include the establishment of rogue access points, packet sniffing, and the exploitation of vulnerabilities in wireless encryption protocols. Defense mechanisms involve the use of strong encryption, regularly updating wireless security protocols, monitoring for unauthorized access points, and employing intrusion detection systems for wireless network protection.

Another sophisticated attack vector is Advanced Persistent Threats (APTs), characterized by prolonged and targeted cyber-espionage campaigns. APTs involve stealthy infiltration into a network, often remaining undetected for extended periods to exfiltrate sensitive data. Attackers employ advanced techniques, including custom malware, social engineering, and lateral movement within the network to avoid detection. Defending against APTs requires a multifaceted approach, combining threat intelligence, network segmentation, user education, and advanced endpoint protection to detect and mitigate the threat.

DNS Spoofing, also known as DNS Cache Poisoning, exploits vulnerabilities in the Domain Name System (DNS) to redirect users to malicious websites. By corrupting the DNS cache with false information, attackers can divert legitimate traffic to fraudulent websites, enabling phishing, data theft, or the dissemination of malware. Implementing secure DNS configurations, employing DNS Security Extensions (DNSSEC), and regularly monitoring DNS traffic can help prevent and detect DNS spoofing attacks.

The Threat of Internet of Things (IoT) Exploitation adds a layer of complexity to network security, given the proliferation of connected devices with varying levels of security. Insecure IoT devices can serve as entry points for attackers to infiltrate networks, leading to potential data breaches or disruption of services. Robust security practices for IoT environments involve strong authentication mechanisms, regular firmware updates, network segmentation, and monitoring for anomalous device behavior.

Network Sniffing, a technique employed by both ethical network administrators and malicious actors, involves capturing and analyzing network traffic to glean information about the data being transmitted. While legitimate network sniffing aids in troubleshooting and network optimization, malicious network sniffing can lead to the unauthorized interception of sensitive information, including passwords and other confidential data. Encryption, secure protocols, and network monitoring are essential countermeasures to mitigate the risks associated with network sniffing.

Intrusion attempts are prevalent in the form of Brute Force Attacks, wherein attackers systematically attempt to gain unauthorized access by trying various combinations of usernames and passwords. These attacks exploit weak or easily guessable credentials, emphasizing the importance of enforcing strong password policies, implementing account lockout mechanisms, and employing multi-factor authentication to thwart brute force attempts.

Social Engineering attacks exploit human psychology to manipulate individuals into divulging sensitive information or performing actions that compromise security. Techniques include pretexting, phishing, and baiting, with attackers often posing as trusted entities to deceive targets. User education, awareness training, and implementing strict access controls are critical components in mitigating the risk of social engineering attacks.

The landscape of network-based attacks is dynamic and continuously evolving, necessitating a comprehensive and adaptive approach to cybersecurity. As technologies advance, so do the tactics employed by malicious actors, underscoring the importance of proactive defenses, continuous monitoring, and a holistic security posture to safeguard against the multifaceted threats posed to networked systems. The integration of advanced threat intelligence, behavioral analysis, and collaborative efforts within the cybersecurity community are essential elements in staying ahead of the ever-evolving threat landscape.

Vulnerabilities in Network Infrastructure

Vulnerabilities in network infrastructure represent critical points of exposure that can be exploited by malicious actors to compromise the confidentiality, integrity, and availability of systems and data. One fundamental vulnerability lies in the software and firmware that power networking devices, including routers, switches, and firewalls. Software vulnerabilities, often arising from coding errors or design flaws, can be exploited by attackers to gain unauthorized access, execute arbitrary code, or perform denial-of-service attacks. The complexity of networking software, coupled with the frequent release of patches and updates, poses a challenge for organizations to maintain a secure and up-to-date infrastructure. Failure to promptly address these vulnerabilities leaves networks susceptible to exploitation.

Hardware vulnerabilities in network infrastructure encompass weaknesses in the physical components of networking devices. These vulnerabilities may stem from manufacturing defects, compromised supply chains, or the presence of hidden backdoors. Adversaries can exploit hardware vulnerabilities to compromise the overall security of a network, potentially leading to unauthorized access or the interception of sensitive data. Securing network hardware requires rigorous quality assurance processes, supply chain integrity measures, and regular assessments to identify and mitigate potential vulnerabilities in the physical infrastructure.

Default configurations and weak security settings in networking devices introduce vulnerabilities that attackers often exploit. Manufacturers often ship devices with default settings that prioritize ease of deployment over security. Failing to modify default credentials, enable encryption, or configure proper access controls leaves networks susceptible to unauthorized access and manipulation. Robust security practices necessitate the customization of default settings, the implementation of strong authentication mechanisms, and the adherence to security best practices to mitigate the risk of exploitation.

Inadequate access controls within network infrastructure constitute a significant vulnerability that can be exploited by attackers to gain unauthorized access or escalate privileges. Weak password policies, improperly configured user permissions, and the absence of multifactor authentication mechanisms create openings for adversaries to compromise network security. Implementing strong access controls, enforcing the principle of least privilege, and regularly auditing user permissions are essential measures to mitigate the risks associated with access control vulnerabilities.

The pervasive use of encryption in network communication introduces a vulnerability when improperly configured or when leveraging weak cryptographic algorithms. Misconfigurations in encryption protocols, such as the use of outdated algorithms or insufficient key lengths, can expose sensitive data to eavesdropping and decryption by attackers. To address encryption vulnerabilities, organizations must ensure the proper configuration of encryption protocols, employ strong cryptographic algorithms, and stay abreast of advancements in encryption standards to enhance the security of data in transit.

Network devices often communicate using various protocols, and vulnerabilities within these protocols can be exploited by attackers to manipulate or intercept data. For instance, vulnerabilities in the Border Gateway Protocol (BGP) can lead to route hijacking, enabling attackers to redirect traffic to malicious destinations. Similarly, vulnerabilities in the Domain Name System (DNS) can result in DNS spoofing attacks, compromising the integrity of domain resolution. Regularly updating and patching networking protocols, implementing security mechanisms like DNS Security Extensions (DNSSEC), and monitoring for anomalous protocol behavior are crucial in mitigating protocol-related vulnerabilities.

The proliferation of Internet of Things (IoT) devices within network infrastructures introduces a new dimension of vulnerability. Insecure IoT devices with weak security controls can serve as entry points for attackers to compromise network integrity. Manufacturers often prioritize functionality and ease of use over security in IoT device design, leaving them susceptible to exploitation. Securing IoT devices involves implementing strong authentication, ensuring regular firmware updates, and segregating IoT networks from critical infrastructure to limit potential risks.

Software-defined networking (SDN) and cloud-based infrastructures, while offering enhanced flexibility and scalability, introduce their own set of vulnerabilities. In SDN environments, the centralized control plane becomes a critical point of vulnerability, and an attacker gaining control over this plane can manipulate network behavior. Cloud-based infrastructures are susceptible to misconfigurations, unauthorized access to cloud consoles, and insecure application programming interfaces (APIs). To mitigate vulnerabilities in SDN and cloud environments, organizations must implement robust security controls, conduct regular audits, and adhere to best practices for cloud security.

Social engineering attacks, such as phishing and spear phishing, exploit human vulnerabilities within an organization to gain unauthorized access to network infrastructure. Through deceptive tactics, attackers trick individuals into revealing sensitive information, such as login credentials, or clicking on malicious links. Employee awareness and training programs, coupled with the implementation of email filtering solutions, play a critical role in mitigating the risks associated with social engineering attacks.

The interconnectivity of networked systems also introduces vulnerabilities related to third-party dependencies. The use of third-party software, libraries, or services may inadvertently expose networks to vulnerabilities present in these external components. Regularly assessing and monitoring third-party dependencies, staying informed about security updates and patches, and establishing clear security requirements in vendor contracts are essential measures to mitigate the risks associated with third-party vulnerabilities.

In summary, vulnerabilities in network infrastructure manifest across various dimensions, including software, hardware, configurations, access controls, encryption, protocols, IoT devices, emerging technologies, social engineering, and third-party dependencies. A comprehensive and proactive approach to network security involves regular vulnerability assessments, prompt patch management, adherence to security best practices, user education, and ongoing monitoring to detect and remediate potential vulnerabilities. The dynamic nature of the cybersecurity landscape necessitates continuous vigilance and adaptation to stay ahead of emerging threats and safeguard the integrity of networked systems.

2.3 Firewalls and Intrusion Detection Systems

Role of Firewalls in Network Security

Firewalls play a pivotal role in the complex and dynamic landscape of network security, serving as a crucial line of defense against unauthorized access, cyber threats, and the potential compromise of sensitive information within networked environments. At its core, a firewall is a network security device or software that monitors and controls incoming and outgoing network traffic based on predetermined security rules. These rules act as a barrier, allowing or blocking data packets based on specified criteria, effectively acting as a gatekeeper that filters and regulates the flow of traffic between networks.

One fundamental function of firewalls is to establish a perimeter defense, defining a barrier between an organization's internal network and the external world, typically the internet. This demarcation is essential in preventing unauthorized access to sensitive internal resources, systems, and data. By examining the characteristics of incoming and outgoing traffic, firewalls can enforce policies that dictate which communication is permitted and which is denied, thereby creating a secure boundary that safeguards against external threats.

Firewalls operate at different layers of the OSI (Open Systems Interconnection) model, providing a multi-layered defense mechanism. At the network layer, traditional firewalls examine packet headers, source and destination IP addresses, and port numbers to make filtering decisions. This network layer filtering ensures that only legitimate traffic is allowed to traverse the network, enhancing overall security. Additionally, firewalls can operate at the transport layer, inspecting data payloads and enforcing rules based on the specifics of the data being transmitted. This granular inspection capability adds an extra layer of scrutiny, preventing the transmission of malicious payloads.

Stateful inspection is a crucial feature of modern firewalls, enabling them to monitor the state of active connections and make dynamic decisions based on the context of network traffic. By maintaining a state table that tracks the state of connections, firewalls can intelligently allow or block traffic, ensuring that only legitimate connections are established. This capability is particularly effective in preventing unauthorized access and blocking malicious activities, such as unauthorized data exfiltration or the initiation of malware-related communications.

Application-layer filtering represents an advanced firewall capability that scrutinizes network traffic at the application layer, allowing or blocking specific applications or services. This level of granularity enables organizations to enforce policies that govern the use of particular applications, ensuring compliance with security and regulatory requirements. Application-layer firewalls are adept at identifying and mitigating threats associated with specific protocols, applications, or services, contributing to a more comprehensive defense against diverse cyber threats.

Virtual Private Networks (VPNs) leverage firewalls to establish secure and encrypted communication channels over public networks. Firewalls play a critical role in VPN implementations by encrypting data traffic, authenticating users, and ensuring the secure transmission of information between geographically dispersed locations. By enforcing encryption standards and VPN protocols, firewalls contribute to the confidentiality and integrity of data as it traverses potentially insecure networks.

Intrusion Prevention Systems (IPS) are often integrated with firewalls to provide real-time threat detection and prevention capabilities. IPS functionality involves the analysis of network traffic for known and emerging threats, enabling the firewall to take proactive measures in blocking or mitigating potential attacks. This integration enhances the security posture of networks by actively identifying and thwarting malicious activities, reducing the window of vulnerability to cyber threats.

Firewalls also contribute to network segmentation, a crucial aspect of network security that involves dividing a network into distinct segments or zones. By creating separate network segments based on business functions, security requirements, or user roles, firewalls can enforce stringent access controls between these segments. This segmentation limits the lateral movement of attackers within a network, containing potential breaches and minimizing the impact of security incidents.

Logging and monitoring capabilities embedded in firewalls provide organizations with visibility into network activities, allowing for the detection of suspicious or anomalous behavior. Firewalls generate logs that capture information about permitted and denied traffic, potential security incidents, and rule violations. Security Information and Event Management (SIEM) solutions can aggregate and analyze firewall logs, offering organizations insights into potential security threats, compliance violations, and overall network health.

The role of firewalls extends beyond traditional network boundaries to address emerging challenges associated with mobile devices and remote workforces. Next-Generation Firewalls (NGFWs) integrate advanced features, such as deep packet inspection, intrusion prevention, and application-level filtering, to adapt to the evolving threat landscape. NGFWs enhance visibility and control over applications, users, and content, offering a more comprehensive defense against sophisticated cyber threats in a dynamic and interconnected digital environment.

Firewalls contribute significantly to the implementation of security policies within organizations. Through the creation and enforcement of access control policies, firewalls dictate which network services and resources users and systems can access. This role in policy enforcement aligns with broader security strategies, ensuring that organizations adhere to regulatory requirements, industry best practices, and internal security policies.

Firewalls also play a vital role in safeguarding against Distributed Denial of Service (DDoS) attacks, a prevalent threat in the cybersecurity landscape. By implementing DDoS mitigation techniques, firewalls can detect and mitigate the impact of volumetric attacks, ensuring that network resources remain available and accessible even in the face of concerted efforts to overwhelm them with traffic.

As organizations increasingly adopt cloud computing and hybrid infrastructure models, cloud-based firewalls become essential components of the overall security strategy. Cloud firewalls extend the protective perimeter to encompass cloud-based resources, ensuring that security policies are consistently applied across on-premises and cloud environments. This cohesive approach enhances security and compliance in the context of evolving IT architectures.

In conclusion, firewalls are foundational elements in network security, providing a critical defense layer against a diverse range of cyber threats. From establishing perimeter defenses and enforcing access control policies to monitoring network activities and thwarting emerging threats, firewalls play a multifaceted role in securing the integrity, confidentiality, and availability of networked systems. As organizations navigate the complexities of an ever-evolving threat landscape, firewalls remain essential components of a robust and adaptive cybersecurity strategy, contributing to the resilience and security of modern digital infrastructures.

Implementing Effective Intrusion Detection and Prevention

Implementing effective intrusion detection and prevention is a cornerstone of modern cybersecurity strategies, crucial for safeguarding networks, systems, and sensitive data from a multitude of evolving cyber threats. Intrusion detection and prevention systems (IDPS) are integral components designed to identify and respond to unauthorized and malicious activities within an information system. The implementation of these systems involves a comprehensive and adaptive approach, encompassing technologies, processes, and human expertise to create a robust defense against cyber threats.

One fundamental aspect of effective intrusion detection and prevention is understanding the distinctive roles each system plays in fortifying cybersecurity defenses. Intrusion Detection Systems (IDS) act as vigilant sentinels, continuously monitoring network traffic and system activities for signs of anomalous behavior or known attack patterns. IDS are designed to raise alerts or notifications when suspicious activities are detected, providing security teams with valuable insights into potential threats. In contrast, Intrusion Prevention Systems (IPS) take a more proactive stance by not only detecting but also actively blocking or mitigating identified threats in real-time. This dynamic response capability enhances the overall security posture, preventing potential security incidents from escalating.

The deployment of intrusion detection and prevention systems involves careful consideration of network architecture, traffic patterns, and potential threat vectors. Network-based IDS are strategically placed at critical points within the network, such as perimeter gateways and internal segments, to monitor incoming and outgoing traffic. Host-based IDS focus on individual systems, analyzing logs, file integrity, and system calls to detect anomalous activities at the host level. The combination of both network-based and host-based IDS provides a comprehensive and layered defense, ensuring that potential threats are identified across different levels of the network infrastructure.

Signature-based detection is a foundational technique employed by intrusion detection and prevention systems, involving the comparison of observed network or system activity against a predefined database of known attack signatures. This approach is effective in identifying well-known and widely documented threats, making it a valuable tool in the cybersecurity arsenal. However, signature-based detection has limitations, particularly in detecting novel or previously unseen threats that lack identifiable patterns. To address this gap, anomaly-based detection methods analyze baseline network or system behavior, triggering alerts when deviations from the established norm are detected. Anomaly-based detection enhances the system's ability to identify previously unknown threats or sophisticated attacks that do not conform to known patterns.

Behavioral analysis is an advanced approach to intrusion detection and prevention, leveraging machine learning and artificial intelligence algorithms to model and predict normal and abnormal behaviors. By continuously learning and adapting to evolving threats, behavioral analysis enhances the system's ability to detect subtle deviations indicative of potential security incidents. This proactive approach enables the identification of zero-day exploits and previously unknown attack vectors, contributing to a more resilient defense against emerging threats.

The integration of threat intelligence feeds into intrusion detection and prevention systems further enhances their efficacy. Threat intelligence provides real-time information about current cyber threats, including indicators of compromise, attack signatures, and tactics, techniques, and procedures (TTPs) employed by threat actors. By incorporating threat intelligence into detection and prevention systems, organizations can stay ahead of evolving threats and proactively adapt their security measures to mitigate potential risks.

A key consideration in implementing effective intrusion detection and prevention is minimizing false positives and negatives. False positives occur when the system incorrectly identifies benign activities as malicious, leading to unnecessary alerts and potentially diverting resources from genuine threats. False negatives, on the other hand, occur when the system fails to detect actual security incidents, leaving the organization vulnerable to attacks. Striking the right balance between sensitivity and specificity in detection algorithms, fine-tuning rule sets, and regularly updating signatures and behavioral models are essential steps in reducing the incidence of false positives and negatives.

The responsiveness and agility of intrusion detection and prevention systems are critical in maintaining an effective security posture. Automated response capabilities, such as blocking malicious IP addresses, isolating compromised systems, or modifying firewall rules, enable rapid and targeted responses to identified threats. Automated responses not only reduce the time to mitigate potential risks but also alleviate the burden on security teams, allowing them to focus on more complex and strategic aspects of cybersecurity.

Continuous monitoring and auditing of intrusion detection and prevention systems contribute to their effectiveness over time. Regularly reviewing system logs, analyzing alerts, and conducting periodic assessments ensure that the systems remain aligned with organizational security policies and adapt to evolving threats. Ongoing training for security personnel is equally crucial, enabling them to stay abreast of the latest attack vectors, tactics, and vulnerabilities.

Network segmentation plays a significant role in enhancing the effectiveness of intrusion detection and prevention. By dividing the network into isolated segments based on business functions or security requirements, organizations can contain potential threats and limit lateral movement within the network. This segmentation reduces the attack surface, making it more challenging for adversaries to traverse the network and compromise critical assets.

Collaboration and information sharing within the cybersecurity community are essential elements in the implementation of effective intrusion detection and prevention. Sharing threat intelligence, indicators of compromise, and best practices among organizations, industry groups, and cybersecurity vendors contribute to a collective defense against common threats. Participating in Information Sharing and Analysis Centers (ISACs) and engaging with the broader cybersecurity community fosters a collaborative approach to identifying and mitigating emerging threats.

The role of human expertise in intrusion detection and prevention cannot be overstated. Security analysts, equipped with a deep understanding of network protocols, system architectures, and threat landscapes, play a crucial role in analyzing alerts, investigating security incidents, and fine-tuning detection mechanisms. Human intuition, critical thinking, and contextual understanding complement the capabilities of automated systems, ensuring a holistic and adaptive defense against cyber threats.

In conclusion, implementing effective intrusion detection and prevention is a multifaceted endeavor that demands a combination of technology, processes, and human expertise. From the deployment of network and host-based systems to the utilization of signature-based, anomaly-based, and behavioral analysis techniques, organizations must adopt a layered and adaptive approach to secure their networked environments. Regular monitoring, threat intelligence integration, automated response capabilities, and collaboration within the cybersecurity community contribute to the resilience of intrusion detection and prevention systems. In an ever-evolving cybersecurity landscape, the proactive and strategic implementation of these systems is essential for organizations seeking to protect their assets and data from an array of sophisticated and persistent cyber threats.

2.4 Secure Network Design

Principles of Secure Network Architecture

The principles of secure network architecture constitute the foundational elements that organizations must adhere to in designing, implementing, and maintaining resilient and robust network infrastructures. Central to these principles is the concept of defense-in-depth, a strategy that involves the layering of multiple security measures to create a comprehensive and dynamic defense against a diverse range of cyber threats. By implementing a layered approach, organizations can mitigate the impact of potential security breaches and provide a resilient defense that extends beyond traditional perimeter protection.

One fundamental principle of secure network architecture is the concept of the least privilege, which advocates granting the minimum level of access or permissions necessary for users, systems, and processes to perform their designated functions. This principle helps minimize the attack surface, reducing the potential impact of security incidents and limiting the lateral movement of adversaries within the network. By adhering to the least privilege principle, organizations ensure that users only have access to the resources essential for their roles, thereby enhancing overall security.

Segmentation is another key principle that underscores the importance of dividing a network into isolated segments or zones based on business functions, security requirements, or user roles. Network segmentation limits the scope of potential security incidents, containing threats to specific segments and preventing the unrestricted lateral movement of attackers within the network. This principle aligns with the defense-in-depth strategy, creating barriers that impede the progress of adversaries and enhance the overall resilience of the network architecture.

Secure network architecture principles also emphasize the importance of thorough and continuous monitoring. Monitoring network activities, traffic patterns, and system behaviors enables organizations to detect and respond to security incidents in real-time. By implementing robust monitoring mechanisms, organizations can identify anomalous activities, potential vulnerabilities, and unauthorized access, allowing for timely intervention and mitigation. Continuous monitoring complements other security measures, providing insights into the evolving threat landscape and helping organizations adapt their defenses accordingly.

Encryption serves as a foundational principle in securing network communications and data. By employing strong encryption algorithms and protocols, organizations can protect sensitive information from eavesdropping, unauthorized access, and tampering during transit. End-to-end encryption ensures the confidentiality and integrity of data, especially in scenarios where data traverses untrusted networks or cloud environments. Encryption principles extend beyond data in transit to encompass data at rest, safeguarding information stored on devices, servers, and databases from unauthorized access.

Authentication and access control principles play a pivotal role in securing network architecture by verifying the identities of users, devices, and systems attempting to access resources. Implementing multi-factor authentication adds an additional layer of security by requiring users to provide multiple forms of identification, such as passwords, tokens, or biometrics. Access control mechanisms enforce the principle of least privilege, ensuring that only authorized entities can access specific resources. By robustly implementing authentication and access controls, organizations fortify their network architecture against unauthorized access and potential compromise.

Regular and timely software patching and updates constitute a critical principle in secure network architecture. Keeping operating systems, applications, and network devices up-to-date with the latest security patches and fixes helps address known vulnerabilities and weaknesses. Timely patch management is essential in reducing the attack surface and preventing exploitation by malicious actors seeking to capitalize on unpatched software. Automated patching solutions, coupled with thorough testing processes, contribute to the efficient and effective implementation of this principle, ensuring that organizations can proactively address security vulnerabilities.

The concept of network visibility is integral to secure network architecture principles. Organizations must have comprehensive visibility into network traffic, user activities, and system behaviors to effectively detect and respond to security incidents. Network monitoring tools, intrusion detection systems, and Security Information and Event Management (SIEM) solutions provide the necessary visibility to identify patterns indicative of potential threats. A transparent and well-documented network infrastructure aids in understanding the normal baseline of network behavior, facilitating the identification of anomalous activities that may indicate security incidents.

Resilience and redundancy principles emphasize the importance of designing network architectures that can withstand disruptions and continue to operate even in the face of failures or attacks. Redundant systems, backup mechanisms, and failover capabilities ensure that critical network services remain available, reducing the impact of potential outages or incidents. By incorporating redundancy into the network design, organizations enhance the reliability and availability of their systems, promoting business continuity and minimizing the impact of unforeseen events.

Security awareness and training principles recognize the human element as a crucial factor in secure network architecture. Educating users and personnel about cybersecurity best practices, the risks associated with social engineering attacks, and the importance of maintaining strong password hygiene contributes to a security-aware culture. Regular training programs keep users informed about emerging threats and equip them with the knowledge and skills to recognize and respond to potential security incidents. Security awareness extends beyond end-users to include network administrators, developers, and other personnel involved in maintaining the security of the network infrastructure.

The principle of continuous improvement emphasizes the dynamic and evolving nature of cybersecurity. Secure network architecture is not a static concept but a dynamic process that requires ongoing evaluation, adaptation, and enhancement. Regular security assessments, penetration testing, and vulnerability assessments contribute to identifying weaknesses and areas for improvement. The feedback loop created by continuous improvement ensures that organizations can adapt their security measures to address emerging threats, technology advancements, and changes in the operational environment.

Collaboration and information sharing principles encourage organizations to participate in collaborative efforts within the cybersecurity community. Sharing threat intelligence, indicators of compromise, and best practices contribute to a collective defense against common threats. Collaboration with industry peers, Information Sharing and Analysis Centers (ISACs), and cybersecurity vendors fosters a community-driven approach to identifying and mitigating emerging threats. The principle of collaboration recognizes that cybersecurity is a shared responsibility, and collective efforts can result in a more resilient and adaptive defense against evolving cyber threats.

In conclusion, the principles of secure network architecture form the bedrock of effective cybersecurity strategies, guiding organizations in the design, implementation, and maintenance of resilient and robust network infrastructures. From defense-in-depth strategies and the principle of least privilege to network segmentation, encryption, and continuous improvement, these principles collectively contribute to a comprehensive and adaptive approach to securing networked environments. By aligning with these principles, organizations can fortify their defenses, minimize the impact of potential security incidents, and navigate the dynamic and evolving landscape of cybersecurity with resilience and confidence.

Best Practices for Securing Network Gateways

Securing network gateways is paramount in establishing a robust defense against a myriad of cyber threats that constantly evolve in sophistication and intensity. Network gateways serve as the entry and exit points for network traffic, making them critical components for enforcing security policies, filtering malicious content, and safeguarding sensitive data. A comprehensive set of best practices is essential for organizations to secure their network gateways effectively, creating a resilient barrier against potential security breaches.

One foundational best practice is the implementation of strong access controls and authentication mechanisms at network gateways. By enforcing the principle of least privilege, organizations can ensure that only authorized users and devices have access to specific network resources. Multi-factor authentication adds an extra layer of security, requiring users to provide multiple forms of identification before gaining access. Access controls extend beyond user authentication to include stringent controls on applications, services, and devices interacting with the network, reducing the attack surface and mitigating the risk of unauthorized access.

Intrusion Prevention Systems (IPS) play a crucial role in enhancing the security posture of network gateways. IPS solutions actively monitor and analyze network traffic for known and emerging threats, blocking or mitigating potential attacks in real-time. By inspecting and filtering traffic based on predefined signatures, patterns, and behavioral anomalies, IPS solutions contribute to the early detection and prevention of malicious activities. Regular updates to IPS signatures and continuous monitoring ensure that the system remains effective against evolving threats, reinforcing the defense at the gateway.

The integration of robust antivirus and anti-malware solutions is a fundamental best practice for securing network gateways. These solutions scan incoming and outgoing traffic for malicious code, preventing the spread of malware, ransomware, and other forms of malicious software. Regular signature updates, heuristic analysis, and behavioral monitoring enhance the effectiveness of antivirus solutions in identifying and neutralizing emerging threats. By deploying a multi-layered approach that combines antivirus, anti-malware, and IPS capabilities, organizations establish a comprehensive defense against a wide range of cyber threats at the gateway level.

Encryption is a critical best practice to safeguard data in transit as it traverses network gateways. Secure Sockets Layer (SSL) and Transport Layer Security (TLS) protocols provide encryption for communications over the internet, ensuring the confidentiality and integrity of sensitive information. Implementing strong encryption standards and regularly updating cryptographic protocols contribute to a secure communication channel. Inspection of encrypted traffic using SSL/TLS decryption mechanisms allows network gateways to analyze the content for potential threats, maintaining visibility into encrypted communications without compromising security.

Network segmentation is an effective best practice that enhances the security of network gateways by dividing the network into isolated segments based on business functions, security requirements, or user roles. Segmentation limits lateral movement within the network, preventing attackers from easily traversing between different segments. By implementing segmentation at the gateway, organizations can contain potential security incidents and mitigate the impact of breaches, enhancing overall network resilience.

Effective content filtering at network gateways is crucial for blocking access to malicious websites, inappropriate content, and potential security threats. Web filtering solutions enable organizations to enforce policies that control internet access based on categories, blacklists, and whitelists. By blocking access to known malicious domains, filtering malicious content, and preventing access to risky websites, content filtering adds a layer of defense against web-based threats at the gateway. Regularly updating content filtering databases and customizing policies based on organizational needs contribute to the efficacy of this best practice.

Next-Generation Firewalls (NGFWs) represent an advanced best practice for securing network gateways, integrating multiple security features beyond traditional firewall capabilities. NGFWs combine firewall functions with intrusion prevention, application-level filtering, and advanced threat detection. These advanced features provide organizations with enhanced visibility into network activities, application usage, and potential security threats. By incorporating NGFWs into their network architecture, organizations can create a more adaptive and resilient defense at the gateway, capable of addressing sophisticated and evolving cyber threats.

Regular monitoring and logging at network gateways contribute to the detection and response to security incidents in real-time. Comprehensive logs capture information about network traffic, user activities, and potential security events, providing valuable data for analysis and investigation. Security Information and Event Management (SIEM) solutions can aggregate, correlate, and analyze gateway logs, facilitating the identification of patterns indicative of potential threats. Regularly reviewing logs, conducting threat hunting, and implementing incident response procedures strengthen the security posture at the gateway, enabling organizations to respond effectively to security incidents.

Effective patch management is a critical best practice to maintain the security of network gateways by addressing vulnerabilities in operating systems, applications, and gateway devices. Regularly applying security patches and updates ensures that known vulnerabilities are promptly mitigated, reducing the risk of exploitation by malicious actors. Automated patch management solutions, combined with thorough testing processes, contribute to the efficient implementation of this best practice, allowing organizations to stay ahead of potential security threats and maintain a secure gateway infrastructure.

The principle of network resilience involves planning for and mitigating the impact of potential disruptions to network services. Redundancy, failover mechanisms, and load balancing contribute to the resilience of network gateways, ensuring continuous availability and performance. By implementing redundant gateway devices, organizations can maintain network operations even in the event of hardware failures or outages. Failover mechanisms automatically redirect traffic to alternate gateways, minimizing downtime and enhancing overall network resilience in the face of unforeseen events.

Collaboration and threat intelligence sharing principles contribute to a collective defense against common threats at the network gateway. Participating in Information Sharing and Analysis Centers (ISACs), sharing threat intelligence with industry peers, and collaborating with cybersecurity vendors enhance the overall security posture. The principle of collaboration recognizes that cyber threats often transcend individual organizations, and collective efforts contribute to a more informed and adaptive defense against evolving threats.

Security awareness and training for users interacting with network gateways are essential best practices to mitigate the risks associated with social engineering attacks. Educating users about phishing, email scams, and other social engineering techniques helps create a security-aware culture. Regular training programs keep users informed about emerging threats and equip them with the knowledge and skills to recognize and respond to potential security incidents.

Security awareness extends beyond end-users to include network administrators, developers, and other personnel involved in maintaining the security of the gateway infrastructure.

Continuous improvement principles emphasize the dynamic and evolving nature of cybersecurity. Secure network gateways require ongoing evaluation, adaptation, and enhancement to address emerging threats, technology advancements, and changes in the operational environment. Regular security assessments, penetration testing, and vulnerability assessments contribute to identifying weaknesses and areas for improvement. The feedback loop created by continuous improvement ensures that organizations can adapt their security measures to evolving threats, maintaining a secure and resilient gateway infrastructure.

In conclusion, best practices for securing network gateways encompass a comprehensive set of measures aimed at establishing a robust defense against a diverse range of cyber threats. From access controls and authentication mechanisms to intrusion prevention, encryption, and network segmentation, organizations must adopt a multi-layered and adaptive approach. By incorporating advanced technologies like NGFWs, monitoring and logging, effective patch management, and collaboration within the cybersecurity community, organizations can fortify their network gateways and navigate the dynamic landscape of cybersecurity with resilience and confidence.

Chapter 3: The Human Firewall: Cyber Hygiene and User Awareness

3.1 Importance of Human Factor in Cybersecurity

The importance of the human factor in cybersecurity cannot be overstated, as individuals play a pivotal role in shaping the overall security posture of organizations. In an era where cyber threats continue to evolve in sophistication and diversity, understanding and addressing the human element is critical for developing effective and resilient cybersecurity strategies. The human factor encompasses a spectrum of elements, including user behavior, awareness, education, psychology, and organizational culture, all of which significantly influence the success or failure of cybersecurity measures.

At the heart of the human factor lies the reality that individuals, whether employees, end-users, or administrators, are not only targets of cyber attacks but also the first line of defense against them. User behavior, shaped by habits, knowledge, and attitudes, directly impacts the security of digital systems. Recognizing the human factor involves acknowledging the potential for both strengths and vulnerabilities within this dynamic landscape. Users can act as active sensors, detecting anomalies, reporting security incidents, and contributing valuable insights to the overall threat intelligence of an organization.

Human behavior often intersects with the realm of social engineering, a tactic frequently employed by cybercriminals to exploit psychological traits and manipulate individuals into divulging sensitive information or performing actions detrimental to security. Phishing, pretexting, and other social engineering techniques leverage human trust, curiosity, and a willingness to assist, highlighting the need for heightened awareness and education. Addressing the importance of the human factor requires comprehensive training programs that empower individuals to recognize and resist social engineering attempts, fostering a culture of skepticism and vigilance.

The human factor is particularly evident in the context of organizational culture, where attitudes, values, and norms shape the collective approach to cybersecurity. A security-aware culture recognizes the shared responsibility of all individuals within an organization to contribute to the protection of information assets. Leadership commitment, clear communication, and positive reinforcement are essential components in cultivating a security-conscious environment. Emphasizing the importance of cybersecurity within the organizational culture encourages individuals to prioritize security considerations in their daily activities, creating a resilient defense against potential threats.

The significance of the human factor extends to the realm of insider threats, where individuals with access to sensitive information may pose risks either intentionally or unintentionally. Malicious insiders seeking to steal data, sabotage systems, or leak information underscore the need for monitoring, user behavior analytics, and proactive risk mitigation strategies. Balancing trust with vigilant oversight is crucial, and recognizing the human factor involves acknowledging that insiders can be both valuable contributors and potential risks to cybersecurity.

The education and awareness component of the human factor is a cornerstone of effective cybersecurity. Well-informed individuals are better equipped to make secure decisions, identify potential threats, and respond appropriately to security incidents. Security awareness programs, encompassing regular training sessions, simulated phishing exercises, and informational campaigns, contribute to building a knowledgeable and security-savvy workforce. Elevating the importance of cybersecurity in educational initiatives ensures that individuals are equipped with the skills to navigate the digital landscape securely.

In the era of remote work and increased reliance on technology, the human factor gains additional prominence. The shift to remote and flexible work arrangements introduces new challenges related to securing home networks, personal devices, and the blending of professional and personal responsibilities. Recognizing the human factor in this context involves providing tailored guidance and support to individuals navigating the complexities of a digital work environment. Education on secure remote practices, the use of virtual private networks (VPNs), and the importance of securing home Wi-Fi networks become integral components of addressing the unique challenges associated with remote work.

Importantly, the human factor is evident in the context of incident response and recovery. Individuals who have firsthand experience or knowledge of security incidents play a critical role in the post-incident review process. Their insights contribute to organizational learning, helping to identify root causes, refine incident response procedures, and enhance overall resilience. Recognizing the human factor in incident response involves creating a collaborative environment where individuals feel empowered to share their experiences, contributing to a continuous improvement cycle in cybersecurity strategies.

The human factor is also intertwined with the concept of usability in cybersecurity. Security measures that are overly complex or burdensome may lead individuals to seek workarounds, potentially compromising security. Recognizing the importance of the human factor involves designing security solutions with usability in mind. Striking a balance between security and user experience ensures that individuals can seamlessly integrate security practices into their workflows, reducing the likelihood of circumvention and enhancing overall compliance with security measures.

In the development and deployment of technology, the human factor plays a crucial role in ensuring the effectiveness and acceptance of security measures. User interfaces, system designs, and authentication mechanisms that align with human cognitive abilities and behaviors contribute to the success of cybersecurity solutions. Recognizing the human factor in technology design involves conducting user-centric assessments, gathering feedback, and iteratively refining security features to enhance usability and effectiveness.

Beyond individual behaviors, the human factor is evident in the collaborative efforts within the cybersecurity community. Information sharing, collaboration between organizations, and collective responses to emerging threats emphasize the interconnected nature of the human factor in cybersecurity. Recognizing the importance of collaboration involves active participation in Information Sharing and Analysis Centers (ISACs), industry partnerships, and engaging with the broader cybersecurity ecosystem. The collective intelligence of the community becomes a powerful asset in addressing shared challenges and staying ahead of evolving threats.

Ultimately, recognizing the human factor in cybersecurity is about embracing a holistic and human-centric approach to security. It involves acknowledging that individuals are not merely targets or potential liabilities but active participants and assets in the defense against cyber threats. By elevating the importance of education, fostering a security-aware culture, and integrating the human factor into the design and implementation of cybersecurity strategies, organizations can build a resilient defense that aligns with the dynamic and evolving nature of the digital landscape. In doing so, the human factor becomes a strength, contributing to the adaptive and collective response needed to navigate the complex challenges of cybersecurity effectively.

Recognizing Humans as a Security Asset

Recognizing humans as a security asset represents a paradigm shift in cybersecurity philosophy, acknowledging the pivotal role that individuals play in fortifying the overall security posture of organizations. In traditional cybersecurity models, humans were often viewed as potential weak links, susceptible to falling victim to social engineering attacks and inadvertently introducing security vulnerabilities. However, a more contemporary and human-centric approach reframes this perspective, recognizing that well-informed, trained, and engaged individuals can serve as a formidable line of defense against a diverse range of cyber threats.

Education and awareness form the cornerstone of harnessing humans as a security asset. Empowering individuals with a deep understanding of cybersecurity best practices, threat landscapes, and the importance of their role in the security ecosystem is fundamental. Security awareness programs aim to educate employees about the evolving tactics employed by cybercriminals, emphasizing the significance of vigilance, skepticism, and responsible online behavior. By fostering a culture of cybersecurity awareness, organizations equip their workforce with the knowledge and skills to recognize, report, and mitigate potential security risks.

The human element is particularly critical in the context of social engineering attacks, where adversaries exploit psychological and behavioral traits to manipulate individuals into divulging sensitive information or performing actions detrimental to security. Recognizing humans as a security asset involves training individuals to identify and resist social engineering tactics such as phishing, pretexting, and baiting. Simulated phishing exercises provide hands-on experience, allowing individuals to recognize the signs of a potential attack and respond appropriately. By arming employees with the ability to discern and resist social engineering attempts, organizations leverage humans as an active defense against one of the most prevalent and effective forms of cyber threats.

Beyond education, individuals contribute to cybersecurity as active sensors, capable of detecting anomalies and potential security incidents. Cultivating a sense of responsibility and ownership among employees encourages them to report suspicious activities, unexpected system behaviors, or any deviations from the norm. Establishing clear and accessible reporting channels, coupled with a non-punitive approach, encourages individuals to share information about potential security incidents promptly. This collaborative approach transforms employees into proactive contributors to the organization's overall threat detection and response capabilities.

In the realm of endpoint security, recognizing humans as a security asset involves engaging them as partners in the protection of devices and data. Employees are often the end-users of devices connected to the corporate network, and their understanding of basic security hygiene, such as keeping software up-to-date, using strong passwords, and being cautious about downloading or clicking on suspicious links, directly impacts the security of endpoints. Regular training on these fundamentals empowers individuals to actively participate in the defense against malware, ransomware, and other endpoint threats.

The concept of "security champions" within organizations exemplifies the recognition of humans as security assets. These are individuals who, due to their interest, expertise, or role within the organization, take on an active role in promoting and advocating for cybersecurity best practices. Security champions act as ambassadors, helping disseminate knowledge, fostering a security-conscious culture, and encouraging their peers to prioritize and adhere to security guidelines. By leveraging the passion and influence of security champions, organizations amplify the impact of their cybersecurity education and awareness initiatives.

Collaboration between security teams and other departments within an organization further emphasizes the role of humans as security assets. Business units, IT teams, and executive leadership are integral parts of the cybersecurity ecosystem, and their active involvement is crucial for implementing effective security measures. Establishing clear communication channels, breaking down silos, and fostering a collaborative mindset enable organizations to harness the collective intelligence and resources of their human assets in addressing cybersecurity challenges comprehensively.

Recognizing humans as a security asset extends to the realm of incident response and crisis management. Equipping employees with the knowledge and skills to respond effectively to security incidents, report anomalies, and adhere to incident response procedures transforms them into active participants in the organization's resilience strategy. Conducting regular tabletop exercises and simulations involving employees from various departments enhances their preparedness and ensures a coordinated and well-executed response in the event of a security incident.

The concept of "gamification" has emerged as an innovative strategy to engage and motivate individuals in their cybersecurity responsibilities. By incorporating elements of gaming, such as challenges, rewards, and competition, organizations create an interactive and enjoyable environment for learning and practicing cybersecurity skills. Gamification not only makes cybersecurity training more engaging but also fosters a sense of camaraderie and healthy competition among employees, encouraging them to actively participate in enhancing the organization's security posture.

In the realm of insider threat mitigation, recognizing humans as a security asset involves balancing trust and vigilance. While employees are essential contributors to organizational success, they also have the potential to pose insider threats, either intentionally or unintentionally. Implementing robust user behavior analytics, monitoring access patterns, and conducting periodic risk assessments contribute to recognizing and addressing potential insider threats. Balancing a culture of trust with the need for continuous monitoring and risk mitigation ensures that humans remain valuable assets without compromising security.

The concept of "security culture" encapsulates the idea of recognizing humans as a foundational element of cybersecurity. Building a security-conscious culture involves instilling a sense of shared responsibility for security across all levels of an organization. Leadership commitment, regular communication, and positive reinforcement contribute to the development of a security culture where individuals actively contribute to the protection of information assets. In such a culture, security becomes ingrained in the organization's values, and individuals naturally prioritize security considerations in their day-to-day activities.

The human element is particularly vital in the context of incident recovery and learning from security incidents. Post-incident reviews and debriefings involve individuals who were directly or indirectly impacted by the incident, providing valuable insights into the incident's root causes and lessons learned. Engaging employees in this reflective process not only contributes to organizational learning but also empowers individuals with a deeper understanding of cybersecurity risks and the importance of their role in maintaining a resilient security posture.

In conclusion, recognizing humans as a security asset represents a paradigm shift that emphasizes the proactive and positive role individuals play in cybersecurity. From education and awareness to active participation in incident response and the cultivation of a security culture, organizations that leverage the human element as a strategic asset enhance their overall security posture. By empowering individuals with knowledge, fostering a sense of responsibility, and creating a collaborative and security-conscious environment, organizations can navigate the dynamic and evolving landscape of cybersecurity with resilience and confidence.

Common Human-Related Security Risks

Common human-related security risks pose significant challenges to organizations, highlighting the need for comprehensive cybersecurity strategies that address the dynamic interplay between human behavior and digital threats. Social engineering stands out as a pervasive and sophisticated risk, leveraging psychological manipulation to exploit individuals for unauthorized access or information. Phishing, a prevalent form of social engineering, involves deceptive emails, messages, or websites that trick individuals into divulging sensitive information. Beyond phishing, pretexting, baiting, and quid pro quo attacks rely on human trust and cooperation, exploiting the innate willingness to assist or share information.

Weak password practices present another widespread human-related security risk. Individuals often choose weak passwords, reuse them across multiple accounts, or fail to update them regularly. This creates opportunities for attackers to compromise accounts through brute-force attacks, credential stuffing, or password spraying. The human tendency to prioritize convenience over security contributes to the prevalence of weak password practices, emphasizing the importance of user education and enforcing robust password policies.

Inadequate awareness and training among users represent a critical vulnerability. Many security incidents stem from users' lack of understanding about cybersecurity threats, safe online practices, and the potential consequences of their actions. Without proper education, individuals may inadvertently download malware, click on malicious links, or fall victim to scams. Comprehensive security awareness programs that include simulated phishing exercises, regular training sessions, and informational campaigns are essential to mitigate this risk and empower individuals to make informed security decisions.

Insider threats, whether intentional or unintentional, pose a complex human-related security risk. Employees, contractors, or partners with access to sensitive information may compromise security through malicious actions or inadvertent mistakes. Malicious insiders may steal data, sabotage systems, or leak sensitive information, while unintentional insiders may inadvertently expose sensitive data through negligence or lack of awareness. Balancing trust with vigilant monitoring, implementing user behavior analytics, and fostering a culture of security awareness are crucial for addressing insider threats effectively.

BYOD (Bring Your Own Device) and the use of personal devices for work purposes introduce additional human-related security risks. Individuals accessing corporate networks and data from personal devices may inadvertently expose sensitive information to potential security threats. The lack of control over personal devices, varying security configurations, and the potential for unauthorized access increase the risk of data breaches. Organizations must establish clear policies, implement mobile device management solutions, and educate users on the risks associated with BYOD to mitigate these challenges effectively.

Negligence and complacency among employees contribute to human-related security risks. Failure to follow security policies, disregarding warning signs, and overlooking the importance of cybersecurity measures can lead to security incidents. Negligence may manifest in actions such as leaving devices unattended, using unsecured Wi-Fi networks, or failing to apply security patches promptly. Creating a security-conscious culture, emphasizing the consequences of negligence, and promoting a sense of shared responsibility are essential for addressing this human-related risk.

Lack of understanding about the risks associated with removable media, such as USB drives, poses another human-related security challenge. Individuals may unknowingly introduce malware or unauthorized software into corporate networks by using untrusted or compromised removable media. Organizations need to educate users about the risks associated with external devices, implement controls to restrict their use, and regularly scan for potential threats introduced through removable media.

Overreliance on social media and oversharing of personal information online expose individuals and organizations to heightened security risks. Attackers leverage publicly available information on social media platforms to conduct reconnaissance, launch targeted attacks, or engage in impersonation. Individuals may inadvertently share sensitive details about their work, relationships, or routines, providing attackers with valuable insights. Promoting responsible social media use, restricting access to sensitive information, and raising awareness about the risks associated with oversharing are crucial components of addressing this human-related security risk.

Unsecured or public Wi-Fi networks represent a common human-related security risk, as individuals may connect to untrusted networks without considering the potential security implications. Attackers can exploit vulnerabilities in unsecured Wi-Fi to intercept communications, launch man-in-the-middle attacks, or distribute malware. Educating users about the risks associated with public Wi-Fi, encouraging the use of virtual private networks (VPNs), and implementing strong network security measures help mitigate the threats posed by unsecured Wi-Fi networks.

The human tendency to resist or delay software updates and patches introduces vulnerabilities that attackers can exploit. Individuals may ignore update notifications or postpone system patches due to concerns about disruptions or inconvenience. This resistance allows attackers to target known vulnerabilities and exploit unpatched systems. Organizations must emphasize the importance of timely updates, automate patch management processes, and provide user-friendly mechanisms to encourage individuals to keep their software and systems up-to-date.

In conclusion, common human-related security risks underscore the intricate relationship between human behavior and the cybersecurity landscape. From social engineering and weak password practices to insider threats, negligence, and the challenges associated with BYOD, organizations must adopt multifaceted strategies that blend technical measures with comprehensive user education and awareness programs. Recognizing the human factor as both a potential vulnerability and a valuable asset, organizations can build a resilient cybersecurity posture that actively involves and empowers individuals in the collective effort to combat evolving digital threats.

3.2 Cyber Hygiene Best Practices

Cyber hygiene, akin to personal hygiene in the physical world, encompasses a set of practices and habits designed to maintain the health and security of digital systems. In a constantly evolving cyber threat landscape, cyber hygiene serves as a fundamental and proactive approach to safeguarding individuals, organizations, and their digital assets. These best practices are essential for minimizing vulnerabilities, reducing the risk of cyber attacks, and fostering a culture of security awareness.

A cornerstone of cyber hygiene is the regular and systematic practice of software updates and patch management. Keeping operating systems, applications, and software components up-to-date ensures that known vulnerabilities are promptly addressed. Cybercriminals often exploit outdated software to launch attacks, making timely updates a critical line of defense. Automated patch management tools facilitate this process, streamlining the deployment of security patches and reducing the window of opportunity for potential attackers.

Secure password practices constitute another vital aspect of cyber hygiene. Individuals are often the first line of defense against unauthorized access to digital accounts, systems, and networks. Implementing strong, unique passwords for each account, regularly updating them, and avoiding password reuse are foundational principles. Encouraging the use of passphrase combinations, incorporating a mix of characters, and leveraging multi-factor authentication (MFA) further fortify the resilience of password-based security measures.

Effective endpoint security is integral to cyber hygiene, particularly in the context of the diverse devices connected to corporate networks. Employing reputable antivirus and anti-malware solutions helps detect and neutralize malicious software, protecting endpoints from potential threats. Regular scans, heuristic analysis, and behavioral monitoring enhance the capabilities of endpoint security solutions in identifying and mitigating evolving forms of malware and ransomware. By establishing a robust defense at the endpoint, organizations bolster their overall cyber hygiene posture.

Practicing safe browsing habits is a fundamental cyber hygiene best practice. Individuals should exercise caution when navigating the internet, avoid clicking on suspicious links, and verify the legitimacy of websites before entering sensitive information. Web filtering solutions, which restrict access to known malicious sites and filter inappropriate content, contribute to safe browsing practices. Cyber hygiene emphasizes the importance of user education and awareness to empower individuals with the skills to discern potential threats and make secure decisions while online.

Regular data backups are an essential component of cyber hygiene, providing a means to recover from data loss due to accidental deletion, hardware failure, or cyber attacks such as ransomware. Automated backup solutions, combined with a well-defined backup strategy, ensure that critical data is regularly and securely duplicated.

Cyber hygiene recognizes the significance of data resilience and recovery as an integral part of maintaining business continuity in the face of unexpected events.

Securing Wi-Fi networks is a cyber hygiene practice crucial for preventing unauthorized access and potential breaches. Implementing strong encryption standards, such as WPA3, regularly updating Wi-Fi passwords, and configuring routers to use secure authentication protocols contribute to the protection of wireless networks. Cyber hygiene extends to raising awareness about the risks associated with public Wi-Fi and encouraging the use of virtual private networks (VPNs) when connecting to untrusted networks.

The principle of least privilege is a foundational cyber hygiene concept that emphasizes restricting user access to the minimum level necessary for their roles and responsibilities. By limiting access privileges, organizations reduce the attack surface and mitigate the potential impact of security incidents. Cyber hygiene recognizes that user permissions should align with job requirements, preventing unnecessary exposure to sensitive information and reducing the risk of insider threats.

Email security practices are integral to cyber hygiene, given the prevalence of phishing and other email-based attacks. Individuals should exercise caution when opening email attachments, clicking on links, or responding to unsolicited emails. Implementing email filtering solutions that detect and block malicious content helps protect against phishing attempts. Regular cybersecurity training, including simulated phishing exercises, enhances users' ability to recognize and report suspicious emails, reinforcing the human element of cyber hygiene.

Device encryption is a cyber hygiene best practice that safeguards sensitive data stored on devices such as laptops, smartphones, and tablets. Full disk encryption protects data from unauthorized access in the event of device loss or theft. Cyber hygiene recognizes the importance of encrypting data at rest to maintain confidentiality and prevent unauthorized disclosure. Device encryption should be complemented by strong access controls, including secure login mechanisms and multi-factor authentication, for comprehensive data protection.

Effective incident response planning is a proactive cyber hygiene measure that prepares organizations to address and mitigate the impact of security incidents. Establishing an incident response team, defining response procedures, and conducting regular drills contribute to the organization's readiness to handle cyber threats. Cyber hygiene acknowledges that incident response is not only a reactive measure but an integral part of a comprehensive cybersecurity strategy that aims to minimize the time to detect, respond, and recover from security incidents.

Implementing a robust cyber hygiene program involves continuous monitoring of network activities, user behaviors, and system events. Security Information and Event Management (SIEM) solutions play a key role in aggregating and analyzing data from various sources, enabling organizations to detect and respond to potential security incidents in real-time. Cyber hygiene recognizes the importance of visibility into the network environment, leveraging monitoring tools and threat intelligence feeds to stay ahead of emerging threats.

Education and awareness training are ongoing cyber hygiene practices designed to keep individuals informed about evolving cybersecurity threats and best practices. Regular training sessions, workshops, and awareness campaigns contribute to a security-aware culture within organizations. Cyber hygiene emphasizes the need for individuals to stay vigilant, adapt to new threats, and actively participate in maintaining the security of digital environments. This human-centric approach ensures that the human factor becomes an asset rather than a liability in the realm of cybersecurity.

Secure coding practices constitute a crucial aspect of cyber hygiene, particularly for organizations involved in software development. Adhering to secure coding principles, conducting code reviews, and integrating security testing into the development lifecycle contribute to the creation of resilient and secure software. Cyber hygiene extends to the proactive identification and remediation of vulnerabilities in applications, preventing potential exploitation by attackers.

Adopting a risk-based approach is integral to cyber hygiene, aligning security measures with the specific risks and priorities of an organization. Conducting regular risk assessments, vulnerability scans, and penetration testing contributes to identifying and addressing potential weaknesses in the cybersecurity posture. Cyber hygiene recognizes that the threat landscape is dynamic, and adapting security measures based on risk assessments ensures a proactive and adaptive defense against evolving cyber threats.

In conclusion, cyber hygiene best practices form the foundation of a proactive and adaptive cybersecurity strategy. From software updates and secure password practices to endpoint security, safe browsing habits, and incident response planning, these practices collectively contribute to reducing vulnerabilities and mitigating the impact of cyber threats. Cyber hygiene recognizes the importance of user education, ongoing awareness training, and a risk-based approach to cybersecurity. By integrating these best practices into organizational culture and workflows, individuals and organizations can navigate the dynamic and evolving cyber threat landscape with resilience and confidence.

Password Management and Complexity

Password management and complexity are integral aspects of cybersecurity, playing a crucial role in safeguarding digital identities, sensitive information, and critical systems from unauthorized access. As the digital landscape continues to evolve, the importance of robust password practices becomes increasingly evident, requiring individuals and organizations to adopt strategies that balance usability and security.

Central to password management is the concept of creating and maintaining strong, unique passwords for each digital account or system. A strong password is characterized by its complexity, typically including a combination of uppercase and lowercase letters, numbers, and special characters. The goal is to create a password that is resistant to brute-force attacks, where an attacker systematically attempts to guess the password by trying different combinations. Strong, unique passwords serve as a frontline defense, mitigating the risk of unauthorized access and protecting against the compromise of one account leading to a cascade of security breaches.

The principle of password uniqueness is paramount in password management. Reusing passwords across multiple accounts introduces significant vulnerabilities, as a security breach in one service could potentially compromise multiple accounts. This practice, known as password reuse, is exploited by cybercriminals who leverage stolen credentials from one platform to gain unauthorized access to other accounts. Password managers emerge as valuable tools in addressing this challenge, facilitating the generation and storage of unique, complex passwords for each account while relieving users of the burden of memorizing them.

The adoption of multi-factor authentication (MFA) enhances password management by adding an additional layer of security beyond the traditional username and password combination. MFA typically involves the use of a second authentication factor, such as a temporary code sent to a mobile device or generated by a hardware token. By requiring users to provide multiple forms of identification, MFA significantly raises the bar for unauthorized access, even if passwords are compromised. Organizations and individuals alike are encouraged to embrace MFA as a complementary strategy to bolster password management efforts.

Managing passwords effectively also involves regular updates and changes. Periodic password changes are a common practice, aiming to mitigate the impact of potential compromises and limit the window of opportunity for attackers. However, the effectiveness of this approach has been debated, with some experts suggesting that frequent password changes may lead to weaker passwords as users resort to predictable patterns or incremental adjustments. Striking a balance between regular updates and avoiding predictable password changes is essential for maintaining robust password management practices.

Password expiration policies are often implemented as part of password management strategies, requiring users to change their passwords after a predefined period. While intended to enhance security, such policies can inadvertently lead to weaker passwords, as users may opt for easily memorable variations to comply with frequent changes. The effectiveness of password expiration policies should be evaluated in the context of the organization's specific risk landscape, with a focus on encouraging the use of strong, unique passwords rather than simply adhering to a fixed schedule of changes.

The concept of passphrase complexity introduces a human-centric element to password management. Instead of relying on a string of unrelated characters, passphrases involve combining multiple words or a sentence. Passphrases can be both easier to remember and more resistant to certain types of attacks, provided they are of sufficient length and complexity. Encouraging users to create memorable yet complex passphrases contributes to improved password management practices, aligning security measures with human behaviors.

Educating users about password security is an essential component of effective password management. Security awareness training should cover the importance of strong, unique passwords, the risks associated with password reuse, and the role of MFA in enhancing authentication security. By fostering a culture of security awareness, organizations empower individuals to make informed decisions about password management and actively participate in safeguarding digital assets.

The integration of biometric authentication represents a technological advancement in password management, offering an alternative or complementary method to traditional password-based authentication. Biometric identifiers, such as fingerprints, facial recognition, or iris scans, provide a unique and inherent form of authentication tied to an individual's physical characteristics. While biometrics enhance the user experience by eliminating the need to remember complex passwords, their adoption introduces considerations related to privacy, data security, and the potential for biometric data breaches.

Password management extends beyond individual practices to encompass organizational strategies for securely storing and handling passwords. Hashing and salting are cryptographic techniques employed to protect stored passwords in databases. Hashing involves converting passwords into irreversible, fixed-length strings of characters, while salting introduces a unique random value for each user before hashing. This prevents attackers from using precomputed tables, known as rainbow tables, to efficiently crack passwords. Organizations should prioritize the secure storage of passwords, employing encryption and access controls to safeguard sensitive authentication data.

Password management tools, such as password managers and vaults, play a significant role in promoting secure password practices. These tools generate, store, and automatically fill in complex passwords for users, eliminating the need for individuals to memorize multiple passwords. Password managers also provide a centralized platform for managing credentials, facilitating the secure sharing of passwords within teams without compromising security. However, organizations and users should carefully evaluate the security of chosen password management tools, considering factors such as encryption strength, authentication methods, and the vendor's reputation.

In the realm of enterprise cybersecurity, privileged account management (PAM) is a specialized aspect of password management that focuses on securing accounts with elevated access rights. Privileged accounts, often targeted by attackers seeking to escalate privileges, require stringent management practices. PAM solutions enforce policies for secure password storage, rotation, and access controls for privileged accounts. Robust PAM strategies contribute to limiting the exposure of privileged credentials and mitigating the risk of unauthorized access to critical systems.

The proliferation of Internet of Things (IoT) devices introduces new considerations for password management. Many IoT devices come with default or hardcoded passwords, posing security risks if these passwords are not changed upon installation. Effective password management for IoT devices involves setting strong, unique passwords, updating default credentials, and ensuring that devices support secure authentication protocols. Organizations must consider IoT devices as potential entry points for attackers and incorporate them into comprehensive password management strategies.

In conclusion, password management and complexity are foundational elements of cybersecurity, representing a critical line of defense against unauthorized access and potential breaches. From the adoption of strong, unique passwords and the use of multi-factor authentication to the integration of passphrase complexity and the secure storage of credentials, effective password management requires a multifaceted approach. Balancing security with usability, fostering a culture of security awareness, and leveraging technological advancements contribute to building robust password management practices that align with the evolving nature of the digital landscape.

As organizations and individuals navigate the complex challenges of cybersecurity, prioritizing effective password management remains an essential pillar of their defense strategy.

Software Updates and Patch Management

Software updates and patch management are essential components of cybersecurity strategies, playing a critical role in maintaining the health, security, and resilience of digital systems. In a landscape where cyber threats continually evolve, software vulnerabilities are prime targets for exploitation by malicious actors. Software updates, also known as patches, address identified vulnerabilities, introduce new features, and enhance the overall performance of software applications. Effective patch management ensures that these updates are systematically and promptly applied to mitigate potential risks, safeguard sensitive data, and fortify the overall cybersecurity posture of individuals and organizations.

The primary objective of software updates and patch management is to address security vulnerabilities identified in software applications. As software is developed and deployed, security researchers and vendors continuously analyze its code to identify potential weaknesses that could be exploited by cybercriminals. Once vulnerabilities are discovered, vendors release patches—software updates specifically designed to fix these vulnerabilities. Patch management involves the systematic deployment of these updates to ensure that the software remains secure and resilient against emerging threats.

Timeliness is a critical factor in patch management, as the window of vulnerability—the time between the discovery of a vulnerability and the deployment of a corresponding patch—represents a period of heightened risk. Cybercriminals actively exploit this window to launch attacks, knowing that systems are susceptible until patches are applied. Organizations and individuals must prioritize the timely installation of patches to minimize exposure and reduce the likelihood of falling victim to exploits targeting known vulnerabilities.

The scope of patch management extends beyond addressing security vulnerabilities to include the improvement of software functionality and performance. Software updates often introduce new features, enhance user experience, and optimize the efficiency of applications. Organizations and users alike benefit from these improvements, as updated software not only bolsters security but also provides access to the latest capabilities and enhancements, contributing to a more robust and efficient digital environment.

Patch management is a multifaceted process that requires careful planning and execution. Automated patch management tools play a crucial role in streamlining this process, enabling organizations to efficiently deploy patches across large-scale IT environments. These tools automate the detection of available patches, prioritize them based on severity and impact, and facilitate their distribution to endpoints. Automation ensures that patches are applied consistently, reducing the risk of human error and ensuring that no vulnerable systems are overlooked.

The diversity of software applications used in modern computing environments poses a challenge for patch management. Organizations must contend with a wide range of software vendors, each with its own release cycles and update mechanisms. Coordinating the deployment of patches across diverse software portfolios requires a comprehensive approach that encompasses collaboration with vendors, effective communication, and adherence to industry best practices. Standardizing patch management processes helps organizations navigate the complexity of software diversity and ensures a cohesive strategy for maintaining security across all applications.

Cloud computing introduces additional considerations for patch management, as organizations increasingly rely on cloud services and infrastructure. In cloud environments, the responsibility for certain aspects of patch management may be shared between the cloud service provider and the customer. Understanding these shared responsibilities is crucial for implementing effective patch management in the cloud. Cloud-native patching solutions, automated deployment pipelines, and continuous monitoring contribute to a dynamic and responsive approach to patch management in cloud environments.

Mobile devices, including smartphones and tablets, represent a significant aspect of contemporary computing, and patch management is equally vital for securing these devices. Mobile operating systems, applications, and firmware require regular updates to address security vulnerabilities and enhance functionality. However, mobile devices pose unique challenges, as users may delay or avoid installing updates due to concerns about data usage, device performance, or inconvenience. Educating users about the importance of mobile device updates and implementing policies to encourage timely installations are critical components of mobile patch management.

Internet of Things (IoT) devices constitute another frontier for patch management, as the proliferation of connected devices introduces new challenges. Many IoT devices, ranging from smart thermostats to industrial sensors, come with embedded software that may lack robust update mechanisms. In some cases, IoT devices are shipped with default credentials and firmware versions that are seldom updated by users. Patch management for IoT devices requires collaboration between manufacturers, vendors, and end-users to ensure that devices remain secure throughout their lifecycle.

While automated patch management tools enhance efficiency, organizations must carefully plan and test patches before deployment to avoid unintended consequences. Patch testing involves assessing the compatibility of patches with existing software configurations, identifying potential conflicts, and evaluating the impact of patches on system performance. Testing helps mitigate the risk of disruptions caused by incompatible patches and ensures that organizations can confidently apply updates without compromising operational stability.

Patch management is inherently intertwined with risk management, as organizations must balance the need to secure systems with the potential for disruptions introduced by patches. Risk assessments help organizations prioritize patches based on the severity of vulnerabilities, the criticality of affected systems, and the potential impact of disruptions. This risk-based approach enables organizations to allocate resources efficiently, focusing on patches that address the most significant security risks while minimizing potential operational disruptions.

In addition to addressing known vulnerabilities, proactive organizations adopt a vulnerability management approach that involves continuous monitoring, identification, and prioritization of potential vulnerabilities. Vulnerability management complements patch management by providing insights into emerging threats and potential weaknesses in the IT infrastructure. Integrating vulnerability management into the overall cybersecurity strategy allows organizations to proactively address security risks before patches are available or deployed.

Patch management is not a one-time activity but an ongoing process that requires continuous monitoring and adaptation. Threat landscapes evolve, new vulnerabilities emerge, and cyber threats become more sophisticated over time. Organizations must remain vigilant, staying informed about emerging threats and promptly addressing newly discovered vulnerabilities. Continuous monitoring, threat intelligence feeds, and proactive engagement with the cybersecurity community contribute to a dynamic and adaptive patch management strategy.

The human factor is a critical consideration in patch management, as end-users play a pivotal role in the timely installation of updates. Organizations must educate users about the importance of patching, the potential risks associated with delaying updates, and the role they play in maintaining a secure digital environment. User awareness campaigns, clear communication about the impact of patches, and user-friendly update processes contribute to a collaborative approach where individuals actively contribute to the organization's cybersecurity resilience.

In conclusion, software updates and patch management are foundational elements of effective cybersecurity, addressing vulnerabilities, enhancing functionality, and safeguarding digital systems against evolving threats. From automated tools and risk-based approaches to considerations for diverse computing environments, patch management requires a comprehensive strategy that adapts to the complexities of modern IT landscapes. By prioritizing timely and systematic patch deployment, organizations and individuals alike contribute to a more secure digital ecosystem, resilient against the ever-evolving challenges posed by cyber threats.

3.3 User Awareness Training

User awareness training is a cornerstone of cybersecurity, recognizing that individuals play a pivotal role in safeguarding digital environments against evolving threats. In an era where cyber attacks frequently target human vulnerabilities, educating users becomes a strategic imperative for organizations and individuals alike. User awareness training goes beyond imparting technical knowledge; it aims to cultivate a security-conscious culture, empower individuals with the skills to recognize and respond to potential threats, and foster a collective sense of responsibility for cybersecurity.

At its core, user awareness training seeks to bridge the gap between technology and human behavior. While technological solutions provide essential layers of defense, the human factor remains a dynamic and often unpredictable element in the cybersecurity landscape. Recognizing this, user awareness training engages individuals in understanding the risks, adopting secure practices, and becoming active contributors to the overall security posture of the organization. By imparting knowledge about common cyber threats, attack vectors, and protective measures, user awareness training equips individuals with the awareness needed to make informed decisions in the digital realm.

Phishing, a prevalent and deceptive form of social engineering, underscores the importance of user awareness training. Phishing attacks often leverage psychological manipulation to trick individuals into divulging sensitive information, clicking on malicious links, or downloading malware. User awareness training educates individuals about the characteristics of phishing attempts, emphasizing the importance of scrutinizing emails, verifying the legitimacy of links, and exercising caution when sharing sensitive information. Simulated phishing exercises, integrated into user awareness programs, provide hands-on experience and help reinforce the lessons learned.

Weak password practices represent a significant vulnerability in cybersecurity, and user awareness training addresses this by emphasizing the importance of creating strong, unique passwords. Individuals are educated about the risks associated with password reuse, the significance of regular password updates, and the role of multi-factor authentication (MFA) in enhancing account security. By instilling best practices for password management, user awareness training contributes to reducing the likelihood of unauthorized access due to weak or compromised credentials.

Social engineering tactics extend beyond phishing to include various manipulative techniques that exploit human trust and cooperation. User awareness training explores scenarios such as pretexting, where attackers create fabricated stories to extract information, or baiting, where malicious content is disguised as something enticing. By illustrating real-world examples and providing practical guidance, user awareness training empowers individuals to recognize and resist social engineering attempts, fostering a culture of skepticism and vigilance.

The human element in cybersecurity is further underscored by the prevalence of insider threats—both intentional and unintentional. User awareness training addresses the complexities of insider threats by educating employees about the potential risks associated with malicious actions or inadvertent mistakes. It emphasizes the importance of user behavior analytics, monitoring for unusual activities, and reporting any suspicious behavior. By promoting a sense of shared responsibility, user awareness training encourages individuals to actively contribute to the detection and mitigation of insider threats.

As remote work becomes increasingly prevalent, user awareness training adapts to address the unique challenges of securing home networks and personal devices. Individuals are educated about the risks associated with unsecured Wi-Fi networks, the importance of keeping software and devices updated, and the need for secure practices in remote work environments. By tailoring training content to the specific concerns of remote work, user awareness programs empower individuals to navigate the complexities of a digital work environment securely.

The effectiveness of user awareness training relies on the alignment of training content with the real-world threats individuals may encounter. Training modules often cover topics such as malware awareness, ransomware prevention, and secure online browsing. The goal is not only to convey technical information but also to provide practical insights that individuals can apply in their daily digital interactions. User awareness training aims to demystify cybersecurity concepts, making them accessible and relevant to individuals regardless of their technical background.

Simulated cybersecurity exercises and tabletop drills form an integral part of user awareness training. These exercises create realistic scenarios that allow individuals to apply their knowledge and skills in a controlled environment. By simulating cyber incidents, organizations assess the readiness of their workforce to respond effectively, identify areas for improvement, and reinforce the importance of incident response procedures. Simulated exercises enhance the practical application of user awareness training, turning theoretical knowledge into actionable responses.

The role of leadership in shaping a security-aware culture cannot be overstated, and user awareness training extends its impact by engaging leadership in cybersecurity initiatives. Executives and managers set the tone for organizational culture, and their understanding of cybersecurity risks influences the behavior of the entire workforce. User awareness training for leadership focuses on strategic aspects of cybersecurity, risk management, and the role of leadership in promoting a security-conscious environment. By aligning leadership perspectives with cybersecurity goals, user awareness training creates a cohesive approach that permeates all levels of the organization.

Continuous learning is a fundamental principle of user awareness training, reflecting the dynamic nature of cybersecurity threats. Training programs evolve to address emerging threats, new attack vectors, and changes in technology. By staying current with the latest trends and incorporating real-world examples into training content, user awareness programs ensure that individuals are equipped to adapt to the evolving threat landscape. Regular updates, refresher courses, and ongoing communication channels contribute to a culture of continuous improvement in cybersecurity awareness.

User awareness training extends beyond the confines of organizational boundaries to encompass the broader cybersecurity community. Information sharing, collaboration with industry peers, and participation in cybersecurity forums contribute to a collective understanding of evolving threats. User awareness programs encourage individuals to engage with the cybersecurity community, stay informed about emerging risks, and actively contribute to the shared knowledge base. By fostering a sense of community, user awareness training reinforces the interconnected nature of cybersecurity efforts.

In conclusion, user awareness training is a dynamic and integral element of cybersecurity, recognizing the human factor as both a potential vulnerability and a valuable asset. From phishing and social engineering to insider threats and the complexities of remote work, user awareness training addresses a spectrum of challenges individuals may encounter in the digital landscape. By combining technical knowledge with practical insights, fostering a culture of shared responsibility, and adapting to the evolving threat landscape, user awareness training empowers individuals to navigate the complexities of cybersecurity confidently. As organizations and individuals recognize the significance of the human element, user awareness training becomes a strategic investment in building a resilient defense against the ever-evolving cyber threats.

Educating Users on Social Engineering Tactics

Social engineering tactics represent a multifaceted and evolving threat that poses significant challenges to the security of individuals, organizations, and society at large. At its core, social engineering is a manipulation technique that exploits human psychology to gain unauthorized access, extract sensitive information, or manipulate individuals into performing actions that may compromise security. One prevalent avenue through which social engineers operate is by leveraging the inherent trust and reliance people place in digital communication and technology. Phishing, a widely employed social engineering tactic, involves deceptive emails, messages, or websites that mimic legitimate sources to trick users into revealing confidential information such as passwords or financial details. The art of persuasion plays a pivotal role in social engineering, as attackers often exploit human emotions, fears, or desires to manipulate targets. By impersonating trustworthy figures, such as colleagues, tech support personnel, or even friends, social engineers seek to create a false sense of familiarity, lowering the target's guard and increasing the likelihood of compliance. The effectiveness of these tactics is amplified by the vast amount of personal information available online, enabling attackers to craft convincing narratives tailored to their victims.

Moreover, pretexting, another facet of social engineering, involves the creation of a fabricated scenario or pretext to elicit specific information or actions from the target. This may involve posing as a colleague seeking assistance, a service provider requesting sensitive details for verification, or any scenario designed to manipulate the target's willingness to share information. Social engineers often exploit common cognitive biases, such as authority bias or urgency, to manipulate individuals into acting against their better judgment. Authority bias, for example, occurs when individuals are more likely to comply with requests from perceived figures of authority, whether real or fabricated. Social engineers frequently impersonate executives, IT administrators, or other authoritative figures to exploit this psychological tendency.

In addition to exploiting trust and authority, social engineers often prey on the human tendency to reciprocate favors or comply with social norms. The principle of reciprocity is harnessed when attackers offer false assistance, creating a sense of indebtedness in the target, who may then be more inclined to divulge sensitive information or perform actions against their own interests. Similarly, conformity to social norms is manipulated by social engineers who create scenarios that align with expected behavior, making it more likely for individuals to follow through with requests that appear to be commonplace. Understanding these psychological vulnerabilities is crucial for users to recognize and resist the manipulative techniques employed by social engineers.

The digital landscape has provided social engineers with an expansive playground, allowing them to exploit various communication channels and platforms. Social media, in particular, has become a fertile ground for reconnaissance, enabling attackers to gather extensive personal information about potential targets. By aggregating data from public profiles, social engineers can craft highly personalized and convincing messages, increasing the likelihood of successful manipulation. Additionally, the anonymity afforded by the internet empowers social engineers to conceal their true identities and intentions, further complicating the task of identifying and thwarting these attacks.

Furthermore, the sophistication of social engineering attacks has evolved in tandem with advancements in technology. Spear phishing, a targeted form of phishing, involves tailoring attacks to specific individuals or organizations, often using information gleaned from previous reconnaissance efforts. This personalized approach makes spear phishing more challenging to detect, as attackers leverage contextually relevant details to enhance the credibility of their messages. Moreover, vishing (voice phishing) and smishing (SMS phishing) exploit telephone and text messaging channels, respectively, adding another layer of complexity to the landscape of social engineering tactics. As technology continues to advance, social engineers are likely to leverage emerging platforms and communication channels to refine their techniques and increase the efficacy of their attacks.

It is imperative for users to adopt a proactive and informed approach to mitigate the risks associated with social engineering. Education and awareness play pivotal roles in empowering individuals to recognize and resist manipulation attempts. Users should cultivate a healthy skepticism, particularly when faced with unsolicited communications or requests for sensitive information. Verifying the legitimacy of messages through alternative channels, such as contacting the supposed sender through known and trusted means, can help users confirm the authenticity of requests and thwart potential social engineering attacks. Additionally, organizations should implement comprehensive security awareness training programs to educate employees about the tactics employed by social engineers and instill a security-first mindset.

Moreover, the implementation of robust security measures, such as multi-factor authentication, can add an extra layer of defense against unauthorized access. By requiring multiple forms of verification, even if credentials are compromised, attackers face additional barriers to gaining access. Regular security audits, vulnerability assessments, and incident response drills are essential components of a comprehensive security strategy. These measures help organizations identify and address potential weaknesses in their security posture, ensuring a proactive rather than reactive approach to social engineering threats.

In conclusion, social engineering tactics represent a persistent and adaptive threat that exploits the inherent vulnerabilities of human psychology. By understanding the manipulation techniques employed by social engineers and fostering a culture of security awareness, individuals and organizations can fortify their defenses against these insidious attacks. As technology continues to advance, the landscape of social engineering will undoubtedly evolve, necessitating a continuous commitment to education, awareness, and proactive security measures to safeguard against the ever-changing tactics of those seeking to exploit human trust and behavior for malicious purposes.

Promoting a Security-Conscious Culture

Promoting a security-conscious culture within an organization is a multifaceted and integral aspect of ensuring the resilience and protection of sensitive information in today's complex digital landscape. At the core of this endeavor is the recognition that security is not solely the responsibility of an organization's IT department but a shared commitment that involves every individual within the organization. Establishing a security-conscious culture begins with fostering awareness and education among employees about the importance of cybersecurity, the potential risks, and the role each individual plays in safeguarding the organization's assets.

Central to building a security-conscious culture is the acknowledgment that human behavior is both a critical asset and a potential vulnerability in the realm of cybersecurity. Educating employees about the various cyber threats they may encounter, such as phishing, social engineering, and malware, is essential. This education should extend beyond the workplace, encouraging individuals to practice safe cybersecurity habits in their personal digital lives as well. By understanding the evolving nature of cyber threats, employees can become more adept at recognizing and mitigating potential risks both at work and in their everyday online activities.

Communication is a key driver in cultivating a security-conscious culture. Organizations must establish clear and accessible channels for disseminating information about cybersecurity policies, best practices, and any emerging threats. Regular communication through newsletters, workshops, and training sessions helps keep security at the forefront of employees' minds, reinforcing the importance of vigilance and adherence to established security protocols. Emphasizing the real-world consequences of security lapses, both for the individual and the organization, can provide a compelling incentive for employees to prioritize cybersecurity in their daily activities.

Leadership plays a pivotal role in setting the tone for a security-conscious culture. Executives and managers must demonstrate a strong commitment to cybersecurity by visibly incorporating it into the organization's values and mission. This commitment should be reflected in the allocation of resources, both in terms of budget and personnel, to support robust cybersecurity measures. When leadership prioritizes and invests in cybersecurity initiatives, it sends a clear message throughout the organization that security is not merely a checkbox but an integral part of the organizational ethos.

Creating a culture of transparency and accountability is equally crucial. Employees should feel empowered to report potential security incidents or concerns without fear of reprisal. Establishing a reporting mechanism, such as a dedicated email address or a confidential hotline, encourages the free flow of information and allows organizations to respond promptly to potential threats. Recognizing and rewarding individuals for their contributions to the organization's security posture further reinforces the importance of each employee's role in maintaining a secure environment.

In addition to communication and leadership, the implementation of robust policies and procedures is fundamental to a security-conscious culture. Clearly defined and regularly updated cybersecurity policies should address aspects such as password management, data handling, remote work protocols, and the use of personal devices within the corporate network. Regular training sessions can help reinforce these policies and ensure that employees remain informed about any updates or changes. Simulated phishing exercises and other hands-on activities provide valuable opportunities for employees to practice identifying and responding to potential threats in a controlled environment.

Technological solutions are integral to a comprehensive security strategy, but they should be viewed as one component of a broader cultural approach. Firewalls, antivirus software, and intrusion detection systems are essential tools, but their effectiveness is significantly enhanced when complemented by a vigilant and security-aware workforce. Encouraging employees to adopt multi-factor authentication, keep software and systems up to date, and use secure channels for communication are simple yet effective practices that contribute to the overall security posture of an organization.

Moreover, fostering collaboration between different departments within an organization is vital. The IT and security teams must work closely with human resources, legal, and other departments to ensure that security policies and practices are aligned with the organization's overall goals and objectives. Legal and compliance teams can provide guidance on industry regulations and legal requirements, helping to shape security policies that not only protect the organization but also ensure compliance with relevant laws.

Continuous improvement is a hallmark of a mature security-conscious culture. Regular assessments, audits, and evaluations of the organization's security posture are essential to identify areas for improvement and address emerging threats. An agile and adaptive approach to cybersecurity enables organizations to evolve their strategies in response to the ever-changing threat landscape. Encouraging employees to provide feedback on security practices and protocols fosters a sense of ownership and investment in the organization's overall security posture.

In conclusion, promoting a security-conscious culture is a dynamic and ongoing effort that requires a holistic approach encompassing education, communication, leadership, policies, and collaboration. By recognizing the crucial role that human behavior plays in cybersecurity, organizations can empower their employees to become active participants in the defense against cyber threats. Through clear communication, leadership commitment, and the implementation of effective policies and procedures, organizations can create an environment where security is not just a compliance requirement but a shared responsibility and a fundamental aspect of the organizational culture. In this way, a security-conscious culture becomes a powerful defense against the evolving and sophisticated challenges presented by the modern cybersecurity landscape.

3.4 Building a Resilient Human Firewall

Building a resilient human firewall is a comprehensive and strategic approach to fortifying an organization's defenses against the myriad cyber threats that constantly evolve in the digital landscape. The term "human firewall" underscores the critical role that individuals within an organization play in safeguarding sensitive information and systems. Unlike traditional firewalls that rely on technology to block malicious activities, a human firewall leverages the collective awareness, knowledge, and behavior of employees to create a formidable line of defense against cyber threats. At its core, building a resilient human firewall involves cultivating a culture of cybersecurity consciousness that permeates every level of an organization.

The foundation of a resilient human firewall lies in education and awareness. Employees need to be well-informed about the various cyber threats they may encounter, ranging from phishing and social engineering to malware and ransomware attacks. Regular and targeted training programs are essential to ensure that employees not only understand the potential risks but also develop the skills needed to recognize and respond effectively to security threats. This educational effort should extend beyond theoretical knowledge, incorporating practical scenarios and real-world examples to enhance the relevance and applicability of the training.

Simulated exercises and drills form an integral part of human firewall building. By exposing employees to realistic scenarios that mimic potential cyber threats, organizations can assess their readiness and effectiveness in responding to security incidents. These exercises not only help employees practice applying their knowledge but also serve as valuable learning experiences that reinforce the importance of remaining vigilant and proactive in the face of evolving threats. The lessons learned from simulations can inform and refine organizational policies, procedures, and training programs to better align with the dynamic nature of the cybersecurity landscape.

Communication is a linchpin in building a resilient human firewall. Clear and transparent communication channels must be established to disseminate information about cybersecurity policies, best practices, and any emerging threats. Regular communication through newsletters, email updates, and internal messaging platforms helps to keep security at the forefront of employees' minds. Moreover, encouraging an open dialogue where employees feel comfortable reporting potential security incidents or seeking clarification on security matters fosters a culture of transparency and accountability.

Leadership plays a crucial role in setting the tone for a resilient human firewall. Executives and managers must champion the cause of cybersecurity, demonstrating a commitment to creating a secure environment. When leadership prioritizes and invests in cybersecurity initiatives, it sends a powerful message throughout the organization that security is not just an IT concern but a fundamental aspect of the organizational ethos. Leading by example, executives should actively participate in training programs, adhere to security policies, and promote a culture where cybersecurity is viewed as a shared responsibility.

Policies and procedures form the backbone of a resilient human firewall. Clearly defined and regularly updated cybersecurity policies should cover a spectrum of areas, including password management, data handling, acceptable use of technology, and incident response protocols. These policies should be easily accessible to all employees, and regular training sessions should be conducted to ensure that everyone understands and adheres to them. Importantly, policies should not be overly restrictive; instead, they should strike a balance between security and usability to encourage compliance.

Technology is an essential enabler in building a resilient human firewall. While human awareness and behavior are critical, technology provides additional layers of defense. Implementing advanced threat detection tools, firewalls, and antivirus solutions can help to identify and block malicious activities. Moreover, the use of multi-factor authentication (MFA) adds an extra layer of protection by requiring multiple forms of verification for access. Continuous monitoring of network traffic and systems allows organizations to detect and respond promptly to potential security incidents.

The human firewall extends beyond the confines of the office. With the increasing prevalence of remote work, organizations need to adapt their strategies to secure a dispersed workforce. This involves educating remote employees on secure practices for home networks, the use of personal devices, and the importance of maintaining the same level of vigilance outside the office environment. Remote workers should be included in training programs and simulations to ensure that they are well-equipped to navigate the unique cybersecurity challenges associated with working from diverse locations.

Collaboration between different departments within an organization is paramount in building a resilient human firewall. The IT and security teams must work closely with human resources, legal, and other departments to ensure that security policies align with the organization's overall goals and objectives. Legal and compliance teams can provide guidance on industry regulations and legal requirements, helping to shape security policies that not only protect the organization but also ensure compliance with relevant laws.

Moreover, fostering a sense of ownership and accountability among employees is vital. Recognizing and rewarding individuals for their contributions to the organization's security posture reinforces the importance of each employee's role in maintaining a secure environment. Encouraging employees to report security concerns or suggestions for improvement fosters a culture where everyone feels empowered to contribute to the ongoing enhancement of the human firewall.

A resilient human firewall is not a static entity; it requires continuous improvement and adaptation to the evolving threat landscape. Regular assessments, audits, and evaluations of the organization's security posture are essential to identify areas for improvement and address emerging threats. An agile and adaptive approach to cybersecurity enables organizations to evolve their strategies in response to new challenges. Encouraging employees to stay informed about the latest cybersecurity trends and to remain curious and proactive in their approach to security ensures that the human firewall remains robust and effective over time.

In conclusion, building a resilient human firewall is a holistic and dynamic process that involves education, communication, leadership, policies, technology, and collaboration. By recognizing the crucial role that individuals play in cybersecurity and fostering a culture where security is viewed as a shared responsibility, organizations can fortify their defenses against the evolving and sophisticated challenges presented by the modern cybersecurity landscape. In doing so, they not only protect their assets and information but also create an environment where every employee is an active participant in the ongoing effort to maintain a secure and resilient organization.

Integrating Security into Employee Onboarding

Integrating security into employee onboarding is a critical component of establishing a robust and proactive cybersecurity posture within an organization. As new employees join the workforce, they represent both potential assets and vulnerabilities to the overall security framework. Hence, incorporating security awareness and training into the onboarding process is essential to instill a culture of cybersecurity from the very beginning of an employee's tenure. This integration begins with the recognition that employees are often the first line of defense against cyber threats and that their knowledge and behavior play a pivotal role in safeguarding the organization's sensitive information and systems.

To start, the onboarding process should include comprehensive security training sessions that cover a range of topics, from the basics of cybersecurity hygiene to specific organizational policies and procedures. New hires should gain an understanding of the potential cyber threats they may encounter, including phishing attacks, social engineering tactics, and the importance of maintaining the confidentiality and integrity of sensitive information. These training sessions should not only provide theoretical knowledge but also incorporate practical examples and scenarios relevant to the organization's industry and specific threats it may face.

Additionally, new employees should be educated about the organization's acceptable use policies for technology and the proper handling of sensitive data. This includes guidance on the secure use of email, collaboration tools, and other digital resources. By setting clear expectations from the outset, organizations can help prevent inadvertent security breaches caused by employees unknowingly engaging in risky behavior. Incorporating real-world examples of security incidents and their consequences can make the training more relatable and impactful, emphasizing the importance of adhering to security protocols.

Leadership plays a crucial role in signaling the significance of security during onboarding. Executives and managers should actively participate in these training sessions, underscoring the organization's commitment to creating a secure environment. Their involvement not only emphasizes the importance of security but also sets a precedent for the entire workforce. Furthermore, executives should communicate the organization's security priorities, the role each employee plays in maintaining a secure environment, and the potential consequences of security lapses.

In addition to training, onboarding materials should include clear documentation of the organization's cybersecurity policies. New employees should receive a comprehensive handbook or digital resource that outlines security best practices, incident reporting procedures, and guidelines for secure communication and collaboration. This documentation serves as a reference point for employees to revisit whenever they have questions about security protocols. Regular updates to this documentation ensure that employees are informed about any changes to policies or procedures, keeping them aligned with evolving security requirements.

Technology is a crucial enabler in integrating security into employee onboarding. Organizations can leverage e-learning platforms, interactive modules, and other digital tools to deliver engaging and effective security training. These platforms allow employees to learn at their own pace and provide assessments to measure their understanding of key security concepts. Additionally, incorporating gamification elements, such as quizzes or interactive scenarios, can make the training more engaging and memorable, enhancing its effectiveness in reinforcing security principles.

The onboarding process should also include the implementation of security measures on individual devices used by new employees. This may involve installing and configuring antivirus software, enabling firewalls, and ensuring that operating systems and software are up to date with the latest security patches. By integrating these measures during onboarding, organizations establish a baseline level of security on employee devices, reducing the risk of vulnerabilities that could be exploited by cyber threats.

Furthermore, new employees should be introduced to the organization's incident response plan as part of the onboarding process. Understanding the steps to take in the event of a security incident, including whom to contact and how to report suspicious activities, empowers employees to respond effectively in critical situations. This proactive approach not only enhances the organization's overall security posture but also contributes to a culture where employees feel confident and capable in dealing with security incidents.

Integration of security into employee onboarding extends beyond the physical workplace, especially with the rise of remote and hybrid work environments. Organizations must adapt their onboarding strategies to address the unique security challenges associated with remote work. This involves educating remote employees about secure practices for home networks, the use of personal devices, and the importance of maintaining the same level of vigilance outside the office environment. Providing remote employees with the necessary tools and resources to secure their remote work setups is crucial for maintaining a consistent and effective security posture.

Regular assessments and evaluations are integral to ensuring the effectiveness of security integration into employee onboarding. Periodic reviews of training programs, documentation, and technology tools help identify areas for improvement and adaptation to emerging threats. Surveys or feedback sessions with new hires can provide valuable insights into the onboarding experience, allowing organizations to refine their approach and address any gaps in security education or awareness.

In conclusion, integrating security into employee onboarding is a strategic imperative for organizations seeking to establish a resilient and proactive cybersecurity culture. By providing comprehensive training, clear documentation, involving leadership, leveraging technology, and addressing the unique challenges of remote work, organizations can instill a sense of responsibility and awareness in employees from the very beginning of their tenure. This approach not only strengthens the human firewall but also contributes to a workforce that is well-equipped to navigate the evolving and sophisticated landscape of cybersecurity threats. Ultimately, the investment in integrating security into employee onboarding pays dividends in the form of a more secure, vigilant, and resilient organization.

Monitoring and Measuring User Awareness Programs

Monitoring and measuring user awareness programs are crucial aspects of maintaining and enhancing an organization's cybersecurity posture. In an era where cyber threats continue to evolve in sophistication and frequency, it is essential for organizations to gauge the effectiveness of their efforts in educating and empowering users to be vigilant against potential risks. Monitoring involves the ongoing assessment of user awareness activities, while measuring aims to quantify the impact and outcomes of these programs. Together, these processes form a dynamic feedback loop that informs continuous improvement and adaptation to the ever-changing cybersecurity landscape.

To begin, monitoring user awareness programs involves the real-time observation and evaluation of various elements within the program. This includes tracking participation rates in training sessions, engagement with educational materials, and the frequency of interactions with simulated phishing exercises. By actively monitoring these metrics, organizations can assess the level of user engagement and identify areas that may require additional focus or reinforcement. For instance, low participation rates in specific training modules may indicate the need for a more targeted and compelling approach to certain cybersecurity topics.

In addition to quantitative measures, qualitative feedback from users is a valuable component of the monitoring process. Surveys, focus groups, or interviews can provide insights into the user experience, allowing organizations to understand the effectiveness of communication strategies, the relevance of training content, and the overall impact on user behavior. This qualitative data offers a more nuanced understanding of how users perceive and respond to cybersecurity awareness initiatives, enabling organizations to tailor their programs to better meet the needs and expectations of their workforce.

Moreover, tracking the success of simulated phishing exercises is a key element of monitoring user awareness. These exercises mimic real-world phishing attempts to test users' ability to recognize and respond to phishing threats. Metrics such as click rates, reporting rates, and the types of phishing scenarios that are most effective provide valuable insights into the organization's susceptibility to phishing attacks. By analyzing these metrics, organizations can refine their training content, adjust the frequency of simulations, and target specific areas where users may need additional support in recognizing and avoiding phishing attempts.

The measurement phase of user awareness programs involves assessing the impact and effectiveness of the initiatives over time. This goes beyond monitoring activities by quantifying outcomes and benchmarking against predefined goals. One common metric is the reduction in the click rates observed in simulated phishing exercises over successive iterations of the program. A declining click rate indicates an improvement in users' ability to identify and avoid phishing attempts, reflecting the program's success in enhancing user awareness.

Similarly, measuring the overall improvement in security posture, such as a decrease in the number of security incidents attributed to user-related errors, provides a tangible indicator of the program's impact. Organizations can track trends in incident reports, analyzing data to identify correlations between user awareness efforts and the reduction of incidents related to social engineering, unauthorized access, or data breaches. This quantitative assessment serves as a key performance indicator for the success of user awareness programs in mitigating cybersecurity risks.

User behavior analytics (UBA) is another powerful tool for measuring the impact of awareness programs. By analyzing patterns of user behavior within an organization's digital environment, UBA can identify deviations from normal behavior that may indicate potential security threats. Monitoring user behavior post-awareness training allows organizations to detect anomalies and assess whether users are applying their knowledge and skills in practice. This insight helps organizations refine their training strategies and address any persisting gaps in user awareness.

Furthermore, organizations can leverage incident response metrics to measure the effectiveness of user awareness in minimizing the impact of security incidents. The time it takes to detect and respond to incidents involving user-related errors, as well as the success rate in containing and mitigating the impact of such incidents, provides valuable data for assessing the practical implications of user awareness programs. A decrease in incident resolution times and an increase in the effectiveness of response efforts are indicative of improved user awareness and a more resilient security posture.

Benchmarking against industry standards and best practices is an essential aspect of measurement. Organizations can compare their user awareness programs to recognized frameworks, such as the National Institute of Standards and Technology (NIST) Cybersecurity Framework or industry-specific standards, to assess their maturity and effectiveness. This benchmarking process provides organizations with a broader perspective on their cybersecurity awareness initiatives and helps identify areas for improvement to align with industry-leading practices.

Moreover, the integration of metrics related to employee morale and job satisfaction into the measurement process is valuable. A positive correlation between engagement in user awareness programs and overall employee satisfaction may indicate that the organization's approach is not only enhancing security but also contributing to a positive workplace culture. Conversely, if user awareness efforts are perceived as burdensome or ineffective, organizations may need to reevaluate their strategies to ensure a balanced and positive impact on the workforce.

Continuous improvement is a fundamental principle underlying both monitoring and measuring user awareness programs. Organizations should regularly revisit and update their training content to address emerging threats and technological advancements. Feedback from monitoring activities, user surveys, and incident data should inform iterative improvements to training materials, delivery methods, and the overall user experience. This adaptive approach ensures that user awareness programs remain relevant and effective in the face of evolving cybersecurity challenges.

In conclusion, the dynamic processes of monitoring and measuring user awareness programs are integral to the success of an organization's cybersecurity strategy. By actively monitoring user engagement, leveraging qualitative feedback, and measuring outcomes against predefined goals and industry benchmarks, organizations can assess the effectiveness of their awareness initiatives. The insights gained from this continuous evaluation inform iterative improvements, ensuring that user awareness programs remain responsive to the ever-changing threat landscape. Ultimately, a well-monitored and measured user awareness program contributes not only to a more vigilant and informed workforce but also to an organization's overall resilience against cyber threats.

Chapter 4: Code Bastions: Fortifying Software and Applications

4.1 Software Security Fundamentals

Software security fundamentals encompass a comprehensive set of principles, practices, and methodologies designed to mitigate vulnerabilities, safeguard data, and protect systems from potential cyber threats. At its core, software security is an integral aspect of the broader field of cybersecurity, emphasizing the importance of building secure, resilient software systems. The fundamentals of software security revolve around the recognition that software applications are susceptible to a myriad of threats and attacks, ranging from common exploits like injection attacks and cross-site scripting to more sophisticated threats exploiting design flaws and misconfigurations. In this intricate landscape, understanding and implementing software security fundamentals are crucial for developers, architects, and organizations striving to create robust and trustworthy software.

The foundation of software security lies in secure coding practices. Developers play a pivotal role in writing code that not only fulfills functional requirements but also adheres to security best practices. This involves understanding and mitigating common coding vulnerabilities, such as buffer overflows, injection flaws, and insecure cryptographic practices. Training developers to follow secure coding guidelines, leveraging static code analysis tools, and conducting code reviews are essential components of establishing a secure coding culture. By integrating security into the development process, organizations can identify and address potential vulnerabilities early in the software development lifecycle.

Authentication and authorization are fundamental aspects of software security, ensuring that users and systems can be verified and granted appropriate levels of access. Robust authentication mechanisms involve secure storage and transmission of credentials, multi-factor authentication, and effective session management. Authorization, on the other hand, entails defining and enforcing access controls to restrict user privileges based on their roles and responsibilities. Implementing the principle of least privilege ensures that users and systems only have access to the resources necessary for their specific tasks, minimizing the potential impact of security breaches.

Encryption is a cornerstone of software security, safeguarding data both in transit and at rest. Secure communication protocols, such as TLS (Transport Layer Security), ensure the confidentiality and integrity of data during transmission. Similarly, encrypting sensitive information stored in databases or on disk prevents unauthorized access and protects against data breaches. Understanding encryption algorithms, key management, and the proper implementation of cryptographic protocols are critical aspects of software security fundamentals.

Input validation and output encoding are essential for mitigating injection attacks, a prevalent threat in the software security landscape. Input validation involves scrutinizing user inputs to ensure they conform to expected formats and do not contain malicious content. Similarly, output encoding ensures that data presented to users is properly sanitized to prevent cross-site scripting attacks. By validating inputs and encoding outputs, developers can thwart attempts to inject malicious code into applications, safeguarding against various forms of injection vulnerabilities.

Security is not solely the responsibility of developers; it also involves secure configuration and deployment practices. Ensuring that software and systems are configured with security in mind requires attention to settings, permissions, and default configurations. Regular security assessments and vulnerability scanning during the deployment phase help identify misconfigurations and weaknesses that may expose systems to potential exploits. Automated tools and frameworks facilitate secure deployment practices, enabling organizations to maintain a consistent and secure configuration across their software ecosystem.

Security awareness and training programs are integral components of software security fundamentals. Educating developers, administrators, and other stakeholders about the latest security threats, best practices, and compliance requirements helps create a security-conscious culture within an organization. By fostering a deep understanding of security principles and instilling a proactive mindset, organizations can empower their teams to make informed decisions and contribute to the overall security of the software they develop and maintain.

Secure software development extends beyond the initial coding and deployment phases; it also encompasses robust maintenance and patching practices. Keeping software up to date with the latest security patches is crucial for addressing known vulnerabilities and safeguarding against exploits. Establishing a systematic and timely process for applying patches helps organizations maintain the security of their software ecosystem, reducing the risk of exploitation by attackers seeking to exploit known vulnerabilities.

Secure design principles are foundational to building software that can withstand evolving threats. Threat modeling, a proactive approach to identifying and mitigating potential threats during the design phase, helps architects and developers anticipate and address security concerns early in the development lifecycle. By considering security requirements alongside functional requirements, organizations can design systems that are inherently more resilient to a wide range of threats, reducing the need for reactive security measures.

In the realm of software security, the principle of defense-in-depth is crucial. This approach involves layering multiple security measures throughout a system, creating a robust and redundant defense against potential attacks. Defense-in-depth encompasses a combination of technical controls, secure coding practices, access controls, and monitoring mechanisms. By implementing a multi-layered defense strategy, organizations can minimize the impact of security breaches and create a more resilient software infrastructure.

The integration of security into the software development lifecycle (SDLC) is a fundamental practice in software security fundamentals. Embedding security considerations at each phase of the SDLC, from requirements and design to coding, testing, and deployment, helps ensure that security is not treated as an afterthought. Security assessments, code reviews, and automated testing tools should be seamlessly integrated into the development process, allowing for the continuous identification and remediation of security vulnerabilities.

Monitoring and incident response are critical components of software security fundamentals. Continuous monitoring of software systems helps organizations detect and respond to security incidents in real-time. Security information and event management (SIEM) tools, log analysis, and anomaly detection mechanisms contribute to proactive threat identification. In the event of a security incident, a well-defined incident response plan guides organizations in containing, mitigating, and recovering from the impact of the incident. Regular drills and simulations help ensure that the incident response team is well-prepared to address potential security breaches effectively.

Compliance with industry standards and regulations is an essential aspect of software security fundamentals. Many industries have specific security requirements and compliance frameworks that organizations must adhere to. Whether it is the Payment Card Industry Data Security Standard (PCI DSS), Health Insurance Portability and Accountability Act (HIPAA), or General Data Protection Regulation (GDPR), understanding and implementing the necessary security controls is imperative for organizations to meet legal and regulatory obligations and protect sensitive data.

In conclusion, software security fundamentals are a comprehensive set of principles and practices that underpin the creation of secure and resilient software systems. From secure coding practices to encryption, authentication, and secure deployment, these fundamentals form the backbone of a proactive and holistic approach to software security. By integrating security considerations throughout the software development lifecycle, fostering a security-conscious culture, and staying abreast of evolving threats and best practices, organizations can build software that not only meets functional requirements but also withstands the challenges posed by an ever-changing cybersecurity landscape.

Understanding Software Vulnerabilities

Understanding software vulnerabilities is a critical aspect of cybersecurity, encompassing the identification, analysis, and mitigation of weaknesses within software systems that could be exploited by malicious actors. Software vulnerabilities represent unintended flaws or weaknesses in the design, implementation, or configuration of software, creating potential entry points for security breaches. These vulnerabilities can manifest at various levels, from programming errors and logical flaws to misconfigurations and design flaws, exposing systems to a range of cyber threats. In comprehending software vulnerabilities, it is essential to delve into the different types, their root causes, and the methodologies used for discovery and remediation.

One common category of software vulnerabilities is coding vulnerabilities, arising from errors or oversights during the development process. Buffer overflows, for instance, occur when a program attempts to write more data into a fixed-size buffer than it can hold, potentially leading to unauthorized access or the execution of arbitrary code. Similarly, injection vulnerabilities, such as SQL injection or cross-site scripting (XSS), involve the insertion of malicious code into input fields, exploiting the software's inability to distinguish between legitimate and malicious input. Understanding coding vulnerabilities requires a deep comprehension of programming languages, secure coding practices, and the potential risks associated with common programming mistakes.

Logical vulnerabilities, often rooted in the software's design or business logic, represent another facet of software weaknesses. These vulnerabilities may not necessarily involve coding errors but rather flaws in how the software processes and validates user inputs or performs critical operations. For instance, authentication bypass vulnerabilities can occur when the software fails to adequately verify a user's identity, allowing unauthorized access to privileged functionalities. Understanding logical vulnerabilities requires a comprehensive analysis of the software's intended behavior, threat modeling, and consideration of potential abuse scenarios that could circumvent intended security controls.

Configuration vulnerabilities stem from misconfigurations in software settings, leading to unintended security weaknesses. These vulnerabilities often result from default configurations that prioritize ease of use over security or from overlooking specific security settings during deployment. An example of a configuration vulnerability is leaving default login credentials unchanged, allowing unauthorized access to sensitive systems. Understanding configuration vulnerabilities involves assessing the security implications of different configuration settings, adhering to security best practices during deployment, and conducting regular audits to identify and rectify misconfigurations.

Design flaws represent vulnerabilities embedded in the fundamental architecture or structure of a software system. These weaknesses are often more challenging to address, as they may result from decisions made early in the development lifecycle. For instance, inadequate input validation at the design level can lead to a range of vulnerabilities, such as injection attacks. Understanding design flaws necessitates a holistic view of the software architecture, threat modeling during the design phase, and a proactive approach to addressing potential security implications before implementation.

The process of discovering and identifying software vulnerabilities involves various methodologies and tools. Automated vulnerability scanners, for example, can analyze software code or deployed applications to identify known vulnerabilities, coding errors, or misconfigurations. Manual code reviews by skilled security professionals are essential for uncovering complex vulnerabilities that automated tools may overlook. Additionally, penetration testing involves simulating real-world attacks to identify and exploit vulnerabilities, providing a comprehensive assessment of a system's security posture. Understanding the nuances of these discovery methodologies is crucial for organizations seeking to proactively identify and address vulnerabilities before they can be exploited by malicious actors.

The Common Vulnerabilities and Exposures (CVE) system is a widely used standardized method for identifying and naming software vulnerabilities. Each vulnerability is assigned a unique identifier (CVE ID), facilitating consistent communication and collaboration across the cybersecurity community. The National Vulnerability Database (NVD) serves as a repository for these identified vulnerabilities, providing detailed information on each vulnerability, including its severity, impact, and available remediation measures. Cybersecurity professionals and organizations regularly monitor the CVE and NVD databases to stay informed about emerging threats and vulnerabilities relevant to their software environments.

The severity of a software vulnerability is often categorized using the Common Vulnerability Scoring System (CVSS), which assigns a numerical score based on factors such as the exploitability of the vulnerability, the potential impact on confidentiality, integrity, and availability, and whether the vulnerability requires user interaction for exploitation. Understanding the CVSS scoring system aids organizations in prioritizing their efforts to address the most critical vulnerabilities that pose the highest risk to their systems.

The remediation of software vulnerabilities involves implementing patches, updates, or configuration changes to eliminate or mitigate the identified weaknesses. Software vendors regularly release security patches to address known vulnerabilities, and organizations must promptly apply these patches to reduce the risk of exploitation. However, the remediation process extends beyond applying patches; organizations must also address configuration vulnerabilities, review and update security policies, and conduct thorough testing to ensure that remediation efforts do not inadvertently introduce new issues.

The concept of "zero-day vulnerabilities" adds an additional layer of complexity to the understanding of software vulnerabilities. Zero-day vulnerabilities are those for which no patch or fix is available at the time of discovery. These vulnerabilities pose a heightened risk, as malicious actors can exploit them before the software vendor has an opportunity to release a patch. Mitigating the risk of zero-day vulnerabilities involves implementing proactive security measures, such as intrusion detection systems, network segmentation, and behavioral analysis, to detect and respond to potential exploitation attempts in real-time.

A crucial aspect of understanding software vulnerabilities is the importance of a coordinated and responsible disclosure process. Security researchers and ethical hackers often discover vulnerabilities and, rather than exploiting them maliciously, follow a responsible disclosure process. This involves notifying the software vendor or relevant authorities about the vulnerability, allowing them time to develop and release a patch before the details are publicly disclosed. Responsible disclosure helps ensure that vulnerabilities are addressed promptly, minimizing the window of opportunity for malicious exploitation.

Security awareness and training play a pivotal role in addressing software vulnerabilities. Educating developers, IT professionals, and end-users about secure coding practices, the implications of different types of vulnerabilities, and the importance of timely patching enhances the overall security posture of an organization. By fostering a culture of security awareness, organizations empower their personnel to contribute actively to the identification and remediation of vulnerabilities, creating a collaborative and proactive approach to software security.

In conclusion, understanding software vulnerabilities is a multifaceted endeavor that involves recognizing coding, logical, configuration, and design flaws within software systems. It requires a comprehensive understanding of various discovery methodologies, the significance of vulnerability databases, and the intricacies of vulnerability scoring systems. The remediation process involves timely patching, configuration adjustments, and proactive security measures. Emphasizing responsible disclosure, addressing zero-day vulnerabilities, and promoting security awareness contribute to a holistic approach to managing software vulnerabilities. In a rapidly evolving cybersecurity landscape, continuous vigilance, proactive measures, and a collaborative approach are essential for organizations seeking to fortify their software systems against potential threats and attacks.

Importance of Secure Coding Practices

The importance of secure coding practices in software development cannot be overstated, as it serves as a foundational pillar in building resilient and trustworthy software systems. Secure coding goes beyond merely achieving functional requirements; it involves incorporating principles and practices that mitigate vulnerabilities, protect against cyber threats, and uphold the confidentiality, integrity, and availability of sensitive data. At its core, secure coding is a proactive approach that prioritizes security considerations throughout the software development lifecycle, from the initial design phase to deployment and ongoing maintenance.

One of the primary reasons secure coding practices are indispensable lies in their role in preventing and mitigating security vulnerabilities. Software vulnerabilities, ranging from common coding errors to more sophisticated design flaws, provide potential entry points for attackers seeking to exploit weaknesses in a system. Secure coding practices, such as input validation, proper error handling, and adherence to secure coding guidelines, act as a robust defense against vulnerabilities like injection attacks, buffer overflows, and other common exploits. By instilling secure coding habits, developers contribute to the creation of software that is inherently more resistant to exploitation, reducing the risk of security breaches and unauthorized access.

Furthermore, secure coding practices play a pivotal role in protecting against the prevalent and pervasive threat of injection attacks. Injection vulnerabilities, such as SQL injection and cross-site scripting (XSS), occur when untrusted data is improperly handled within a software application, allowing attackers to inject malicious code. Secure coding practices, such as parameterized queries, input validation, and output encoding, act as effective countermeasures against injection attacks. By validating and sanitizing input data, developers can ensure that user inputs are processed safely, mitigating the risk of injecting malicious code into the application.

Secure coding practices also contribute significantly to the creation of robust authentication and authorization mechanisms within software systems. Authentication vulnerabilities, such as weak password policies or improper session management, can lead to unauthorized access and compromise user accounts. Authorization vulnerabilities, on the other hand, may result in insufficiently enforced access controls, allowing users to access functionalities or data beyond their intended privileges. Through secure coding practices, developers can implement strong authentication mechanisms, enforce proper session management, and establish granular access controls, ensuring that users are verified and authorized appropriately.

In the context of encryption and data protection, secure coding practices are paramount in safeguarding sensitive information. Inadequate cryptographic practices, such as using weak algorithms or improperly managing encryption keys, can expose data to unauthorized disclosure or tampering. Secure coding entails implementing robust encryption algorithms, managing cryptographic keys securely, and ensuring the proper use of encryption throughout the software application. By adhering to secure coding principles in the handling of sensitive data, developers contribute to the creation of software that protects the confidentiality and integrity of information, even in the event of a security breach.

Secure coding practices also address the ever-evolving challenge of securing web applications against various threats. Cross-site scripting (XSS) and cross-site request forgery (CSRF) are common web application vulnerabilities that can lead to the compromise of user data or the execution of unauthorized actions on behalf of authenticated users. Through secure coding practices such as input validation, output encoding, and anti-CSRF tokens, developers can fortify web applications against these threats. Secure coding in the context of web applications involves understanding the unique challenges posed by the web environment and implementing measures to mitigate the associated risks effectively.

Moreover, the importance of secure coding practices is underscored by their role in reducing the attack surface of software applications. Attack surface refers to the potential points of entry that an attacker could exploit to compromise a system. Through secure coding, developers minimize unnecessary functionality, reduce the use of insecure libraries, and eliminate unnecessary access points, thereby narrowing the attack surface. By adopting the principle of least privilege, secure coding practices ensure that users and components of the software have only the necessary permissions, limiting the potential impact of security breaches.

Additionally, the significance of secure coding practices extends to compliance with regulatory requirements and industry standards. Many industries have specific regulations and standards that mandate the protection of sensitive information and the implementation of secure coding practices. For example, the Payment Card Industry Data Security Standard (PCI DSS) includes requirements for secure coding to protect payment card data. Adhering to secure coding practices not only helps organizations meet regulatory obligations but also instills a security-minded culture that aligns with industry best practices.

In the context of the evolving landscape of software development, where agile methodologies and DevOps practices are prevalent, secure coding becomes an integral part of the continuous integration and continuous deployment (CI/CD) pipeline. Incorporating security checks, static code analysis, and automated testing for security vulnerabilities into the CI/CD process ensures that security is not sacrificed in the pursuit of rapid development and deployment. By integrating secure coding practices into the DevOps lifecycle, organizations can achieve a balance between speed and security, fostering a culture of collaboration between development and security teams.

Furthermore, secure coding practices contribute significantly to the resilience of software applications in the face of emerging threats and evolving attack vectors. Cybersecurity threats are dynamic, and attackers continuously develop new techniques to exploit vulnerabilities. Secure coding practices involve staying abreast of the latest security trends, understanding emerging threats, and adapting coding practices to address new challenges. By fostering a proactive and adaptive approach to security, developers contribute to the creation of software that can withstand the test of time and remain resilient against the evolving threat landscape.

In terms of cost-effectiveness, the importance of secure coding practices is evident in their role in minimizing the potential impact and financial consequences of security breaches. The cost of remediating security vulnerabilities and addressing data breaches is significantly higher than the investment required to implement secure coding practices from the outset. By prioritizing security during the development phase, organizations can avoid the substantial costs associated with incident response, legal consequences, and reputational damage that may result from a security breach.

Secure coding practices also promote a culture of security awareness and responsibility among developers. Educating developers about the implications of their coding decisions, the potential security risks, and the importance of adhering to secure coding guidelines fosters a mindset where security is considered an integral part of software development. By instilling a sense of ownership and accountability for security, organizations create a collaborative environment where developers actively contribute to the overall security posture of the software they build.

In conclusion, the importance of secure coding practices is multifaceted and integral to the overall success of software development efforts. Secure coding not only mitigates vulnerabilities, protects against cyber threats, and upholds data confidentiality but also contributes to compliance with regulatory requirements, reduces the attack surface, and enhances the resilience of software applications. As a proactive and cost-effective approach, secure coding practices play a crucial role in maintaining the trust of users, minimizing the risk of security breaches, and fostering a culture of security awareness within organizations. In the ever-evolving landscape of cybersecurity, secure coding practices stand as a foundational element in building software that is not only functional and innovative but also secure and resilient.

4.2 Threats to Software Security

Threats to software security represent a diverse and dynamic array of risks that continually challenge the integrity, confidentiality, and availability of digital assets. These threats, originating from various sources, exploit vulnerabilities within software systems, creating potential avenues for unauthorized access, data breaches, and service disruptions. Understanding the landscape of threats to software security is paramount for individuals and organizations involved in software development, deployment, and maintenance. From common threats that exploit coding vulnerabilities to sophisticated attacks leveraging social engineering and advanced persistent threats, the spectrum of risks underscores the need for comprehensive security measures throughout the software development lifecycle.

One prevalent category of threats to software security stems from coding vulnerabilities that arise during the development phase. These vulnerabilities include buffer overflows, injection attacks, and insecure cryptographic practices, among others. Buffer overflows occur when a program attempts to write more data into a fixed-size buffer than it can hold, potentially leading to the execution of arbitrary code or unauthorized access. Injection attacks, such as SQL injection and cross-site scripting (XSS), involve the insertion of malicious code into input fields, exploiting the software's inability to distinguish between legitimate and malicious input. Insecure cryptographic practices, such as the use of weak algorithms or inadequate key management, can compromise the confidentiality and integrity of sensitive data. Mitigating these coding vulnerabilities requires a proactive approach, incorporating secure coding practices, regular code reviews, and automated tools to identify and remediate weaknesses before deployment.

Web applications face a distinct set of threats due to their ubiquitous presence and the nature of user interactions. Cross-site scripting (XSS) and cross-site request forgery (CSRF) are common threats targeting web applications. XSS occurs when attackers inject malicious scripts into web pages viewed by other users, potentially leading to the theft of sensitive information or the compromise of user accounts. CSRF involves tricking authenticated users into performing unintended actions without their consent, leading to unauthorized changes or transactions. Web application firewalls, input validation, and secure session management are essential countermeasures to address these threats. Additionally, the rise of client-side technologies and rich web interfaces introduces new attack vectors, such as client-side injection attacks and security implications associated with asynchronous communication.

Phishing attacks represent a persistent and pervasive threat to software security, exploiting human vulnerabilities rather than technical weaknesses. In a phishing attack, malicious actors attempt to deceive individuals into divulging sensitive information, such as usernames, passwords, or financial details, by posing as trustworthy entities. Phishing techniques continue to evolve, encompassing email phishing, spear phishing targeting specific individuals, and vishing (voice phishing) over phone calls. Education and awareness programs are crucial in mitigating the risk of phishing, as individuals need to recognize the signs of deceptive communication and avoid falling victim to social engineering tactics. Implementing email filtering, multi-factor authentication, and regularly updating security policies can also fortify defenses against phishing threats.

Software security is further jeopardized by the emergence of advanced persistent threats (APTs), which represent sophisticated and targeted attacks typically orchestrated by well-funded and organized adversaries. APTs involve a prolonged and stealthy approach to infiltrate and compromise specific targets, often with the objective of espionage, intellectual property theft, or political influence. These threats leverage various techniques, including zero-day vulnerabilities, social engineering, and malware, to persistently evade detection and maintain unauthorized access. Detecting and mitigating APTs require advanced threat detection mechanisms, continuous monitoring, and a comprehensive incident response strategy. Organizations must adopt a proactive stance, anticipating the potential presence of APTs and implementing security measures that extend beyond traditional perimeter defenses.

The evolving landscape of software security is also shaped by the increasing prevalence of ransomware attacks. Ransomware is malicious software that encrypts a victim's files, rendering them inaccessible, and demands a ransom payment in exchange for the decryption key. Ransomware attacks often target individuals, businesses, and critical infrastructure, causing significant disruptions and financial losses. The tactics employed by ransomware attackers include phishing emails, exploiting unpatched vulnerabilities, and leveraging social engineering to gain access to systems. Defending against ransomware requires a combination of robust backup strategies, regular software updates, and user education to prevent the inadvertent execution of malicious payloads.

Supply chain attacks have emerged as a prominent and sophisticated threat vector, exploiting vulnerabilities within the interconnected ecosystem of software development and distribution. Adversaries compromise the software supply chain by infiltrating the development process, introducing malicious code into legitimate software, or exploiting dependencies within the supply chain. The SolarWinds supply chain attack is a notable example where attackers compromised a software update to distribute a backdoor to thousands of organizations. Mitigating supply chain threats necessitates enhanced scrutiny of third-party components, secure coding practices, and the implementation of integrity checks to verify the authenticity of software updates. Organizations must establish robust measures to ensure the integrity and security of the entire software supply chain.

The Internet of Things (IoT) introduces a new dimension of software security challenges, as the proliferation of connected devices expands the attack surface and introduces vulnerabilities that can be exploited. IoT devices, ranging from smart home appliances to industrial control systems, often lack stringent security controls and are susceptible to attacks such as device hijacking, data interception, and unauthorized access. The interconnected nature of IoT ecosystems poses unique challenges, as vulnerabilities in one device can potentially impact the entire network. Secure coding practices specific to IoT, device authentication, and encryption are essential in addressing these threats. Additionally, ongoing efforts to establish industry standards and regulatory frameworks for IoT security aim to enhance the overall resilience of IoT ecosystems.

Social engineering remains a persistent threat vector that exploits human psychology to manipulate individuals into divulging sensitive information or performing actions that compromise security. Techniques such as pretexting, baiting, and quid pro quo involve creating deceptive scenarios to manipulate individuals into revealing confidential information or taking unauthorized actions. Phishing, a form of social engineering, often combines deceptive communication with malicious links or attachments to trick individuals into providing credentials or installing malware. Combating social engineering threats requires a combination of awareness training, user education, and the implementation of technical controls such as email filtering and multi-factor authentication. Organizations must foster a culture of skepticism and empower individuals to question unexpected or suspicious requests.

Cryptocurrency-related threats have gained prominence in the cyber threat landscape, with attackers leveraging cryptocurrency mining malware and ransomware to exploit computing resources and demand ransom payments. Cryptocurrency mining malware infects systems, utilizing their computational power to mine cryptocurrencies without the owner's consent. Ransomware attacks often demand ransom payments in cryptocurrency due to its pseudonymous nature, making transactions difficult to trace. Defending against cryptocurrency-related threats involves securing systems against malware, implementing robust backup strategies, and educating users about the risks associated with cryptocurrency payments. Organizations must also prioritize the patching of vulnerabilities exploited by cryptocurrency mining malware to prevent unauthorized use of computing resources.

In conclusion, the multifaceted landscape of threats to software security necessitates a holistic and adaptive approach to defense. From coding vulnerabilities that can be mitigated through secure coding practices to sophisticated APTs and supply chain attacks that require advanced threat detection, the spectrum of risks is broad and dynamic. Addressing threats involves a combination of technical controls, user education, proactive monitoring, and collaboration within the cybersecurity community. As software continues to play a pivotal role in our interconnected digital world, the vigilance and resilience of software security measures are paramount in mitigating risks, protecting sensitive information, and ensuring the overall integrity of digital ecosystems.

Exploitation of Software Vulnerabilities

The exploitation of software vulnerabilities represents a pervasive and sophisticated facet of cyber threats, where malicious actors seek to capitalize on weaknesses within software systems for unauthorized access, data manipulation, or system compromise. This exploitation occurs at various levels, from common coding errors to intricate design flaws, and it poses a continuous challenge to the security posture of organizations, individuals, and entire digital ecosystems. Understanding the mechanisms and motivations behind the exploitation of software vulnerabilities is crucial for developing effective defense strategies, implementing proactive security measures, and fortifying software systems against evolving cyber threats.

At its core, the exploitation of software vulnerabilities often begins with the identification of weaknesses within the codebase or design of a software application. Common coding vulnerabilities, such as buffer overflows, injection attacks, and insecure cryptographic practices, provide entry points for attackers to manipulate the intended behavior of the software. For instance, a buffer overflow vulnerability occurs when an attacker sends more data than a program's buffer can handle, leading to the execution of arbitrary code. Injection attacks, such as SQL injection or cross-site scripting (XSS), involve injecting malicious code into input fields, exploiting the software's failure to distinguish between legitimate and malicious inputs. Exploiting these coding vulnerabilities requires a thorough understanding of the software's implementation details, the ability to craft malicious inputs, and the knowledge of techniques to bypass security controls.

Sophisticated attackers often leverage zero-day vulnerabilities, which are flaws in software that are unknown to the vendor or the cybersecurity community. These vulnerabilities provide a unique advantage to attackers as there are no available patches or mitigations at the time of exploitation. The discovery and exploitation of zero-day vulnerabilities involve a combination of reverse engineering, vulnerability research, and, in some cases, insider knowledge. Once a zero-day vulnerability is identified, attackers can craft exploits to take advantage of the specific weakness, potentially allowing them to gain unauthorized access, execute arbitrary code, or compromise the confidentiality of data. The clandestine nature of zero-day exploits makes them particularly challenging to defend against, emphasizing the importance of rapid detection and response capabilities.

The exploitation of software vulnerabilities extends beyond traditional coding weaknesses to encompass logical flaws in the design or business logic of an application. Logical vulnerabilities may not involve traditional coding errors but instead exploit flaws in how the software processes and validates user inputs or executes critical operations. For example, an authentication bypass vulnerability could allow an attacker to access privileged functionalities without proper verification of user identity. Identifying and exploiting logical vulnerabilities often requires a deep understanding of the software's intended behavior, potential abuse scenarios, and an ability to manipulate inputs or interactions to subvert the intended security controls.

Injection attacks, a prevalent method of exploiting software vulnerabilities, take various forms depending on the context of the application. SQL injection involves injecting malicious SQL queries into input fields, potentially leading to unauthorized access to databases or data manipulation. Cross-site scripting (XSS) targets web applications by injecting malicious scripts into web pages viewed by other users, enabling the theft of sensitive information or the compromise of user accounts. The exploitation of injection vulnerabilities involves crafting inputs that evade input validation and execute malicious commands within the application's context. Attackers leverage a variety of techniques, such as encoding, obfuscation, and evasion tactics, to bypass security measures and successfully inject and execute malicious code.

Web applications, given their widespread use and accessibility, are particularly susceptible to exploitation. Cross-site scripting (XSS) and cross-site request forgery (CSRF) are common threats that target web applications, compromising the security and privacy of users. XSS occurs when attackers inject malicious scripts into web pages viewed by other users, allowing them to steal sensitive information or perform actions on behalf of the user without their consent. CSRF involves tricking authenticated users into performing unintended actions without their knowledge, leading to unauthorized changes or transactions. The exploitation of web application vulnerabilities often involves the manipulation of user interactions, session management, and the injection of malicious payloads into web forms. Web application firewalls, secure coding practices, and regular security assessments are essential countermeasures to defend against these threats.

Moreover, the exploitation of software vulnerabilities frequently involves the deployment of malware, which can take various forms and serve diverse purposes. Malware encompasses a broad category of malicious software designed to disrupt, damage, or gain unauthorized access to computer systems. Exploiting vulnerabilities to deliver malware may involve the use of malicious attachments in emails, drive-by downloads from compromised websites, or the exploitation of unpatched software vulnerabilities to execute arbitrary code. Once deployed, malware can enable remote control of compromised systems, exfiltration of sensitive data, or the creation of botnets for large-scale attacks. Defending against the exploitation of vulnerabilities to deliver malware requires a combination of robust endpoint protection, network monitoring, and user education to mitigate the risk of infection.

Supply chain attacks represent a sophisticated form of exploitation, where adversaries compromise the software supply chain to introduce malicious code into legitimate software or manipulate dependencies. The SolarWinds supply chain attack is a prominent example where attackers compromised a software update to distribute a backdoor to thousands of organizations. Exploiting the software supply chain involves infiltrating development environments, introducing malicious code into code repositories, or compromising the distribution mechanisms for software updates. These attacks highlight the interconnected nature of the software ecosystem, where vulnerabilities in one component can have cascading effects throughout the supply chain. Defending against supply chain attacks requires enhanced scrutiny of third-party components, secure coding practices, and the implementation of integrity checks to verify the authenticity of software updates.

Advanced Persistent Threats (APTs) represent a high-profile and persistent form of exploitation where well-funded and organized adversaries conduct targeted attacks over an extended period. APTs typically involve multiple stages, including initial compromise, lateral movement, privilege escalation, and data exfiltration. The exploitation of vulnerabilities within the targeted environment enables APTs to maintain persistent access and avoid detection. APTs often leverage zero-day vulnerabilities, social engineering, and sophisticated malware to achieve their objectives. Detecting and mitigating APTs require advanced threat detection mechanisms, continuous monitoring, and a comprehensive incident response strategy. Organizations must adopt a proactive stance, anticipating potential APT presence and implementing security measures that extend beyond traditional perimeter defenses.

Furthermore, the exploitation of software vulnerabilities is frequently associated with ransomware attacks, where attackers encrypt files or entire systems and demand a ransom payment for their release. Ransomware exploits vulnerabilities in software or human behavior, often leveraging phishing emails, unpatched software, or insecure remote desktop protocols. Once a system is compromised, the ransomware encrypts files, rendering them inaccessible, and displays a ransom note demanding payment in cryptocurrency. The exploitation of vulnerabilities in this context emphasizes the critical importance of timely software updates, secure configurations, and user education to prevent the successful deployment of ransomware.

Cryptocurrency-related threats have emerged as a form of exploitation where attackers leverage cryptocurrency mining malware to exploit computing resources for mining without the owner's consent. Cryptocurrency mining malware infects systems, utilizing their computational power to mine cryptocurrencies, often leading to degraded system performance and increased energy consumption. The exploitation of vulnerabilities to deploy cryptocurrency mining malware may involve exploiting unpatched software vulnerabilities, leveraging social engineering, or compromising web applications. Defending against these threats requires securing systems against malware, implementing robust backup strategies, and educating users about the risks associated with cryptocurrency mining.

Social engineering, a tactic that exploits human psychology to manipulate individuals into divulging sensitive information or performing actions that compromise security, is often intertwined with the exploitation of software vulnerabilities. Techniques such as phishing, pretexting, and baiting involve creating deceptive scenarios to manipulate individuals. Phishing, in particular, combines deceptive communication with malicious links or attachments to trick individuals into providing credentials or installing malware. The success of social engineering tactics often relies on exploiting the trust or curiosity of individuals, emphasizing the importance of security awareness training, user education, and the implementation of technical controls such as email filtering and multi-factor authentication to mitigate these threats.

In conclusion, the exploitation of software vulnerabilities is a multifaceted and persistent challenge that spans a spectrum of techniques, motivations, and targets. From common coding errors to advanced persistent threats, attackers continually seek to capitalize on weaknesses within software systems for various malicious purposes. Mitigating the risk of exploitation requires a combination of secure coding practices, timely software updates, user education, and advanced threat detection mechanisms. As software plays an increasingly central role in our digital lives, the vigilance and resilience of defenses against the exploitation of vulnerabilities are paramount in safeguarding the integrity, confidentiality, and availability of digital assets.

Common Attacks on Applications

Common attacks on applications represent a persistent and evolving threat landscape in the realm of cybersecurity, where malicious actors employ diverse techniques to exploit vulnerabilities and compromise the security of software systems. These attacks, ranging from traditional methods to more sophisticated strategies, target applications at various layers, including the application code, network communication, and user interfaces. Understanding the nature and characteristics of these common attacks is crucial for developers, security professionals, and organizations to fortify their applications against potential risks and safeguard sensitive data.

One prevalent category of attacks on applications involves injection attacks, where malicious code is injected into the input fields of an application to manipulate its behavior. SQL injection (SQLi) is a classic example, where attackers insert malicious SQL queries into input fields, exploiting the application's failure to properly validate and sanitize user inputs. This can lead to unauthorized access, data manipulation, or even the execution of arbitrary commands on the underlying database. Similarly, cross-site scripting (XSS) attacks target web applications, injecting malicious scripts into web pages that are then served to other users. This enables attackers to steal sensitive information, such as user credentials or session tokens, and compromise the integrity of the application's content.

Cross-site request forgery (CSRF) is another type of attack that exploits the trust a web application has in a user's browser. In CSRF attacks, malicious actors trick authenticated users into unknowingly executing unwanted actions on a web application where the user is already authenticated. This could lead to unauthorized changes in user settings, initiation of financial transactions, or other unintended actions, as the attacker is able to forge requests that the application processes as legitimate.

Authentication-related attacks pose significant threats to applications, aiming to compromise user credentials and gain unauthorized access. Brute-force attacks involve systematically attempting various combinations of usernames and passwords until the correct credentials are discovered. Credential stuffing attacks leverage previously leaked or stolen credentials to gain unauthorized access to accounts where users have reused passwords across multiple services. Additionally, phishing attacks target users directly, tricking them into revealing their login credentials through deceptive emails or websites designed to mimic legitimate login pages. Effective countermeasures include implementing multi-factor authentication, secure password policies, and user education programs to raise awareness about phishing threats.

Denial-of-service (DoS) and distributed denial-of-service (DDoS) attacks aim to disrupt the availability of an application by overwhelming its resources or infrastructure. In a DoS attack, a single source overwhelms a target application with a flood of requests, causing it to become unresponsive. DDoS attacks, on the other hand, involve coordinated efforts from multiple sources to amplify the volume of traffic, making it even more challenging to mitigate. These attacks can lead to service outages, degraded performance, and financial losses. Mitigation strategies include implementing traffic filtering, load balancing, and leveraging content delivery networks (CDNs) to distribute the load and absorb malicious traffic.

Man-in-the-middle (MitM) attacks exploit vulnerabilities in communication channels to intercept and manipulate data exchanged between two parties. In the context of applications, MitM attacks can occur during data transmission, potentially exposing sensitive information such as login credentials or financial transactions. Techniques used in MitM attacks include packet sniffing, session hijacking, and the use of rogue Wi-Fi access points. Employing encryption through protocols like HTTPS helps secure communication channels and prevent unauthorized interception. Additionally, certificate pinning and secure session management can further enhance the resilience of applications against MitM attacks.

Session management attacks target the mechanisms by which applications maintain user sessions, aiming to compromise user identities and permissions. Session fixation attacks involve an attacker setting a user's session identifier, potentially allowing them to hijack the user's session. Session hijacking attacks, also known as session sniffing, occur when an attacker intercepts and steals an active session identifier, gaining unauthorized access to the victim's account. Implementing secure session management practices, such as using random and long-lived session identifiers, employing secure cookies, and regularly rotating session keys, helps mitigate the risk of these attacks.

File inclusion vulnerabilities can be exploited by attackers to manipulate the files accessed by an application, potentially leading to unauthorized access or the execution of arbitrary code. Inclusion attacks come in two main forms: local file inclusion (LFI) and remote file inclusion (RFI). LFI occurs when an application allows the inclusion of files that are already present on the server, potentially leading to the disclosure of sensitive information. RFI involves the inclusion of files from a remote server, allowing attackers to execute malicious code. Preventive measures include input validation, using whitelists to restrict file inclusion, and avoiding dynamic file inclusion whenever possible.

Security misconfigurations represent a common yet often overlooked attack vector where misconfigured settings or default configurations expose vulnerabilities in an application. This can include default usernames and passwords, unnecessary open ports, or overly permissive access controls. Attackers exploit these misconfigurations to gain unauthorized access, escalate privileges, or perform other malicious activities. Implementing a thorough security review process, regularly auditing configurations, and following security best practices help identify and remediate misconfigurations, strengthening the overall security posture of applications.

Cryptographic attacks leverage weaknesses in the implementation or usage of cryptographic mechanisms within an application. Common cryptographic attacks include ciphertext-only attacks, where attackers intercept and analyze encrypted data without access to the encryption key, and chosen ciphertext attacks, where attackers can choose specific ciphertexts for decryption. Additionally, cryptographic vulnerabilities can lead to the compromise of digital signatures, exposing sensitive information or enabling unauthorized access. Ensuring the proper implementation of cryptographic algorithms, using secure key management practices, and staying informed about the latest cryptographic vulnerabilities are essential for mitigating these risks.

Code injection attacks exploit vulnerabilities in an application's code to inject and execute malicious code. Beyond injection attacks like SQL injection and XSS, other forms of code injection include operating system command injection and LDAP injection. In OS command injection, attackers inject malicious commands into commands executed by the underlying operating system, potentially leading to unauthorized access or system compromise. LDAP injection attacks target applications that use Lightweight Directory Access Protocol (LDAP) for authentication, allowing attackers to manipulate LDAP queries and gain unauthorized access. Preventive measures involve input validation, using parameterized queries, and avoiding the direct concatenation of user inputs into code execution contexts.

As applications increasingly leverage third-party components and libraries, supply chain attacks have gained prominence. These attacks involve compromising the software supply chain to introduce malicious code into legitimate software or manipulate dependencies. Attackers may infiltrate development environments, compromise code repositories, or tamper with software updates to distribute backdoors or other malicious payloads. The SolarWinds supply chain attack exemplifies the potential impact of such exploits. Defending against supply chain attacks requires enhanced scrutiny of third-party components, secure coding practices, and the implementation of integrity checks to verify the authenticity of software updates.

Social engineering attacks exploit human psychology to manipulate individuals into divulging sensitive information or performing actions that compromise security. Techniques such as phishing, pretexting, and baiting are commonly used to trick individuals into revealing credentials, clicking on malicious links, or downloading malware. Phishing, in particular, often combines deceptive communication with malicious payloads to compromise both individuals and organizations. Robust user education programs, phishing awareness training, and the implementation of email filtering mechanisms are essential for mitigating the risk of social engineering attacks.

In conclusion, the landscape of common attacks on applications is diverse and continually evolving, reflecting the dynamic nature of cybersecurity threats. From injection attacks that exploit coding vulnerabilities to social engineering tactics targeting human vulnerabilities, attackers employ a wide array of techniques to compromise the security of applications. Robust defense strategies involve secure coding practices, regular security assessments, user education, and the implementation of security controls tailored to mitigate specific threats. As applications play an increasingly central role in our interconnected digital world, the vigilance and resilience of defenses against these common attacks are paramount in ensuring the integrity, confidentiality, and availability of digital assets.

4.3 Secure Software Development Life Cycle (SDLC)

The Secure Software Development Life Cycle (SDLC) is a comprehensive and proactive approach to integrating security measures into every phase of the software development process, aiming to create robust and secure applications. This approach recognizes that addressing security considerations solely at the end of the development cycle is insufficient and may result in overlooking critical vulnerabilities. Instead, it emphasizes the incorporation of security principles and practices from the initial planning stages through to deployment and ongoing maintenance. The Secure SDLC aligns with the broader SDLC phases, including requirements gathering, design, implementation, testing, deployment, and maintenance, with the overarching goal of minimizing security risks and building resilient software systems.

The first phase of the Secure SDLC is the requirements gathering stage, where security considerations are integrated into the definition of functional and non-functional requirements. This involves identifying potential security threats, defining security controls, and establishing security-related user stories. By incorporating security requirements at the outset, development teams lay the foundation for a security-focused development process and ensure that security is an integral part of the application's design and functionality.

In the design phase, security architecture and design principles are crucial components of the Secure SDLC. Security architects collaborate with development teams to define the overall system architecture, identify potential security risks, and design security controls. Threat modeling is a valuable practice during this phase, allowing teams to systematically analyze and prioritize potential threats and vulnerabilities. Security controls, such as encryption, access controls, and secure APIs, are integrated into the design to mitigate identified risks. The Secure SDLC emphasizes the importance of creating a robust security architecture that can withstand potential attacks and ensure the confidentiality, integrity, and availability of sensitive information.

As the development phase commences, secure coding practices become a focal point in the Secure SDLC. Developers are trained in secure coding principles and guidelines, encouraging practices that mitigate common vulnerabilities such as injection attacks, buffer overflows, and insecure data storage. Code reviews and static analysis tools are employed to identify and address security flaws early in the development process. By emphasizing secure coding from the outset, the Secure SDLC aims to prevent vulnerabilities from being introduced into the codebase, reducing the likelihood of security breaches during the application's lifecycle.

The testing phase within the Secure SDLC is multifaceted, incorporating a variety of testing methodologies to assess the security posture of the application. Static Application Security Testing (SAST) and Dynamic Application Security Testing (DAST) are employed to identify and remediate vulnerabilities in the source code and runtime environment, respectively. Additionally, penetration testing simulates real-world attacks to uncover potential weaknesses and assess the effectiveness of security controls. Security-focused testing also includes assessments of authentication mechanisms, authorization controls, and data protection measures. Automated testing tools and manual testing by security professionals play a crucial role in identifying and addressing security vulnerabilities before the application is deployed.

The deployment phase in the Secure SDLC involves ensuring that security controls remain effective in a production environment. Secure deployment practices, such as the use of secure configuration settings, encryption for data in transit, and strong authentication mechanisms, are implemented to fortify the application against potential threats. Continuous monitoring and incident response procedures are established to detect and respond to security incidents promptly. Additionally, secure deployment practices encompass the validation of third-party components and dependencies to mitigate the risk of supply chain attacks. By integrating security into the deployment process, the Secure SDLC aims to create a secure and resilient production environment for the application.

Post-deployment maintenance is a critical aspect of the Secure SDLC, acknowledging that security is an ongoing process. Regular security updates, patches, and vulnerability assessments are conducted to address emerging threats and vulnerabilities. Incident response plans are continually refined based on lessons learned from security incidents. Continuous monitoring of the application's security posture helps identify and respond to potential issues in real-time. Moreover, the Secure SDLC encourages a culture of security awareness among developers and stakeholders, fostering an environment where security is considered an integral part of the software development lifecycle.

Integration of security awareness and training is a cross-cutting theme throughout the Secure SDLC. Developers, architects, and other stakeholders receive ongoing education about the latest security threats, attack vectors, and mitigation strategies. This proactive approach to security awareness ensures that all individuals involved in the development process are well-equipped to make security-conscious decisions and contribute to the overall security of the application. Security champions within development teams play a crucial role in promoting security best practices and fostering a culture of security within the organization.

The Secure SDLC also emphasizes the importance of documentation in capturing security-related decisions, processes, and configurations. This documentation serves as a valuable resource for developers, security professionals, and other stakeholders, providing insights into the security architecture, threat models, and mitigation strategies implemented throughout the development lifecycle. Comprehensive documentation contributes to knowledge sharing, facilitates audits and compliance assessments, and enables effective incident response by providing a clear understanding of the application's security posture.

Moreover, the Secure SDLC aligns with industry standards and regulatory requirements, ensuring that security measures implemented during the development process meet compliance obligations. Adherence to standards such as ISO/IEC 27001, NIST Cybersecurity Framework, or industry-specific regulations demonstrates a commitment to robust security practices and helps organizations build trust with customers, partners, and regulatory bodies.

The Secure SDLC promotes collaboration between development, security, and operations teams, fostering a DevSecOps culture where security is integrated into every stage of the development pipeline. Automation tools for security testing, continuous integration, and continuous deployment enable rapid and secure delivery of software updates. Collaboration between cross-functional teams ensures that security considerations are not siloed but are seamlessly integrated into the development process, aligning with the principles of agility and DevOps.

In conclusion, the Secure Software Development Life Cycle is a holistic and proactive approach to building secure applications. By integrating security measures throughout the entire development process, from requirements gathering to deployment and ongoing maintenance, the Secure SDLC aims to minimize security risks and create resilient software systems. This approach emphasizes secure coding practices, robust testing methodologies, security-aware deployment procedures, ongoing maintenance, and a culture of security awareness. In a rapidly evolving threat landscape, the Secure SDLC provides organizations with a strategic framework to build and maintain secure applications that can withstand the challenges posed by cyber threats and safeguard sensitive information.

Integrating Security into Development Processes

Integrating security into development processes is a fundamental and proactive approach to building resilient and secure software applications. This paradigm shift recognizes that cybersecurity is not a standalone consideration or a task reserved for specific phases but an integral part of the entire software development lifecycle. By embedding security measures into every stage, from planning and design to implementation, testing, and deployment, organizations can better defend against evolving threats, minimize vulnerabilities, and enhance the overall security posture of their applications.

At the outset, the integration of security into development processes begins with the planning phase. Traditionally, security considerations might have been addressed later in the development lifecycle, but a security-centric approach advocates for early and continuous involvement. During the planning phase, development teams collaborate with security experts to identify potential threats, risks, and compliance requirements. Security-focused user stories and requirements are established, outlining the security controls, data protection measures, and access controls needed to safeguard the application. By incorporating security considerations from the project's inception, organizations lay the foundation for a security-aware development process.

The design phase of development is a critical juncture for integrating security measures. Security architects work closely with development teams to define a robust security architecture. This involves conducting threat modeling exercises to identify and prioritize potential risks, considering factors such as data flow, entry points, and trust boundaries. Security controls, including encryption mechanisms, authentication protocols, and authorization models, are incorporated into the application's design. This proactive approach ensures that security is not an afterthought but an inherent aspect of how the application functions, promoting a defense-in-depth strategy.

As development progresses to the implementation phase, secure coding practices take center stage. Developers are trained in security principles and guided by secure coding standards to write code that is resilient to common vulnerabilities. Static code analysis tools are employed to scan code for potential security flaws, and peer code reviews involve a security perspective to identify and address issues early in the development process. Integrating secure coding practices ensures that the application's codebase is robust against threats such as injection attacks, buffer overflows, and other common vulnerabilities, laying the groundwork for a more secure final product.

The testing phase is a cornerstone of any development process, and integrating security into testing practices is paramount for identifying and addressing vulnerabilities. Static Application Security Testing (SAST) and Dynamic Application Security Testing (DAST) tools are utilized to scan code for potential weaknesses and assess the runtime environment for security flaws. Penetration testing, which simulates real-world attacks, is employed to evaluate the effectiveness of security controls and identify potential gaps. Security-focused testing also includes assessments of authentication mechanisms, authorization controls, and data protection measures. This thorough testing approach ensures that security vulnerabilities are discovered and remediated before the application reaches production.

Furthermore, integrating security into development processes extends to the deployment phase. Secure deployment practices involve configuring the production environment with security in mind. This includes the use of secure configuration settings, the implementation of encryption for data in transit, and the deployment of strong authentication mechanisms. Continuous monitoring and incident response procedures are established to detect and respond to security incidents promptly. Additionally, secure deployment practices encompass the validation of third-party components and dependencies to mitigate the risk of supply chain attacks. By addressing security considerations during deployment, organizations ensure that the application remains secure in a live environment.

Post-deployment maintenance is an ongoing facet of integrating security into development processes. Regular security updates, patches, and vulnerability assessments are conducted to address emerging threats and vulnerabilities. Incident response plans are continually refined based on lessons learned from security incidents. Continuous monitoring of the application's security posture helps identify and respond to potential issues in real-time. Moreover, the integration of security into post-deployment maintenance involves a culture of security awareness among developers and stakeholders, fostering an environment where security is considered an integral part of ongoing operations.

Integration of security awareness and training is a cross-cutting theme throughout the development process. Developers, architects, and other stakeholders receive ongoing education about the latest security threats, attack vectors, and mitigation strategies. This proactive approach to security awareness ensures that all individuals involved in the development process are well-equipped to make security-conscious decisions and contribute to the overall security of the application. Security champions within development teams play a crucial role in promoting security best practices and fostering a culture of security within the organization.

Moreover, documentation plays a key role in integrating security into development processes. Comprehensive documentation captures security-related decisions, processes, and configurations. This documentation serves as a valuable resource for developers, security professionals, and other stakeholders, providing insights into the security architecture, threat models, and mitigation strategies implemented throughout the development lifecycle. Effective documentation contributes to knowledge sharing, facilitates audits and compliance assessments, and enables effective incident response by providing a clear understanding of the application's security posture.

The integration of security into development processes also aligns with industry standards and regulatory requirements. Adherence to standards such as ISO/IEC 27001, NIST Cybersecurity Framework, or industry-specific regulations demonstrates a commitment to robust security practices and helps organizations build trust with customers, partners, and regulatory bodies. By aligning development processes with established security standards, organizations ensure that security measures implemented during development meet compliance obligations, providing a structured and validated approach to cybersecurity.

Furthermore, the integration of security into development processes extends to fostering collaboration between development, security, and operations teams. This collaborative approach embodies the DevSecOps culture, where security is seamlessly integrated into every stage of the development pipeline. Automation tools for security testing, continuous integration, and continuous deployment enable rapid and secure delivery of software updates. Collaboration between cross-functional teams ensures that security considerations are not siloed but are seamlessly integrated into the development process, aligning with the principles of agility and DevOps.

In conclusion, integrating security into development processes is a paradigm shift that recognizes the need for a proactive and comprehensive approach to building secure applications. By incorporating security measures from the planning phase through to deployment and ongoing maintenance, organizations create a more resilient software development lifecycle. This approach emphasizes secure coding practices, robust testing methodologies, security-aware deployment procedures, ongoing maintenance, and a culture of security awareness. In a rapidly evolving threat landscape, the integration of security into development processes provides organizations with a strategic framework to build and maintain secure applications that can withstand the challenges posed by cyber threats and safeguard sensitive information.

Code Review and Security Testing

Code review and security testing are integral components of a robust software development process, working in tandem to identify and rectify vulnerabilities, enhance code quality, and fortify the overall security posture of an application. Code review, a collaborative process involving peers scrutinizing source code changes, aims to ensure conformity to coding standards, enhance readability, and catch logic errors. In the context of security, code review plays a pivotal role in identifying potential vulnerabilities and adherence to secure coding practices. Security testing, on the other hand, encompasses a range of methodologies to assess an application's security, including static analysis, dynamic analysis, and penetration testing. The combination of code review and security testing contributes to the early detection and remediation of security issues, fostering a proactive approach to software security.

Code review serves as a crucial quality assurance step in the software development lifecycle. It involves developers systematically examining source code changes to identify bugs, ensure adherence to coding standards, and promote consistency in the codebase. While the primary goal of code review is to improve code quality, it also presents an opportune moment to address security concerns. Security-focused code review involves scrutinizing code changes for common vulnerabilities such as injection attacks, insecure data storage, and authentication weaknesses. Peer reviewers, often possessing diverse perspectives and experiences, contribute to a collective effort in identifying potential security risks that might have eluded the original developer. This collaborative approach helps instill a culture of shared responsibility for security within development teams.

Static Application Security Testing (SAST) is a key element of security testing, focusing on the analysis of source code or compiled binaries without executing the application. SAST tools scan the source code for potential vulnerabilities, such as SQL injection, cross-site scripting (XSS), and insecure cryptographic practices. By examining the codebase during the development phase, SAST identifies issues early in the lifecycle, enabling developers to address them before the code reaches production. This proactive approach aligns with the principles of secure coding, where vulnerabilities are remediated during the development process, reducing the likelihood of security incidents in later stages.

Dynamic Application Security Testing (DAST) complements SAST by assessing an application in its runtime environment. DAST tools simulate real-world attacks by interacting with the application as an external attacker would. This approach identifies vulnerabilities that might only manifest in specific runtime conditions and provides insights into the application's overall security posture. DAST is particularly valuable for web applications, where it can uncover issues like input validation flaws, session management vulnerabilities, and misconfigurations. The combination of SAST and DAST offers a comprehensive perspective on an application's security, addressing both code-level vulnerabilities and runtime risks.

Penetration testing, another facet of security testing, involves simulating cyberattacks to identify and exploit vulnerabilities in an application or system. Penetration testers, often external security professionals, attempt to breach security defenses to assess the system's resilience against real-world threats. Unlike automated testing tools, penetration testing brings a human element to the assessment, allowing for the identification of nuanced vulnerabilities that may evade automated scans. This approach provides a holistic view of an application's security by evaluating not only technical vulnerabilities but also potential weaknesses in configurations, user access controls, and business logic.

The synergy between code review and security testing lies in their shared objective of identifying and rectifying security vulnerabilities. Code review, with its emphasis on collaboration and knowledge sharing, provides a platform for developers to learn from each other's experiences, share best practices, and collectively improve the security stance of the codebase. It complements security testing methodologies by offering a static analysis of code changes, allowing developers to catch and address potential vulnerabilities before they manifest in the runtime environment. This collaborative and iterative process aligns with the principles of continuous improvement and proactive security.

Moreover, security testing, including both SAST and DAST, serves as a valuable automated supplement to code review. Automated testing tools can efficiently analyze large codebases, scanning for known vulnerabilities and potential risks. The speed and scalability of automated testing make it a valuable asset in scenarios where manual code review might be impractical. However, it is essential to acknowledge the limitations of automated tools, as they may not capture certain nuanced vulnerabilities or contextual intricacies that human reviewers in a code review might identify. Therefore, the combination of both automated testing and manual code review presents a comprehensive strategy to ensure a more resilient and secure codebase.

The effectiveness of code review and security testing is further enhanced when integrated into the continuous integration and continuous deployment (CI/CD) pipeline. By automating code review processes and incorporating security testing into the CI/CD pipeline, organizations can identify and address security issues in real-time. Automated code analysis tools can be configured to run as part of the CI/CD process, providing instant feedback to developers on the security implications of their code changes. This integration ensures that security is not a bottleneck but an inherent part of the development workflow, promoting a DevSecOps culture where security is seamlessly woven into every stage of the development lifecycle.

One of the challenges in integrating code review and security testing is striking a balance between thoroughness and efficiency. Code review requires time and attention from developers and reviewers, and an overly exhaustive process may lead to delays in the development timeline. Conversely, an overly expedited process might overlook critical security considerations. Striking this balance involves setting clear expectations, leveraging automation where feasible, and fostering a culture that values both speed and security. Organizations can implement policies and guidelines that define the scope and depth of code reviews, ensuring that they align with security objectives without impeding the development velocity.

Additionally, the success of code review and security testing relies on the collaboration and communication between development, security, and operations teams. Establishing cross-functional teams that include security experts in code review sessions enhances the collective understanding of security requirements and potential risks. Regular communication channels between development and security teams foster a collaborative approach to addressing identified vulnerabilities. The integration of security considerations into daily stand-ups, sprint planning meetings, and retrospective sessions ensures that security remains a constant consideration rather than an occasional checkpoint.

The evolving landscape of security threats and the continuous evolution of software development practices underscore the importance of a proactive and integrated approach to code review and security testing. As applications become more complex, interconnected, and accessible, the need for robust security measures intensifies. Organizations that prioritize the integration of security into their development processes not only mitigate risks but also foster a culture of security awareness and accountability. Code review and security testing, when combined seamlessly into the development lifecycle, contribute to the creation of resilient applications that withstand the challenges posed by a dynamic and ever-evolving cybersecurity landscape.

4.4 Best Practices for Application Security

Best practices for application security are essential guidelines and strategies that organizations should adopt to safeguard their software systems from potential threats and vulnerabilities. These practices encompass a holistic approach, covering various stages of the software development lifecycle, from planning and design to implementation, testing, deployment, and ongoing maintenance. Embracing these best practices is crucial for building resilient applications that prioritize the confidentiality, integrity, and availability of sensitive information.

The foundation of application security begins in the planning phase of the software development lifecycle. Organizations should adopt a security-by-design approach, integrating security considerations into the early stages of project planning and requirements gathering. This involves identifying potential security threats, defining security controls, and establishing security-related user stories. By incorporating security requirements from the outset, development teams set the stage for a security-aware development process.

In the design phase, secure architecture and design principles play a pivotal role in building robust applications. Security architects collaborate with development teams to define an architecture that considers potential risks and incorporates security controls. Threat modeling is a valuable practice during this phase, allowing teams to systematically analyze and prioritize potential threats and vulnerabilities. Security controls, such as encryption, access controls, and secure APIs, are integrated into the design to mitigate identified risks. The emphasis on secure design ensures that applications are resilient to potential security threats.

Secure coding practices are a cornerstone of application security during the implementation phase. Developers should be trained in secure coding principles and adhere to established coding standards. Secure coding practices mitigate common vulnerabilities such as injection attacks, buffer overflows, and insecure data storage. Code reviews and static code analysis tools are employed to identify and address security flaws early in the development process. By integrating secure coding practices, organizations reduce the likelihood of introducing vulnerabilities into the codebase.

Thorough testing is an essential aspect of application security, and it involves various methodologies. Static Application Security Testing (SAST) and Dynamic Application Security Testing (DAST) are employed to assess code vulnerabilities and runtime risks. SAST tools scan the source code for potential vulnerabilities, while DAST tools simulate real-world attacks to assess the application in its runtime environment. Additionally, penetration testing involves ethical hackers attempting to exploit vulnerabilities, providing a realistic evaluation of an application's security posture. The combination of these testing methodologies ensures a comprehensive assessment of an application's security.

The deployment phase is another critical juncture for application security. Secure deployment practices involve configuring the production environment with security in mind. This includes the use of secure configuration settings, the implementation of encryption for data in transit, and the deployment of strong authentication mechanisms. Continuous monitoring and incident response procedures are established to detect and respond to security incidents promptly. Additionally, the validation of third-party components and dependencies is crucial to mitigate the risk of supply chain attacks. By addressing security considerations during deployment, organizations ensure that applications remain secure in a live environment.

Post-deployment maintenance is an ongoing aspect of application security, acknowledging that security is an evolving process. Regular security updates, patches, and vulnerability assessments are conducted to address emerging threats and vulnerabilities. Incident response plans are continually refined based on lessons learned from security incidents. Continuous monitoring of the application's security posture helps identify and respond to potential issues in real-time. Moreover, a culture of security awareness among developers and stakeholders is fostered, creating an environment where security is an integral part of ongoing operations.

Integration of security awareness and training is a cross-cutting theme throughout the software development lifecycle. Developers, architects, and other stakeholders receive ongoing education about the latest security threats, attack vectors, and mitigation strategies. This proactive approach to security awareness ensures that all individuals involved in the development process are well-equipped to make security-conscious decisions and contribute to the overall security of the application. Security champions within development teams play a crucial role in promoting security best practices and fostering a culture of security within the organization.

Documentation is a key component of best practices for application security. Comprehensive documentation captures security-related decisions, processes, and configurations. This documentation serves as a valuable resource for developers, security professionals, and other stakeholders, providing insights into the security architecture, threat models, and mitigation strategies implemented throughout the development lifecycle. Effective documentation contributes to knowledge sharing, facilitates audits and compliance assessments, and enables effective incident response by providing a clear understanding of the application's security posture.

Furthermore, best practices for application security align with industry standards and regulatory requirements. Adherence to standards such as ISO/IEC 27001, NIST Cybersecurity Framework, or industry-specific regulations demonstrates a commitment to robust security practices and helps organizations build trust with customers, partners, and regulatory bodies. By aligning with established security standards, organizations ensure that security measures implemented during development meet compliance obligations, providing a structured and validated approach to cybersecurity.

The best practices for application security also emphasize the importance of collaboration and communication between development, security, and operations teams. Establishing cross-functional teams that include security experts in various stages of the development process enhances the collective understanding of security requirements and potential risks. Regular communication channels between development and security teams foster a collaborative approach to addressing identified vulnerabilities. The integration of security considerations into daily stand-ups, sprint planning meetings, and retrospective sessions ensures that security remains a constant consideration rather than an occasional checkpoint.

Organizations should adopt a risk-based approach to application security, prioritizing efforts based on the severity and potential impact of identified vulnerabilities. Not all vulnerabilities pose the same level of risk, and organizations must allocate resources based on the criticality of the issues at hand. This risk-based approach enables organizations to focus on addressing the most impactful security concerns first, ensuring that resources are utilized efficiently to maximize the security posture of applications.

Implementing secure coding standards and guidelines is crucial for maintaining consistency in the development process. These standards provide developers with clear and actionable guidance on secure coding practices, coding conventions, and potential pitfalls to avoid. Regular training sessions and awareness programs help reinforce these standards, ensuring that developers are equipped with the knowledge and skills to adhere to secure coding practices consistently.

Additionally, the principle of least privilege should be applied across the development and operational environments. Users, systems, and processes should be granted only the minimum level of access required to perform their functions. This reduces the potential attack surface and limits the impact of security incidents. Access controls, authentication mechanisms, and authorization processes should be designed to adhere to the principle of least privilege, mitigating the risk of unauthorized access and privilege escalation.

In conclusion, best practices for application security represent a comprehensive and proactive approach to building resilient software systems. By integrating security considerations throughout the software development lifecycle, organizations can create applications that are robust against potential threats and vulnerabilities. These practices encompass secure coding, testing methodologies, deployment procedures, ongoing maintenance, and a culture of security awareness. In a dynamic and evolving threat landscape, adherence to best practices for application security ensures that organizations can effectively mitigate risks, safeguard sensitive information, and build trust with users and stakeholders.

Implementing Web Application Firewalls

Implementing Web Application Firewalls (WAFs) is a critical strategy in fortifying the security posture of web applications against a myriad of cyber threats. A WAF serves as a protective barrier between web applications and potential attackers, offering a line of defense that complements other security measures. The implementation of WAFs involves deploying specialized security appliances, software, or cloud-based services that analyze and filter HTTP traffic to and from a web application. This process enables the identification and mitigation of various web application attacks, including but not limited to SQL injection, cross-site scripting (XSS), cross-site request forgery (CSRF), and other injection attacks.

One of the primary functions of a WAF is to scrutinize incoming web traffic for malicious patterns and anomalies. By employing various detection mechanisms, such as signature-based detection, anomaly-based detection, and heuristics, a WAF can identify patterns indicative of known attacks or behaviors deviating from the expected norm. Signature-based detection involves comparing incoming requests against a predefined set of patterns or signatures associated with known attacks. Anomaly-based detection, on the other hand, focuses on identifying deviations from established baselines, flagging unusual patterns that might indicate a potential attack. The combination of these detection methods enhances the WAF's ability to recognize and respond to a broad spectrum of web-based threats.

Furthermore, WAFs play a crucial role in mitigating SQL injection attacks, a prevalent and potentially devastating web application vulnerability. SQL injection occurs when attackers manipulate input fields to inject malicious SQL code into database queries, potentially leading to unauthorized access or data manipulation. WAFs equipped with SQL injection protection capabilities analyze incoming requests for SQL-like patterns and employ heuristics to identify and block such malicious attempts. This proactive defense mechanism helps prevent attackers from exploiting vulnerabilities in web applications to compromise databases and exfiltrate sensitive information.

Cross-site scripting (XSS) is another class of attack that WAFs aim to mitigate. XSS attacks involve injecting malicious scripts into web pages viewed by other users. WAFs with XSS protection capabilities inspect web content for potentially malicious script patterns and sanitize or block such content to prevent it from reaching end-users. This defensive measure safeguards users from inadvertently executing malicious scripts that could compromise their accounts or steal sensitive information.

The integration of threat intelligence feeds into WAFs enhances their ability to detect and respond to emerging threats. Threat intelligence feeds provide real-time information about known malicious IP addresses, attack patterns, and indicators of compromise. By incorporating this intelligence, a WAF can dynamically adjust its rules and filters, ensuring that it stays ahead of evolving threats. This level of adaptability is crucial in the ever-changing landscape of web application security, where new attack vectors and techniques constantly emerge.

Effective WAF implementation involves customizing rule sets to align with the specific security requirements and characteristics of the protected web application. WAFs typically offer a set of predefined rules that address common web application vulnerabilities. However, to maximize effectiveness, organizations should tailor these rules and configurations to the unique aspects of their applications. This customization process requires a deep understanding of the application's architecture, user interactions, and potential vulnerabilities. Collaborative efforts between security teams, application developers, and system administrators are vital to creating rule sets that strike the right balance between security and functionality.

Moreover, WAFs often support the creation of positive security models, which define and allow only the expected behavior of web applications. Positive security models specify the legitimate input and behavior of web applications, rejecting anything that deviates from these predefined expectations. This approach helps prevent unknown and unexpected attacks by allowing only the explicitly defined and approved interactions. Positive security models complement traditional negative security models, which focus on identifying and blocking known attack patterns. The combination of both approaches provides a comprehensive defense against a wide range of web application threats.

Cloud-based WAF solutions offer scalability and flexibility, making them particularly suitable for modern, dynamic web applications hosted in cloud environments. Cloud WAF services leverage distributed infrastructure to handle large volumes of web traffic, providing the scalability needed to protect applications with varying levels of demand. Additionally, cloud-based WAFs often offer centralized management interfaces, simplifying the configuration and monitoring of security policies across multiple web applications. This centralized management approach is especially valuable in complex, distributed environments where numerous web applications require consistent and effective security controls.

Continuous monitoring and logging are integral components of a robust WAF implementation. WAFs generate logs that capture details about incoming requests, detected threats, and the actions taken in response. These logs serve multiple purposes, including real-time threat detection, forensic analysis, and compliance reporting. By regularly reviewing WAF logs, security teams can gain insights into emerging attack patterns, identify potential vulnerabilities, and fine-tune security policies to enhance overall protection. Monitoring and logging also contribute to compliance efforts by providing an audit trail of security events and responses.

While WAFs offer a powerful layer of defense, their effectiveness relies on regular updates and maintenance. Security threats evolve, and new vulnerabilities are discovered over time. Keeping WAF signatures, rules, and configurations up-to-date is crucial to ensuring that the WAF can effectively identify and block the latest threats. Organizations should establish processes for regular WAF updates, including testing changes in a controlled environment before applying them to production systems. Additionally, periodic security assessments and penetration testing can help validate the WAF's effectiveness and identify any potential weaknesses or misconfigurations.

Challenges in WAF implementation include the potential for false positives and false negatives. False positives occur when a WAF incorrectly identifies legitimate traffic as malicious and blocks it. Conversely, false negatives occur when a WAF fails to detect and block actual malicious activity. Striking the right balance to minimize false positives without compromising security requires careful tuning of WAF rules and configurations. Organizations should invest time in understanding their web applications, monitoring WAF performance, and refining rules to achieve optimal results.

In conclusion, implementing Web Application Firewalls is a strategic imperative in the contemporary landscape of web application security. WAFs serve as a crucial defense mechanism against a wide array of cyber threats, offering protection at the application layer where vulnerabilities are often exploited. The implementation process involves deploying specialized security measures, customizing rule sets, leveraging threat intelligence, and continuously monitoring and updating configurations. The collaborative efforts of security teams, application developers, and system administrators are vital to tailoring WAFs to the unique characteristics of protected applications. Whether on-premises or in the cloud, the deployment of WAFs represents a proactive and adaptive approach to safeguarding web applications, enhancing overall resilience against evolving cyber threats.

Securing APIs and Microservices

Securing APIs and microservices has become a paramount concern as organizations increasingly adopt modular and distributed architectures to enhance agility and scalability. APIs (Application Programming Interfaces) and microservices facilitate seamless communication between different components of a system, enabling efficient data exchange and functionality. However, the distributed nature of these architectures introduces unique security challenges that require comprehensive strategies to safeguard sensitive information, prevent unauthorized access, and mitigate potential vulnerabilities.

Authentication and authorization are foundational aspects of securing APIs and microservices. Properly implementing strong authentication mechanisms ensures that only authorized entities can access the APIs and microservices. This involves verifying the identity of clients, such as applications or users, before allowing them to interact with the API or microservice. Common authentication methods include API keys, OAuth tokens, and client certificates. Authorization mechanisms, on the other hand, dictate what actions authenticated entities can perform. Role-based access control (RBAC), attribute-based access control (ABAC), and fine-grained permissions contribute to effective authorization, allowing organizations to enforce the principle of least privilege.

The use of secure communication protocols is critical in preventing eavesdropping and tampering of data transmitted between APIs and microservices. Transport Layer Security (TLS) or its predecessor, Secure Sockets Layer (SSL), encrypts data in transit, ensuring that it remains confidential and integral during communication. Implementing strong cipher suites, regularly updating TLS versions, and adhering to best practices in certificate management enhance the overall security of data exchanged between services. Additionally, organizations must enforce the use of HTTPS to encrypt communication channels, especially when dealing with sensitive information.

Considering the dynamic and evolving nature of modern applications, API security should encompass proper management of API keys and secrets. API keys, often used for authentication, should be treated as sensitive information and safeguarded against unauthorized access. Regularly rotating keys, utilizing secure key storage solutions, and implementing measures to detect and respond to key compromises are crucial components of a robust API key management strategy. Secret management involves securing sensitive information, such as database credentials or encryption keys, used by microservices. Leveraging secure vaults or key management services helps protect critical secrets from unauthorized access.

Microservices often communicate with each other through APIs, and securing these interactions requires careful consideration. Implementing mutual TLS (mTLS) authentication between microservices ensures that each service verifies the identity of its communication peers, establishing a secure and authenticated connection. mTLS involves the use of client and server certificates, adding an extra layer of security beyond traditional TLS. This approach is particularly important in preventing man-in-the-middle attacks and unauthorized access to microservices within the internal network.

Another crucial aspect of securing APIs and microservices is input validation and output encoding. Proper input validation helps prevent injection attacks, such as SQL injection and cross-site scripting (XSS), by ensuring that user input is sanitized and validated before being processed by the application. Output encoding further protects against XSS attacks by encoding user-generated content before rendering it in web pages. By validating and encoding both input and output, organizations can significantly reduce the risk of common injection vulnerabilities that might be exploited to compromise the security of APIs and microservices.

API security extends beyond individual authentication and authorization mechanisms to include comprehensive identity management. Implementing identity and access management (IAM) solutions helps organizations manage user identities, roles, and permissions consistently across APIs and microservices. Centralized IAM solutions enable organizations to enforce consistent access policies, streamline user provisioning and de-provisioning, and maintain a unified view of user identities across the entire ecosystem. This centralized approach enhances security and simplifies administration, especially in complex environments with numerous microservices.

Protecting against common web application attacks is essential in securing APIs and microservices. Web Application Firewalls (WAFs) can be deployed to inspect and filter incoming HTTP traffic, detecting and mitigating threats such as SQL injection, cross-site scripting, and other injection attacks. WAFs add an additional layer of defense, complementing the security measures implemented within the microservices themselves. Regularly updating WAF rules and configurations is crucial to adapt to emerging threats and ensure ongoing effectiveness in thwarting potential attacks.

Monitoring and logging play a crucial role in identifying and responding to security incidents in real-time. Organizations should implement comprehensive logging mechanisms to capture relevant security events, including authentication attempts, unauthorized access, and potential vulnerabilities. Centralized logging solutions enable organizations to aggregate logs from various microservices and APIs, facilitating analysis and correlation to identify patterns indicative of security incidents. Integration with Security Information and Event Management (SIEM) systems further enhances the ability to detect and respond to security events across the entire application ecosystem.

Threat modeling is a proactive approach to identifying potential security risks and vulnerabilities early in the development process. Organizations should conduct thorough threat modeling exercises for both APIs and microservices, analyzing potential threats, attack vectors, and weaknesses in the architecture. By identifying and prioritizing potential risks, development teams can implement appropriate security controls and measures during the design and implementation phases. Threat modeling promotes a security-centric mindset, helping organizations build applications with security considerations integrated from the outset.

Containerization and orchestration technologies, such as Docker and Kubernetes, have gained widespread adoption in deploying and managing microservices. Securing containerized environments is crucial to preventing container escapes, privilege escalations, and other security risks. Implementing container security best practices, such as image scanning for vulnerabilities, restricting container privileges, and employing network segmentation, enhances the overall security of microservices running in containerized environments. Continuous monitoring and auditing of containerized applications contribute to identifying and addressing security issues in real-time.

Lastly, compliance with industry regulations and standards is a key consideration in securing APIs and microservices. Organizations operating in regulated industries or handling sensitive data must adhere to relevant standards such as GDPR, HIPAA, or PCI DSS. Ensuring that security measures align with regulatory requirements helps organizations not only protect sensitive information but also demonstrate a commitment to compliance, building trust with customers and stakeholders.

In conclusion, securing APIs and microservices is a multifaceted challenge that requires a comprehensive and adaptive approach. From robust authentication and authorization mechanisms to secure communication, input validation, and identity management, organizations must employ a combination of technical measures and best practices. Implementing thorough monitoring, threat modeling, and compliance measures further enhances the overall security posture of APIs and microservices. In the rapidly evolving landscape of distributed architectures, a proactive and holistic security strategy is essential to safeguarding sensitive data, preventing unauthorized access, and mitigating potential vulnerabilities.

Chapter 5: Cloud Citadel: Ensuring Security in the Virtual Sky

5.1 The Rise of Cloud Computing

The rise of cloud computing marks a transformative epoch in the realm of information technology, reshaping how businesses, individuals, and even governments leverage and manage their computing resources. This paradigm shift represents a departure from traditional on-premises infrastructure models towards a more dynamic, scalable, and accessible computing environment. At its core, cloud computing is a model for delivering computing services over the internet, encompassing a broad spectrum of resources, including storage, processing power, and applications. This evolution has been catalyzed by a confluence of technological advancements, economic considerations, and changing business imperatives.

One of the central tenets of cloud computing is the abstraction of physical infrastructure. In traditional computing setups, organizations invested heavily in procuring, maintaining, and upgrading their own servers, networking equipment, and data centers. Cloud computing disrupts this model by offering a virtualized and shared infrastructure, where users access computing resources on a pay-as-you-go basis. This abstraction not only reduces the upfront capital expenditure for organizations but also allows them to scale their infrastructure dynamically, responding to fluctuating workloads and business demands with unprecedented agility.

The ubiquity of high-speed internet connectivity plays a pivotal role in facilitating the ascendancy of cloud computing. With reliable and fast internet access becoming pervasive, the barriers to accessing computing resources remotely have diminished significantly. Cloud service providers operate vast data centers strategically located around the globe, enabling users to leverage computing power and storage resources seamlessly, regardless of their physical location. This global accessibility has engendered a borderless computing landscape, fostering collaboration, innovation, and market expansion on an unprecedented scale.

Economic considerations underscore the appeal of cloud computing for organizations of all sizes. The shift from a capital-intensive to an operational expenditure model allows businesses to optimize costs and allocate resources more efficiently. Instead of bearing the burden of maintaining and upgrading hardware, organizations pay for the computing services they consume, aligning expenses with actual usage. This financial flexibility is particularly advantageous for startups and small to medium-sized enterprises, democratizing access to advanced computing capabilities that were once the exclusive purview of large enterprises with extensive IT budgets.

The advent of cloud computing has ushered in a panoply of service models that cater to diverse computing needs. Infrastructure as a Service (IaaS) provides fundamental computing resources, such as virtual machines and storage, allowing users to build, deploy, and manage their applications without the complexity of underlying infrastructure. Platform as a Service (PaaS) abstracts even further, offering a comprehensive platform for application development, including tools, frameworks, and middleware. Software as a Service (SaaS) delivers fully-fledged applications over the internet, eliminating the need for users to install, manage, or maintain software locally.

Moreover, the elasticity and scalability inherent in cloud computing redefine how organizations approach resource provisioning. With the ability to scale resources up or down based on demand, businesses no longer need to overprovision infrastructure to accommodate peak loads. This elasticity ensures optimal resource utilization, minimizing waste and enhancing cost efficiency. Auto-scaling mechanisms further automate this process, dynamically adjusting resources in real-time based on predefined criteria. This adaptability is particularly advantageous for applications with variable workloads, allowing organizations to meet performance requirements without compromising on cost-effectiveness.

Security considerations have been a focal point in the discourse surrounding cloud computing. Initially met with skepticism due to concerns about data privacy, regulatory compliance, and the security of shared resources, cloud service providers have invested heavily in fortifying their infrastructures and implementing robust security measures. Encryption, identity and access management, network security, and compliance certifications are integral components of cloud security strategies. The shared responsibility model delineates the division of security responsibilities between cloud service providers and their customers, fostering a collaborative approach to ensuring the integrity and confidentiality of data.

The rise of cloud computing has not only revolutionized IT infrastructure but has also catalyzed a cultural shift in software development methodologies. DevOps, an amalgamation of development and operations, is an approach that emphasizes collaboration, automation, and continuous delivery. Cloud computing provides an ideal environment for implementing DevOps practices, enabling seamless integration and deployment of software, rapid iteration, and enhanced collaboration between development and operations teams. This iterative and collaborative approach accelerates time-to-market, improves software quality, and aligns development efforts more closely with business objectives.

The proliferation of cloud services has spawned a vibrant ecosystem of third-party providers offering specialized services and solutions. From artificial intelligence and machine learning to data analytics, Internet of Things (IoT), and serverless computing, organizations can leverage a myriad of cloud-based services to augment and enhance their capabilities. This extensibility allows businesses to focus on their core competencies while harnessing the expertise and innovation of specialized service providers. The cloud marketplace has become a dynamic marketplace for technological innovation, where organizations can access cutting-edge solutions without the need for substantial upfront investments.

While the benefits of cloud computing are evident, challenges persist, and organizations must navigate considerations such as data residency, vendor lock-in, and evolving regulatory landscapes. Concerns about the potential concentration of power among a few dominant cloud service providers have prompted discussions around fostering a more diverse and competitive cloud ecosystem. Open standards and interoperability initiatives aim to mitigate vendor lock-in and empower organizations to choose the cloud solutions that best align with their needs and preferences.

Looking ahead, the trajectory of cloud computing is poised for continued evolution and refinement. Edge computing, an extension of cloud computing, brings computing resources closer to the point of data generation, reducing latency and enabling real-time processing. Quantum computing, with its potential to revolutionize computation itself, is emerging as an area of exploration within the cloud computing landscape. As the digital landscape evolves, the rise of cloud computing is not merely a technological trend but a transformative force reshaping how individuals and organizations interact with information technology, ushering in a new era of flexibility, efficiency, and innovation.

Understanding Cloud Service Models (IaaS, PaaS, SaaS)

Understanding cloud service models—Infrastructure as a Service (IaaS), Platform as a Service (PaaS), and Software as a Service (SaaS)—is fundamental to navigating the diverse landscape of cloud computing. Each model represents a distinct layer of abstraction, offering varying degrees of control and responsibility to users. IaaS, at the foundational level, provides users with virtualized computing resources over the internet. This includes virtual machines, storage, and networking components, allowing organizations to build, deploy, and manage their applications without the need to invest in and maintain physical hardware. IaaS is characterized by its flexibility and scalability, enabling users to scale resources up or down based on demand while retaining control over the underlying infrastructure.

Moving up the abstraction hierarchy, PaaS provides a more comprehensive platform for application development and deployment. PaaS abstracts not only the underlying infrastructure but also the complexities of middleware, development frameworks, and tools required to build and run applications. This model empowers developers to focus on coding and innovation, leaving the operational intricacies to the PaaS provider. With features such as automated scaling, continuous integration, and a pre-configured development environment, PaaS accelerates the software development lifecycle and fosters collaboration between development and operations teams. This streamlined approach is particularly advantageous for organizations seeking to enhance agility and reduce time-to-market for their applications.

SaaS, positioned at the highest level of abstraction, delivers fully-fledged applications over the internet. Users access software applications hosted and maintained by the SaaS provider without the need for local installation or management. This model encompasses a wide range of applications, from productivity tools like email and office suites to more specialized solutions like customer relationship management (CRM) and enterprise resource planning (ERP) software. SaaS providers handle maintenance, updates, and security, relieving users of the operational burden associated with traditional software deployment. The subscription-based pricing model aligns costs with actual usage, offering a cost-effective and scalable solution for organizations of varying sizes.

Each cloud service model offers distinct advantages and trade-offs, catering to different use cases and organizational requirements. IaaS provides maximum control and customization, making it suitable for scenarios where organizations need to manage specific infrastructure components, have unique security requirements, or run legacy applications. PaaS, with its focus on streamlining development processes, is ideal for organizations prioritizing rapid application development, collaboration, and automation. SaaS, on the other hand, is tailored for end-users seeking hassle-free access to software applications without the burden of infrastructure or software maintenance.

In the realm of IaaS, cloud service providers offer a range of virtualized computing resources. Virtual machines (VMs) form the core of IaaS offerings, providing users with the ability to run applications in isolated environments without the constraints of physical hardware. Users can select VM configurations based on their computational needs, and IaaS providers facilitate the rapid deployment, scaling, and management of these instances. Storage is another critical component of IaaS, allowing users to store and retrieve data seamlessly. Whether it's block storage for databases, object storage for scalable and durable data repositories, or file storage for traditional file systems, IaaS accommodates diverse storage requirements. Networking services in IaaS encompass virtual networks, load balancers, and firewalls, enabling users to architect and manage the network infrastructure that connects their virtual resources.

PaaS, while inheriting the IaaS foundation, abstracts additional layers to simplify the development and deployment of applications. Development frameworks, middleware, and runtime environments are pre-configured and managed by the PaaS provider, allowing developers to focus solely on writing code. The platform automates essential tasks such as scaling, patching, and load balancing, streamlining the deployment and operational aspects of applications. PaaS supports a variety of programming languages and frameworks, providing flexibility for diverse development needs. Database services within PaaS offer scalable and managed database solutions, reducing the administrative burden on users. PaaS encourages collaboration and agility by providing a standardized environment for development, making it easier for teams to work cohesively and deliver applications more efficiently.

In the realm of SaaS, the focus shifts to delivering complete and ready-to-use applications over the internet. SaaS providers host and maintain the software, ensuring that users always have access to the latest features and updates. This model is characterized by its simplicity and accessibility, as users can access applications through web browsers without the need for complex installations or configurations. Email services, collaboration tools, customer management platforms, and enterprise software suites are common examples of SaaS applications. The subscription-based pricing model aligns costs with usage, making SaaS a cost-effective solution for organizations that require ubiquitous access to software without the burden of managing the underlying infrastructure or application lifecycle.

Each cloud service model operates on the principle of shared responsibility between the cloud provider and the user. In IaaS, users retain responsibility for securing their applications and data, managing operating systems, and configuring networking components. The cloud provider ensures the security and availability of the underlying infrastructure. PaaS extends this shared responsibility, with the provider taking on additional responsibilities related to the runtime environment, middleware, and development frameworks. Users focus on coding and application logic, while the PaaS provider manages operational aspects such as scaling, patching, and system updates. In SaaS, the provider assumes even greater responsibility, handling the entire software stack, including application maintenance, security, and updates, while users concentrate solely on using the software to meet their business needs.

Security considerations are paramount across all cloud service models. Cloud providers implement robust security measures to protect physical data centers, networks, and virtualized environments. Encryption, identity and access management, network security, and compliance certifications are integral components of cloud security strategies. Users, in turn, must adopt security best practices to safeguard their applications, data, and access credentials. Collaboration between cloud providers and users is critical to ensuring a secure cloud environment, with shared responsibility extending to aspects such as data encryption, access controls, and security configurations.

The evolution and adoption of cloud service models have transformed the IT landscape, offering unprecedented flexibility, scalability, and accessibility. Organizations can select the model that best aligns with their specific needs and requirements. Whether it's the granular control of IaaS, the streamlined development workflows of PaaS, or the simplicity and accessibility of SaaS, cloud computing provides a versatile toolkit for organizations seeking to innovate, optimize costs, and stay competitive in an increasingly digital and interconnected world.

Cloud Deployment Models (Public, Private, Hybrid)

Cloud deployment models—Public, Private, and Hybrid—constitute the strategic framework through which organizations configure and manage their computing resources in the cloud, each embodying distinct characteristics and catering to specific needs. Public cloud, a prevailing model, involves utilizing computing resources from third-party providers over the internet. Organizations leveraging public clouds benefit from cost efficiency, scalability, and the offloading of infrastructure management responsibilities to the cloud service provider. Services are delivered on a pay-as-you-go basis, enabling organizations to scale resources dynamically based on demand, making it particularly suitable for startups, small to medium-sized enterprises, and businesses with variable workloads.

In contrast, the private cloud deployment model revolves around dedicated infrastructure exclusive to a single organization. This model offers heightened control, customization, and security, making it suitable for businesses with stringent compliance requirements or those handling sensitive data. Private clouds can be hosted on-premises, where organizations maintain and manage their infrastructure, or they can be hosted by third-party providers. While private clouds afford organizations greater control over their computing environment, they often require substantial upfront capital expenditure and ongoing maintenance.

Hybrid cloud, an amalgamation of public and private cloud models, seeks to harness the strengths of both deployment models. Organizations employing a hybrid cloud strategy leverage a combination of on-premises infrastructure, private cloud resources, and public cloud services. This approach provides flexibility and enables businesses to optimize their infrastructure based on specific needs and workloads. Hybrid cloud architectures accommodate scenarios where certain workloads or data must reside on-premises due to regulatory requirements or performance considerations, while others can take advantage of the scalability and cost-effectiveness of public cloud resources.

The public cloud model, represented by major providers such as Amazon Web Services (AWS), Microsoft Azure, and Google Cloud Platform (GCP), has democratized access to cutting-edge computing resources. Public cloud providers operate extensive data centers globally, offering a diverse array of services, including computing power, storage, databases, machine learning, and more. The multi-tenant nature of public clouds allows providers to achieve economies of scale, driving down costs for users. The public cloud is characterized by its agility, rapid scalability, and the ability to leverage a vast ecosystem of services, making it an attractive option for organizations seeking to innovate, experiment, and scale without the burden of significant upfront investments.

Private clouds, by contrast, are tailored for organizations with specific requirements around control, security, and customization. In a private cloud deployment, whether hosted on-premises or by a third-party provider, resources are dedicated exclusively to a single organization. This exclusivity affords organizations greater control over their infrastructure, allowing them to tailor computing resources to meet precise specifications. Private clouds are particularly prevalent in industries with stringent regulatory requirements, such as finance or healthcare, where data sovereignty and compliance are paramount. While private clouds offer a higher degree of control, they may require more substantial upfront investments and ongoing maintenance, limiting the cost efficiencies realized by public cloud users.

Hybrid cloud deployment models have gained traction as organizations seek to strike a balance between the benefits of public and private clouds. Hybrid clouds enable seamless integration and data portability between on-premises infrastructure, private cloud resources, and public cloud services. This flexibility is especially advantageous for organizations with fluctuating workloads or those undergoing digital transformation initiatives. Hybrid cloud architectures facilitate a unified approach to IT management, allowing organizations to leverage the scalability of public clouds for certain workloads while retaining control over critical or sensitive data in private clouds or on-premises infrastructure.

Key considerations in selecting a cloud deployment model include the nature of the organization's workloads, data sensitivity, regulatory requirements, and cost considerations. Public clouds are well-suited for scalable and dynamic workloads, especially for applications that can benefit from the extensive array of services offered by cloud providers. Private clouds are ideal for organizations with specific security or compliance needs, providing the necessary control and customization but often at a higher cost. Hybrid clouds offer a compromise, allowing organizations to optimize infrastructure based on the characteristics of their workloads, balancing scalability, control, and cost efficiency.

Security and data privacy are paramount concerns in cloud deployment models. Public clouds implement robust security measures, including encryption, identity and access management, and compliance certifications, to protect the shared infrastructure and data of multiple users. Private clouds afford organizations more control over their security policies and configurations but require diligent implementation and management. Hybrid clouds demand careful consideration of data movement between environments, necessitating robust encryption and authentication mechanisms to ensure the security of data in transit.

Moreover, cloud deployment models have implications for data residency and sovereignty. Public clouds often span multiple geographic regions, raising concerns about where data is physically stored and processed. Private clouds, especially when hosted on-premises, offer organizations more direct control over the geographic location of their data. Hybrid clouds introduce the challenge of coordinating data movement between different environments while adhering to regulatory requirements and privacy considerations.

The management and orchestration of resources across cloud deployment models are critical aspects of effective cloud governance. Organizations adopting a multi-cloud or hybrid cloud strategy need robust tools and frameworks to manage and monitor resources seamlessly. Cloud management platforms and orchestration tools help optimize resource utilization, automate workflows, and ensure consistent policies across diverse cloud environments. These tools contribute to operational efficiency, cost control, and a unified management experience for organizations leveraging multiple cloud providers or deployment models.

The evolution of cloud deployment models is shaped by ongoing technological advancements and the evolving needs of organizations. Edge computing, an extension of cloud computing, involves processing data closer to the point of generation, reducing latency and enabling real-time processing. Multi-cloud strategies, where organizations leverage services from multiple cloud providers, are gaining prominence as businesses seek to avoid vendor lock-in and tailor their solutions to specific cloud capabilities. As cloud technologies continue to mature, deployment models will likely evolve to accommodate emerging trends and address the ever-changing landscape of IT requirements.

In conclusion, cloud deployment models—Public, Private, and Hybrid—provide organizations with a strategic framework to configure and manage their computing resources according to specific needs. The public cloud offers scalability, agility, and cost efficiency, while private clouds afford control, security, and customization. Hybrid clouds strike a balance, enabling seamless integration between public and private environments. Each deployment model presents trade-offs and considerations, including security, data residency, and management complexities. Organizations must carefully evaluate their requirements, workloads, and regulatory constraints to select the most suitable deployment model or a combination thereof, ensuring that their cloud strategy aligns with their overarching business objectives.

5.2 Security Challenges in the Cloud

Security challenges in the cloud present a complex and dynamic landscape as organizations increasingly migrate their infrastructure, applications, and data to cloud environments. While the cloud offers unparalleled benefits in terms of scalability, flexibility, and cost-efficiency, it also introduces a new set of security considerations that demand careful attention. One of the fundamental challenges is the shared responsibility model inherent in most cloud service providers. While cloud providers are responsible for securing the infrastructure, physical data centers, and the underlying hypervisor, customers retain responsibility for securing their data, applications, identity and access management, and configurations. This division necessitates a clear understanding of roles and responsibilities to avoid security gaps and ensure a comprehensive security posture.

Data breaches and unauthorized access represent significant security challenges in the cloud. With the migration of sensitive data to cloud environments, the potential impact of data breaches has escalated. Organizations must implement robust encryption mechanisms to protect data both in transit and at rest. Effective key management is essential to prevent unauthorized access to encrypted data. Misconfigured access controls, often stemming from oversight or lack of awareness, can lead to unintended exposure of data. Implementing the principle of least privilege and regular auditing of access controls are crucial measures to mitigate the risk of unauthorized access.

Identity and access management (IAM) complexities introduce security challenges as organizations adopt multi-cloud or hybrid cloud architectures. Managing user identities, roles, and permissions consistently across diverse cloud environments requires careful coordination. Identity federation and single sign-on (SSO) solutions help streamline authentication processes, but misconfigurations or vulnerabilities in IAM implementations can be exploited by malicious actors. Strong authentication mechanisms, such as multi-factor authentication (MFA), are essential to bolster the security of user accounts and prevent unauthorized access, especially considering the increased sophistication of cyber threats targeting cloud environments.

Vulnerabilities in cloud configurations pose a significant security risk, often arising from human error or oversight. Cloud resources, such as storage buckets, databases, and virtual machines, are frequently misconfigured, inadvertently exposing sensitive data to the public internet. Automated tools and bots continuously scan for misconfigured cloud instances, making timely detection and remediation critical. Cloud security posture management (CSPM) tools play a crucial role in identifying and addressing misconfigurations, providing organizations with the visibility and control needed to secure their cloud environments effectively.

The dynamic nature of cloud environments introduces challenges in maintaining continuous security monitoring and visibility. Traditional security approaches designed for static, on-premises infrastructure may struggle to adapt to the ephemeral and elastic nature of cloud resources. Organizations must invest in cloud-native security solutions that provide real-time visibility into the security posture of their cloud infrastructure. Security Information and Event Management (SIEM) systems, combined with cloud-specific logging and monitoring tools, enable organizations to detect and respond to security incidents promptly. Additionally, the integration of threat intelligence feeds enhances the ability to identify and mitigate emerging threats in the cloud.

The proliferation of APIs (Application Programming Interfaces) in the cloud introduces a unique set of security challenges. APIs facilitate communication and data exchange between different cloud services and applications, but vulnerabilities in API implementations can be exploited by attackers. Organizations must prioritize API security by implementing proper authentication mechanisms, access controls, and encryption. Regular security assessments and penetration testing of APIs help identify and remediate potential vulnerabilities. API security is a critical component of the overall cloud security strategy, especially as organizations leverage cloud services and microservices architectures.

As organizations embrace containerization and orchestration technologies, securing containerized environments becomes imperative. Containers offer lightweight and scalable deployment, but container security requires a focused approach. Vulnerabilities in container images, insecure configurations, and the potential for container escapes demand proactive measures. Implementing container security best practices, such as scanning images for vulnerabilities, restricting container privileges, and employing network segmentation, helps organizations mitigate the risks associated with containerized deployments. Continuous monitoring and auditing of containerized applications contribute to identifying and addressing security issues in real-time.

Threats related to the supply chain and third-party dependencies pose an escalating risk in the cloud. Cloud service providers rely on a vast ecosystem of third-party vendors for various services, and compromises in the security posture of these vendors can have cascading effects. Organizations must conduct thorough due diligence on the security practices of their cloud service providers and third-party vendors. Contractual agreements and service-level agreements (SLAs) should include clear security requirements and assurances. Regular security assessments of third-party components, including software as a service (SaaS) applications and dependencies, are essential to mitigate the risk of supply chain attacks.

The evolving landscape of cloud-based threats, including advanced persistent threats (APTs) and sophisticated malware, underscores the importance of threat intelligence and proactive security measures. Traditional signature-based security approaches may prove inadequate against polymorphic threats and zero-day vulnerabilities. Cloud-native security solutions that leverage artificial intelligence

(AI) and machine learning (ML) for anomaly detection and be-havioral analysis play a crucial role in identifying and responding to emerging threats. Security teams must adopt a proactive stance, leveraging threat intelligence feeds and collaborating with the broad-er cybersecurity community to stay ahead of evolving threats in the cloud.

Compliance and regulatory challenges are prominent consider-ations in cloud security, particularly for organizations operating in highly regulated industries. Different geographic regions have vary-ing data protection laws and compliance requirements, such as the General Data Protection Regulation (GDPR) in the European Union or the Health Insurance Portability and Accountability Act (HIPAA) in the United States. Ensuring that cloud deployments align with relevant regulatory frameworks requires a nuanced un-derstanding of data residency, privacy, and disclosure requirements. Cloud service providers often offer compliance certifications, but or-ganizations must still take responsibility for understanding and ad-hering to the specific regulatory landscape that applies to their oper-ations.

Incident response and recovery in the cloud present distinct challenges compared to traditional on-premises environments. The dynamic and distributed nature of cloud resources requires organi-zations to have well-defined incident response plans tailored to the cloud environment. This includes processes for identifying and iso-lating compromised resources, preserving digital evidence, and or-chestrating incident response activities across diverse cloud services. Regularly testing incident response plans through simulations and tabletop exercises is essential to ensure preparedness and effective-ness in the event of a security incident.

In conclusion, security challenges in the cloud are multifaceted and require a holistic and adaptive approach. Organizations must navigate the intricacies of shared responsibility models, data protection, identity and access management, and the dynamic nature of cloud environments. Proactive measures, including robust encryption, secure configurations, continuous monitoring, and threat intelligence, are essential components of an effective cloud security strategy. As the cloud landscape evolves, security professionals must stay abreast of emerging threats, leverage cloud-native security solutions, and collaborate across the industry to collectively enhance the security posture of cloud environments.

Shared Responsibility Model

The shared responsibility model represents a foundational concept in cloud computing that delineates the division of security responsibilities between cloud service providers and their customers. This model is instrumental in clarifying the roles each party plays in safeguarding the overall security of data, applications, and infrastructure in the cloud environment. At its core, the shared responsibility model acknowledges that while cloud service providers take on certain responsibilities related to the underlying infrastructure, physical security of data centers, and the global network, customers also bear significant responsibilities concerning the security of their data, applications, access controls, and configurations.

Cloud service providers, such as Amazon Web Services (AWS), Microsoft Azure, and Google Cloud Platform (GCP), assume the responsibility for the security "of" the cloud. This includes ensuring the physical security of data centers, protecting the underlying infrastructure that supports virtualized computing resources, and implementing security measures at the network level. Providers invest heavily in advanced security measures, including encryption, firewalls, and intrusion detection systems, to fortify the overall integrity and availability of the cloud infrastructure. The global reach of cloud providers allows them to establish redundancies, backup systems, and disaster recovery mechanisms, further enhancing the resilience of the cloud environment.

On the other side of the shared responsibility equation, customers are tasked with the security "in" the cloud. This encompasses a broad spectrum of responsibilities, ranging from securing data and applications to configuring access controls and managing identities. Customers retain control over the security settings, configurations, and permissions associated with their cloud resources. For instance, when deploying virtual machines or databases in the cloud, customers are responsible for configuring firewalls, ensuring proper encryption of data, and implementing access controls to prevent unauthorized access. Likewise, in a serverless computing environment, customers are accountable for securing the code and configurations of their serverless functions.

Identity and access management (IAM) is a pivotal aspect of the shared responsibility model, highlighting the joint efforts required to maintain a secure cloud environment. While cloud providers implement robust IAM systems to authenticate and authorize users, customers must define and manage user identities, roles, and permissions within their specific cloud environment. This involves establishing policies that adhere to the principle of least privilege, ensuring that users and applications have only the permissions necessary for their intended tasks. Multi-factor authentication (MFA) is often recommended to enhance the security of user accounts and prevent unauthorized access.

Data security is another critical facet of the shared responsibility model. Cloud providers implement encryption mechanisms to protect data in transit between the customer's environment and the cloud, as well as data at rest within the cloud infrastructure. However, customers are responsible for implementing encryption for their data within the cloud, defining encryption key management practices, and ensuring compliance with industry-specific data protection regulations. This collaborative approach ensures a layered defense strategy, with both the provider and the customer contributing to the overall security posture.

The shared responsibility model is not static; it evolves based on the type of cloud service being utilized. In Infrastructure as a Service (IaaS) scenarios, where customers have more control over the underlying infrastructure, the customer's responsibilities are broader, encompassing tasks such as configuring virtual machines, storage, and network settings. In Platform as a Service (PaaS) and Software as a Service (SaaS) scenarios, where customers focus more on application development and usage, the provider assumes a greater share of the responsibilities related to the underlying infrastructure, with customers concentrating on securing their applications and data.

Education and awareness play a crucial role in the effective implementation of the shared responsibility model. Cloud service providers offer documentation, guidelines, and best practices to help customers understand their specific security responsibilities. However, customers must proactively educate themselves on these guidelines and take steps to implement security measures that align with their organizational requirements. This collaborative approach to security underscores the importance of an informed and engaged customer base in maintaining a secure cloud ecosystem.

The shared responsibility model becomes particularly relevant in incidents involving security breaches or data exposures. When a security incident occurs, determining the root cause and identifying the responsible party relies on a clear understanding of the shared responsibilities. Incidents arising from misconfigurations, unsecured access controls, or inadequately managed identities often fall within the customer's domain of responsibility. In contrast, incidents related to vulnerabilities in the underlying infrastructure, physical security breaches, or global network issues fall within the cloud provider's purview.

As organizations increasingly adopt cloud computing, understanding and adhering to the shared responsibility model becomes paramount for maintaining a robust security posture. Cloud providers and customers must collaborate closely, fostering a shared commitment to security principles. Regular assessments, audits, and continuous monitoring practices help ensure that both parties are fulfilling their respective responsibilities and adapting to the evolving threat landscape. This collaborative and dynamic approach to security underscores the shared responsibility model as a cornerstone in building and maintaining trust in cloud computing environments.

Data Privacy and Compliance Concerns

Data privacy and compliance concerns stand at the forefront of contemporary discussions as individuals, businesses, and governments grapple with the evolving landscape of data-driven technologies. In an era marked by unprecedented digitization and connectivity, the sheer volume and sensitivity of personal and corporate information circulating in the digital realm underscore the critical importance of safeguarding data privacy. At the heart of these concerns lies the intricate balance between the opportunities presented by data-driven innovations and the imperative to protect individuals' privacy rights.

The concept of data privacy revolves around the protection of individuals' personal information, encompassing a spectrum of data points from names and addresses to financial records and online behaviors. In an increasingly interconnected world, where data serves as the lifeblood of digital ecosystems, ensuring the privacy of individuals has become a complex and multifaceted challenge. Individuals rightfully demand transparency, control, and security over the collection, processing, and storage of their personal data. Organizations, in turn, are entrusted with the responsibility of implementing robust data protection measures to honor these expectations.

One of the primary drivers of heightened data privacy concerns is the proliferation of data breaches and cyber-attacks. High-profile incidents, where vast amounts of personal data are compromised, not only result in financial losses but erode trust and raise questions about the ability of organizations to safeguard sensitive information. The frequency and sophistication of cyber threats necessitate a proactive and dynamic approach to cybersecurity, incorporating measures such as encryption, access controls, and threat detection to mitigate the risks associated with data breaches.

In the realm of data privacy, regulatory frameworks play a pivotal role in establishing standards and expectations for organizations that handle personal data. The General Data Protection Regulation (GDPR) in the European Union, for instance, sets a comprehensive and stringent framework for the processing of personal data, outlining principles of transparency, purpose limitation, and data minimization. The GDPR not only empowers individuals with greater control over their data but also imposes significant penalties for non-compliance, prompting organizations worldwide to reassess their data protection practices.

The global nature of data flows and digital interactions necessitates a nuanced understanding of data privacy regulations across different jurisdictions. While the GDPR serves as a prominent example, other regulations, such as the California Consumer Privacy Act (CCPA) in the United States and the Personal Data Protection Act (PDPA) in Singapore, underscore the global trend towards enhancing individuals' rights and holding organizations accountable for responsible data handling. The extraterritorial reach of these regulations means that organizations operating internationally must navigate a complex web of legal requirements to ensure compliance.

Beyond legal considerations, ethical dimensions further shape the discourse on data privacy. Questions about the ethical use of data, especially in the context of emerging technologies like artificial intelligence (AI) and machine learning, highlight the need for responsible data practices. The potential for algorithmic bias, discriminatory outcomes, and invasions of privacy amplifies the urgency for organizations to embed ethical considerations into their data-driven decision-making processes. Ethical frameworks, guidelines, and industry standards are emerging to guide organizations in navigating the ethical complexities of data usage and technology adoption.

Amidst these considerations, the role of individuals in safeguarding their own privacy cannot be understated. Digital literacy and awareness about data privacy rights empower individuals to make informed choices about sharing their personal information. Concepts like informed consent, where individuals understand and agree to how their data will be used, underscore the principle of user autonomy in the digital age. As individuals become more cognizant of their privacy rights, they play an active role in holding organizations accountable for transparent data practices.

The advent of technologies such as the Internet of Things (IoT), which involves the interconnection of devices collecting and exchanging data, introduces new dimensions to data privacy concerns. The sheer ubiquity of IoT devices in everyday life, from smart thermostats to wearable fitness trackers, raises questions about the security of these devices and the potential for unauthorized access to personal data. As the IoT ecosystem continues to expand, the need for robust security measures, standardized protocols, and clear privacy safeguards becomes imperative to mitigate the risks associated with the pervasive collection of data.

In the corporate sphere, data privacy concerns intersect with broader issues of corporate responsibility and reputation management. Organizations that prioritize and champion data privacy as a fundamental value not only comply with regulations but also cultivate trust among their customer base. Privacy-by-design principles, where privacy considerations are integrated into the development of products and services from the outset, signal a commitment to responsible data handling. Transparent communication about data practices, data retention policies, and security measures further strengthens the bond of trust between organizations and their stakeholders.

The advent of Big Data and advanced analytics introduces both opportunities and challenges in the realm of data privacy. The ability to derive valuable insights from vast datasets holds immense potential for innovation, scientific discovery, and societal progress. However, the aggregation of disparate datasets and the potential for re-identification of individuals raise concerns about the de-identification and anonymization of data. Striking a balance between unlocking the benefits of data-driven insights and protecting individual privacy requires a nuanced approach that incorporates anonymization techniques, differential privacy, and a keen understanding of the contextual integrity of data usage.

As the digital landscape continues to evolve, new paradigms such as decentralized identity systems and blockchain technology offer innovative approaches to address data privacy concerns. Decentralized identity solutions, where individuals have greater control over their personal information through the use of self-sovereign identity (SSI), challenge traditional models of data ownership. Blockchain, with its inherent characteristics of transparency and immutability, holds promise for creating verifiable and auditable records of data transactions, potentially enhancing trust and accountability in data ecosystems.

In conclusion, data privacy and compliance concerns represent a dynamic and multifaceted challenge in the digital age. The convergence of technological advancements, regulatory frameworks, ethical considerations, and individual empowerment necessitates a holistic and collaborative approach to safeguarding personal information. Organizations, governments, and individuals must collectively navigate the complexities of data privacy, fostering a culture of responsible data handling, transparency, and ethical decision-making. As data continues to be a driving force in the digital transformation, the ability to strike a balance between innovation and privacy will define the future landscape of a data-centric society.

5.3 Cloud Security Best Practices

Cloud security best practices are paramount in ensuring the integrity, confidentiality, and availability of data and resources in cloud environments. As organizations increasingly leverage the benefits of cloud computing, understanding and implementing robust security measures become essential to mitigate risks associated with cyber threats and data breaches. A foundational principle in cloud security is the adoption of a shared responsibility model, where both the cloud service provider and the customer play distinct but collaborative roles in safeguarding the cloud environment. Organizations should first conduct a comprehensive risk assessment to understand their specific security requirements and potential vulnerabilities. This assessment forms the basis for developing a tailored and effective cloud security strategy.

Identity and access management (IAM) is a cornerstone of cloud security. Implementing robust IAM practices involves defining and managing user identities, roles, and permissions with precision. Organizations should adhere to the principle of least privilege, ensuring that users and applications have only the necessary permissions for their designated tasks. Multi-factor authentication (MFA) should be enforced to add an additional layer of security to user accounts, mitigating the risk of unauthorized access. Regularly reviewing and updating IAM policies, particularly as personnel and roles evolve, is crucial for maintaining a secure access framework.

Encryption is a fundamental practice for protecting data both in transit and at rest. Organizations should leverage encryption protocols such as TLS/SSL for securing data in transit between users and cloud services. For data at rest, robust encryption mechanisms should be implemented, whether through native cloud encryption services or third-party solutions. Key management plays a critical role in encryption, and organizations should employ secure key management practices to safeguard encryption keys. Regularly updating cryptographic protocols and algorithms ensures alignment with the latest security standards.

Securing cloud infrastructure requires a proactive approach to network security. Implementing virtual private clouds (VPCs) or network security groups allows organizations to define and enforce network boundaries, controlling traffic flow and access to resources. Firewalls and intrusion detection/prevention systems should be configured to monitor and filter network traffic, identifying and mitigating potential threats. Regular network vulnerability assessments and penetration testing help organizations identify and address weaknesses in their cloud infrastructure, enhancing overall security posture.

Continuous monitoring and auditing are essential for maintaining visibility into the security posture of cloud environments. Cloud-native monitoring tools, combined with Security Information and Event Management (SIEM) solutions, enable organizations to detect and respond to security incidents promptly. Log management and analysis provide insights into user activities, resource utilization, and potential security anomalies. Automation of security monitoring through the use of security orchestration and response (SOAR) tools enhances the efficiency of incident detection and response.

Regularly updating and patching cloud resources is a fundamental practice for addressing vulnerabilities and ensuring the security of software and operating systems. Cloud service providers often release security patches and updates, and organizations should have a systematic approach to applying these updates promptly. Implementing automated patch management tools helps streamline the process and ensures that cloud resources are protected against known vulnerabilities. Additionally, organizations should conduct regular vulnerability assessments to identify and remediate potential security gaps proactively.

The principle of DevSecOps, integrating security into the entire software development lifecycle, is crucial for maintaining a secure cloud environment. Security considerations should be embedded into the design, development, testing, and deployment phases of cloud-based applications. Code reviews, static analysis, and dynamic analysis tools help identify and rectify security vulnerabilities early in the development process. Automated testing, continuous integration, and continuous deployment (CI/CD) pipelines facilitate the rapid and secure delivery of software updates.

Incident response and recovery planning are critical components of cloud security. Organizations should develop and regularly test incident response plans that outline procedures for identifying, containing, eradicating, recovering from, and learning from security incidents. The cloud environment introduces unique challenges in incident response due to its dynamic nature, and organizations should tailor their plans accordingly. Regularly conducting tabletop exercises and simulations helps ensure that incident response teams are well-prepared to address security incidents effectively.

Data backup and disaster recovery strategies are integral to cloud security. Organizations should implement regular and automated data backup processes, ensuring that critical data is recoverable in the event of data loss or a security incident. Leveraging cloud-native backup and recovery services provides scalability and reliability. Additionally, organizations should define and test disaster recovery plans, ensuring the rapid restoration of services in the event of infrastructure failures or catastrophic events. Regularly reviewing and updating these plans based on changes in cloud environments and business requirements is essential.

Security awareness and training programs are vital for fostering a security-conscious culture within organizations. Educating users about security best practices, the risks associated with phishing and social engineering attacks, and the importance of safeguarding sensitive information contribute to building a resilient human firewall. Training should be ongoing, with periodic updates to address evolving threats and changes in security policies. Simulated phishing exercises can be valuable tools for assessing and improving the effectiveness of security awareness programs.

Compliance with regulatory requirements and industry standards is a key aspect of cloud security. Organizations operating in specific sectors, such as healthcare or finance, must adhere to industry-specific regulations like the Health Insurance Portability and Accountability Act (HIPAA) or the Payment Card Industry Data Security Standard (PCI DSS). Cloud service providers often offer compliance certifications, but organizations must conduct due diligence to ensure alignment with their specific compliance requirements. Regularly conducting internal and third-party audits helps validate adherence to compliance standards and identify areas for improvement.

The adoption of a zero-trust security model is gaining prominence in cloud security best practices. This model challenges the traditional perimeter-based security approach and assumes that threats can originate from both external and internal sources. Zero trust involves verifying the identity and security posture of every user and device attempting to access resources, regardless of their location. Micro-segmentation, network segmentation at a granular level, is a key element of implementing a zero-trust architecture, preventing lateral movement in the event of a security breach.

Collaboration and information sharing within the cybersecurity community contribute to collective defense against emerging threats. Participating in threat intelligence-sharing initiatives and staying informed about the latest vulnerabilities and attack techniques enhance organizations' ability to proactively address security risks. Engaging with industry forums, attending conferences, and fostering partnerships with other organizations and security vendors create a collaborative ecosystem for addressing common challenges and staying ahead of evolving threats.

In conclusion, cloud security best practices encompass a holistic and dynamic approach to safeguarding data and resources in cloud environments. Organizations must integrate security into every aspect of their cloud strategy, from identity and access management to network security, continuous monitoring, and incident response. Adhering to established best practices, staying abreast of evolving threats, and fostering a security-conscious culture contribute to building and maintaining a resilient and secure cloud environment. As the cloud computing landscape continues to evolve, organizations must remain vigilant, adaptive, and proactive in addressing the ever-changing cybersecurity landscape.

Identity and Access Management in the Cloud

Identity and Access Management (IAM) in the cloud is a foundational element of securing digital assets and ensuring that the right individuals have the appropriate level of access to resources within cloud environments. In the dynamic landscape of cloud computing, where resources are virtualized, scalable, and distributed, IAM plays a pivotal role in defining, managing, and securing user identities and their access to various services and data.

The IAM framework in the cloud encompasses a spectrum of functions, beginning with identity provisioning. This involves creating and managing user identities, establishing their roles, and assigning appropriate permissions based on job responsibilities. The cloud IAM system must be agile and responsive to organizational changes, allowing for the seamless onboarding of new users, modifications to roles, and timely removal of access for departing employees. This adaptability is essential for reflecting the dynamic nature of modern enterprises.

Role-based access control (RBAC) is a fundamental concept in cloud IAM, defining permissions based on job functions and responsibilities. By categorizing users into roles and associating specific permissions with those roles, organizations can efficiently manage access at scale. This approach aligns with the principle of least privilege, ensuring that users have the minimum necessary access required to perform their tasks, reducing the risk of unauthorized access and potential security breaches.

Multi-factor authentication (MFA) is a critical component of cloud IAM, adding an extra layer of security beyond traditional username and password authentication. By requiring users to authenticate their identity through multiple factors such as a password, a temporary code, or a biometric verification, MFA enhances the resilience of IAM systems against unauthorized access attempts. Cloud service providers typically offer MFA options, and organizations are encouraged to enforce this security measure, particularly for users with elevated privileges.

The concept of single sign-on (SSO) simplifies the user experience while maintaining robust security. SSO enables users to log in once and gain access to multiple applications or services without the need to re-enter credentials. This not only enhances user convenience but also reduces the likelihood of weak passwords or password reuse. Federated identity management, a form of SSO, extends this capability beyond an organization's boundaries, allowing users to access resources across different cloud platforms seamlessly.

Centralized IAM systems provide a unified view and control over user identities and access across various cloud services and applications. Cloud IAM platforms typically offer dashboards or consoles that allow administrators to manage user accounts, roles, and permissions centrally. This centralized control enhances visibility into access patterns, simplifies auditing and compliance reporting, and facilitates efficient management of security policies.

Automated provisioning and de-provisioning are integral to efficient IAM in the cloud. Automation streamlines the process of granting and revoking access based on predefined rules or workflows. For instance, when a new employee joins an organization, IAM systems can automatically provision the necessary accounts and access rights based on their role, ensuring a timely and consistent onboarding process. Similarly, when an employee leaves or changes roles, de-provisioning automates the removal of unnecessary access, reducing the risk of orphaned accounts or lingering privileges.

IAM in the cloud extends beyond managing human identities to encompass non-human entities such as applications, services, or devices. Service accounts, often used by applications to interact with cloud services programmatically, require careful IAM configuration to ensure secure and controlled access. Managing machine identities involves securing API keys, certificates, or other credentials used by automated processes, and IAM plays a crucial role in orchestrating these machine-to-machine interactions securely.

Fine-grained access controls enable organizations to define specific permissions at the level of individual resources or data elements. This granularity ensures that access is tailored precisely to the needs of users or applications, minimizing the risk of unauthorized data exposure or modifications. Organizations can implement policies that restrict access to sensitive data, ensuring that only authorized individuals or processes can interact with critical information.

Audit trails and logging are essential components of IAM in the cloud, providing visibility into user activities, authentication events, and changes to access permissions. IAM platforms generate logs that organizations can use for security analysis, compliance reporting, and post-incident investigations. Monitoring IAM logs allows for the timely detection of suspicious activities, such as multiple failed login attempts or unauthorized access attempts, enabling organizations to respond proactively to potential security incidents.

IAM in the cloud also addresses the challenge of managing identities and access in hybrid or multi-cloud environments. As organizations embrace diverse cloud services or maintain a combination of on-premises and cloud resources, IAM systems must seamlessly integrate across these environments. Federated identity and IAM interoperability standards enable users to access resources consistently, irrespective of the underlying infrastructure, providing a cohesive and secure experience.

In the context of identity lifecycle management, IAM encompasses the entire journey of a user or entity, from initial onboarding to eventual offboarding. IAM systems must facilitate a smooth onboarding experience by automating the provisioning of accounts and access rights. Conversely, during offboarding or when roles change, IAM systems should promptly de-provision access to prevent security gaps and ensure compliance with least privilege principles.

IAM in the cloud also addresses the challenge of ensuring compliance with regulatory requirements and industry standards. Many industries, such as healthcare or finance, have stringent data protection regulations that mandate specific controls over access to sensitive information. Cloud IAM platforms often provide features that help organizations align with these regulatory frameworks, facilitating audit trails, access reviews, and adherence to data protection principles.

The evolution of IAM in the cloud aligns with the broader trend of digital transformation and the adoption of cloud-native architectures. Cloud-native IAM solutions leverage microservices, APIs, and containerization to provide scalable, flexible, and agile identity services. This enables organizations to adapt to changing business needs, accommodate diverse application architectures, and support the dynamic nature of cloud environments.

Challenges in IAM implementation in the cloud include ensuring the security of IAM configurations. Misconfigurations, such as overly permissive access controls or improperly configured authentication mechanisms, can introduce vulnerabilities. Organizations must conduct regular security assessments and audits of their IAM configurations to identify and rectify potential misconfigurations, reducing the risk of security incidents.

In conclusion, IAM in the cloud is a multifaceted discipline that addresses the complexities of managing identities and access in modern, dynamic computing environments. As organizations transition to cloud-based architectures, IAM becomes a critical enabler of security, compliance, and operational efficiency. By adopting best practices such as RBAC, MFA, centralized management, automation, and robust auditing, organizations can establish a robust IAM framework that balances user convenience with stringent security measures. IAM in the cloud is not merely a technical requirement but a strategic imperative for organizations seeking to navigate the complexities of a digital, interconnected world while safeguarding sensitive information and maintaining regulatory compliance.

Encryption and Key Management

Encryption and key management represent foundational pillars of modern cybersecurity, providing essential mechanisms to safeguard sensitive information in an era marked by pervasive digitization and interconnected systems. Encryption, at its core, is the process of converting plaintext data into ciphertext using cryptographic algorithms. This transformation renders the information unreadable to unauthorized entities and ensures the confidentiality and integrity of the data. The significance of encryption extends across various domains, including communication, storage, and data transmission, serving as a fundamental tool to protect against unauthorized access and mitigate the risk of data breaches.

In the realm of communication, securing data in transit is a paramount concern. Transport Layer Security (TLS) and its predecessor, Secure Sockets Layer (SSL), are cryptographic protocols that implement encryption to secure communication over computer networks. These protocols establish a secure channel between a user's device and a server, encrypting the data exchanged during the communication process. This encryption is particularly crucial for sensitive transactions, such as online banking or e-commerce, where protecting the confidentiality of financial and personal information is paramount.

Data at rest, residing in storage systems, databases, or backup repositories, represents another critical dimension of cybersecurity. Encrypting data at rest ensures that even if unauthorized access is gained to the storage infrastructure, the information remains indecipherable without the appropriate cryptographic keys. Full disk encryption and file-level encryption are common approaches to protect data at rest. In full disk encryption, the entire storage device is encrypted, whereas file-level encryption allows for selective encryption of specific files or directories.

While encryption serves as a robust defense against unauthorized access, effective key management is the linchpin that determines the overall security posture of encrypted systems. The encryption process relies on cryptographic keys, which are mathematical values used to encrypt and decrypt data. Key management involves the generation, distribution, storage, rotation, and revocation of these cryptographic keys throughout their lifecycle. The security of encrypted data hinges on the secure and effective management of these keys.

Key generation is the initial step in key management, involving the creation of cryptographic keys using secure random number generators. Keys may be symmetric or asymmetric, with symmetric keys being used for both encryption and decryption, and asymmetric keys employing a pair of public and private keys for these operations. Asymmetric encryption provides an added layer of security, especially in scenarios where secure key exchange is a concern.

Key distribution is a critical aspect of key management, particularly in systems where multiple entities need access to encrypted data. Securely transmitting cryptographic keys to authorized parties while preventing interception by adversaries is a delicate challenge. Public Key Infrastructure (PKI) is a widely used framework that addresses this challenge by leveraging a hierarchy of certificates and trusted authorities to facilitate secure key distribution. PKI plays a vital role in secure communication over the internet, enabling entities to exchange cryptographic keys and establish trust.

Once cryptographic keys are distributed, secure storage becomes imperative to prevent unauthorized access and ensure the integrity of the keys. Hardware Security Modules (HSMs) are specialized devices designed to securely store and manage cryptographic keys. HSMs provide a dedicated and tamper-resistant environment, adding an extra layer of protection against physical and logical attacks. Cloud service providers often offer cloud-based HSMs, allowing organizations to leverage secure key storage in virtualized environments.

Key rotation is a practice wherein cryptographic keys are periodically replaced with new ones. Regularly rotating keys is a proactive measure to mitigate the impact of potential key compromises. The frequency of key rotation depends on various factors, including the sensitivity of the data and compliance requirements. While key rotation enhances security, it also necessitates careful planning to ensure a smooth transition without disrupting ongoing operations.

Key revocation is a critical component of key management, allowing organizations to invalidate compromised or unauthorized keys. When a key compromise is detected or when an individual with authorized access leaves an organization, revocation ensures that the associated keys are no longer valid. Effective key revocation mechanisms are essential for maintaining control over access to encrypted data and preventing unauthorized parties from exploiting compromised keys.

In scenarios where data needs to be shared securely between parties, key exchange mechanisms come into play. Diffie-Hellman key exchange is a widely used method that allows two parties to establish a shared secret over an insecure communication channel. The parties exchange public keys, and the shared secret is computed independently, enabling secure communication without directly transmitting cryptographic keys. Asymmetric encryption, where a public key is used for encryption and a corresponding private key for decryption, facilitates secure key exchange in a way that mitigates the risks associated with key interception.

Quantum computing represents a potential paradigm shift that could impact the field of encryption. Quantum computers, if realized at scale, have the potential to break widely used encryption algorithms, including those underpinning much of today's internet security. Post-quantum cryptography is an active area of research focused on developing encryption algorithms that remain secure in the face of quantum computing threats. Organizations must anticipate the future landscape and begin preparing for the transition to post-quantum cryptographic algorithms.

In the context of cloud computing, encryption and key management are of paramount importance due to the unique challenges and opportunities presented by cloud environments. Cloud service providers offer native encryption features for data at rest, allowing organizations to encrypt data within cloud storage services. Additionally, cloud providers often offer Key Management Services (KMS) that facilitate the secure management of cryptographic keys in the cloud. Leveraging these native services ensures that data stored in the cloud remains protected against unauthorized access.

The advent of Bring Your Own Key (BYOK) and Hold Your Own Key (HYOK) models provides organizations with greater control over their cryptographic keys in cloud environments. BYOK allows organizations to generate their cryptographic keys and then import these keys into cloud KMS for managing encrypted data. HYOK takes this a step further, enabling organizations to retain complete control over their cryptographic keys, even outside the cloud provider's infrastructure. These models address concerns related to data sovereignty, compliance, and the need for enhanced control over cryptographic keys.

Homomorphic encryption represents an advanced cryptographic technique that allows computations to be performed on encrypted data without decrypting it. This innovation holds significant potential for privacy-preserving data processing in scenarios where secure computation is paramount. While homomorphic encryption is computationally intensive and not yet widely adopted, ongoing research and development efforts aim to make this technology more practical for real-world applications.

The integration of encryption and key management into the broader cybersecurity framework involves considerations of risk management, regulatory compliance, and user experience. Organizations must conduct risk assessments to identify the appropriate level of encryption for different types of data and systems. Regulatory requirements, such as the General Data Protection Regulation (GDPR) or the Health Insurance Portability and Accountability Act (HIPAA), often mandate specific encryption practices for protecting sensitive information.

User experience considerations involve striking a balance between robust security measures and the need for seamless access to encrypted data. Organizations must implement encryption in a way that does not unduly hinder legitimate users' ability to access and interact with data. User education and awareness programs play a crucial role in ensuring that individuals understand the importance of encryption and their role in maintaining a secure computing environment.

In conclusion, encryption and key management represent indispensable components of modern cybersecurity strategies, providing a robust defense against unauthorized access and data breaches. As technology evolves and cybersecurity threats become increasingly sophisticated, organizations must continuously adapt their encryption practices and key management processes to maintain a strong security posture. From securing communication channels to protecting data at rest, encryption is a versatile tool that, when coupled with effective key management, forms a resilient foundation for safeguarding sensitive information in an interconnected and digitized world.

5.4 Continuous Monitoring and Compliance

Continuous monitoring and compliance form a dynamic and integral duo in the realm of cybersecurity, playing a pivotal role in safeguarding digital assets, mitigating risks, and ensuring adherence to regulatory standards. In an era marked by persistent and evolving cyber threats, the traditional approach of periodic security assessments is giving way to continuous monitoring, a proactive and real-time strategy designed to detect and respond to security incidents promptly. This shift is driven by the recognition that cyber threats are not static; they are dynamic, adaptive, and require a continuous and vigilant approach to maintain a resilient security posture.

Continuous monitoring encompasses the systematic and ongoing observation of an organization's information systems, networks, and assets. It involves the collection, analysis, and interpretation of security-related data to provide a real-time understanding of the security status. This data may include logs, network traffic, system configurations, and user activities. By continuously monitoring the digital landscape, organizations gain the ability to detect anomalies, unusual patterns, or potential security incidents as they unfold. This timely detection is crucial for mitigating the impact of security breaches and minimizing the dwell time of adversaries within the network.

One of the foundational elements of continuous monitoring is Security Information and Event Management (SIEM). SIEM solutions aggregate and correlate data from various sources, providing a centralized platform for monitoring and analyzing security events. Through advanced analytics and machine learning, SIEM tools can identify patterns indicative of potential security incidents. Alerts generated by SIEM systems enable security teams to investigate and respond promptly, enhancing the organization's ability to thwart cyber threats effectively.

Continuous monitoring extends beyond traditional on-premises environments to include cloud and hybrid infrastructures. As organizations increasingly migrate to cloud services, the need for visibility into cloud-based activities becomes imperative. Cloud-native monitoring solutions and Cloud Security Posture Management (CSPM) tools play a crucial role in continuous monitoring by providing insights into the security configurations of cloud resources, detecting misconfigurations, and ensuring adherence to security best practices.

Automation is a key enabler of effective continuous monitoring. The sheer volume of data generated by modern IT environments necessitates automated processes for data collection, analysis, and response. Automated monitoring systems can rapidly identify and respond to security incidents, reducing the burden on human analysts and enabling a more agile and proactive security posture. Automated responses, such as blocking malicious IP addresses or isolating compromised systems, contribute to the swift containment of security threats.

Continuous monitoring aligns closely with the concept of the Cybersecurity Continuous Diagnostics and Mitigation (CDM) program, a U.S. government initiative aimed at enhancing the cybersecurity posture of federal agencies. The CDM program emphasizes continuous monitoring as a cornerstone of effective cybersecurity, advocating for a comprehensive and ongoing approach to identify, prioritize, and remediate security vulnerabilities and incidents. This approach recognizes that cybersecurity is not a one-time event but an ongoing process that requires constant attention and adaptation.

The integration of threat intelligence into continuous monitoring adds a proactive dimension to cybersecurity defenses. Threat intelligence feeds provide information about known threats, emerging vulnerabilities, and malicious activities observed globally. By incorporating threat intelligence into continuous monitoring systems, organizations gain a preemptive understanding of potential threats, enabling them to adjust security controls and response strategies accordingly. Threat intelligence also facilitates the attribution of observed activities to specific threat actors or campaigns, aiding in the development of targeted and effective countermeasures.

Compliance, on the other hand, is a critical component of the cybersecurity landscape, driven by the need to adhere to legal, regulatory, and industry-specific requirements. Compliance frameworks, such as the General Data Protection Regulation (GDPR), the Health Insurance Portability and Accountability Act (HIPAA), or the Payment Card Industry Data Security Standard (PCI DSS), establish standards for the protection of sensitive data and define specific security controls that organizations must implement. Achieving and maintaining compliance is not only a legal obligation but also a strategic imperative for organizations aiming to build trust with customers, partners, and stakeholders.

Continuous monitoring and compliance are mutually reinforcing, with continuous monitoring providing the means to enforce and validate compliance requirements. Rather than viewing compliance as a static, checkbox exercise, organizations are increasingly recognizing the value of integrating compliance efforts with continuous monitoring practices. Continuous monitoring helps organizations track their compliance status in real time, identify gaps or deviations from established controls, and promptly address issues to maintain a compliant posture.

Automated compliance management solutions streamline the process of aligning with regulatory requirements. These tools can assess the organization's adherence to specific controls, generate compliance reports, and provide insights into areas that may require attention. Automation not only enhances the efficiency of compliance management but also contributes to the accuracy and consistency of compliance assessments. This is particularly relevant in environments where regulatory landscapes are complex, and adherence to multiple frameworks is required.

The concept of a Risk Management Framework (RMF) aligns closely with continuous monitoring and compliance, providing a structured and iterative approach to managing risks in information systems. RMF integrates security into the system development life cycle, emphasizing continuous monitoring as a core activity. The iterative nature of RMF encourages organizations to assess, authorize, and continuously monitor their systems, fostering a proactive and risk-based approach to cybersecurity.

In addition to regulatory compliance, organizations are increasingly recognizing the importance of aligning cybersecurity efforts with industry best practices and standards. Frameworks such as the National Institute of Standards and Technology (NIST) Cybersecurity Framework or the ISO/IEC 27001 standard provide comprehensive guidelines for establishing, implementing, maintaining, and continually improving an information security management system.

These frameworks emphasize the importance of risk management, continuous monitoring, and a proactive approach to cybersecurity.

The concept of "DevSecOps," which integrates security into the DevOps (Development and Operations) process, is closely tied to continuous monitoring and compliance. DevSecOps advocates for the incorporation of security practices throughout the software development life cycle, from design and coding to testing and deployment. By integrating security into the development process, organizations can identify and address security issues early, reducing the likelihood of vulnerabilities making their way into production environments and enhancing overall compliance with security standards.

Penetration testing, vulnerability assessments, and red teaming activities contribute to both continuous monitoring and compliance efforts. Penetration testing involves simulating real-world cyber-attacks to identify weaknesses in systems, networks, or applications. Vulnerability assessments systematically evaluate systems for known vulnerabilities. Red teaming takes a holistic approach, simulating the tactics, techniques, and procedures of real adversaries to assess the effectiveness of security controls. These activities provide valuable insights into potential security gaps, contribute to continuous monitoring practices, and help organizations maintain a proactive and resilient security posture.

The convergence of continuous monitoring and compliance in the context of incident response is particularly noteworthy. Effective incident response involves the detection, containment, eradication, recovery, and lessons learned from security incidents. Continuous monitoring facilitates the early detection of security incidents, enabling organizations to respond promptly and minimize the impact. Compliance requirements often mandate specific incident response capabilities, emphasizing the need for organizations to develop and test incident response plans to ensure their effectiveness.

In conclusion, continuous monitoring and compliance are inseparable elements of a robust cybersecurity strategy, each reinforcing and enhancing the effectiveness of the other. Continuous monitoring provides real-time visibility into the security posture of an organization, enabling the prompt detection and response to security incidents. Compliance, rooted in legal and regulatory frameworks, establishes a baseline for security controls and practices, guiding organizations in building a resilient defense against cyber threats. The integration of these two concepts is essential for organizations seeking to navigate the complex and evolving landscape of cybersecurity, demonstrating a commitment to proactive risk management, adherence to regulatory standards, and the safeguarding of sensitive information.

Tools and Strategies for Cloud Security Monitoring

Cloud security monitoring is a critical aspect of managing and securing resources in cloud environments, where dynamic and scalable infrastructure requires specialized tools and strategies to detect and respond to potential security threats. As organizations increasingly leverage cloud services, a robust security monitoring approach becomes essential to safeguard data, applications, and networks hosted in the cloud. Various tools and strategies are employed to enhance visibility, threat detection, and incident response capabilities in cloud environments.

A cornerstone of cloud security monitoring is the use of Cloud Security Information and Event Management (Cloud SIEM) solutions. These platforms aggregate and analyze log data from various cloud services, providing a centralized view of security events and activities. Cloud SIEM tools, often offered by cloud service providers or third-party vendors, enable organizations to monitor user activities, resource configurations, and network traffic. The integration of machine learning and behavioral analytics in Cloud SIEM enhances the ability to detect anomalous patterns indicative of potential security incidents.

Cloud-native monitoring solutions, such as Amazon Cloud-Watch, Google Cloud Monitoring, or Azure Monitor, offer comprehensive insights into the performance and health of cloud resources. These tools provide metrics, logs, and alerts for various cloud services, allowing organizations to monitor resource utilization, track changes, and identify potential issues. Cloud-native monitoring is essential for maintaining visibility into the operational aspects of cloud environments and ensuring the optimal performance of hosted applications.

Network monitoring tools designed for cloud environments play a crucial role in detecting and responding to potential security threats. These tools, such as Cisco Stealthwatch Cloud or Palo Alto Networks Prisma Cloud, enable organizations to monitor network traffic, identify anomalies, and detect suspicious activities. Network monitoring in the cloud involves analyzing traffic patterns, identifying potential security misconfigurations, and ensuring that communication between cloud resources adheres to security policies.

Containerized environments, popularized by technologies like Docker and Kubernetes, require specialized monitoring tools to ensure the security of containerized applications. Container security platforms, such as Aqua Security or Sysdig, provide visibility into container activities, monitor container configurations, and detect vulnerabilities or runtime anomalies. Container security tools integrate with orchestration platforms to ensure that security considerations are seamlessly woven into the deployment and management of containerized applications.

Serverless computing, where applications run in ephemeral, event-triggered functions, introduces unique challenges for security monitoring. Serverless security tools, such as AWS Lambda Insights or Azure Functions Monitoring, provide visibility into the execution of serverless functions. These tools monitor function invocations, resource utilization, and runtime behaviors to detect and respond to potential security incidents in serverless environments.

Endpoint detection and response (EDR) tools, which have traditionally been used in on-premises environments, are evolving to address the challenges of monitoring endpoints in cloud environments. Cloud-native EDR solutions, such as CrowdStrike Falcon or Microsoft Defender for Cloud, extend visibility and threat detection capabilities to cloud-based endpoints. These tools monitor endpoint activities, detect malicious behaviors, and enable rapid response to security incidents across both traditional and cloud-based endpoints.

Identity and access management (IAM) monitoring tools are critical for ensuring the security of user identities and permissions in cloud environments. IAM monitoring solutions, such as Okta Identity Cloud or Microsoft Azure Active Directory Identity Protection, provide insights into user activities, authentication events, and changes to access permissions. These tools help organizations detect and respond to unauthorized access attempts, suspicious user behaviors, and potential IAM policy violations.

Threat intelligence feeds play a crucial role in enhancing cloud security monitoring capabilities. Integrating threat intelligence into monitoring tools enables organizations to correlate observed activities with known threats and indicators of compromise. Threat intelligence platforms, such as Recorded Future or ThreatConnect, provide real-time information about emerging threats, enabling organizations to adjust security controls and response strategies based on the latest threat landscape.

Automation is a key strategy for enhancing the efficiency and responsiveness of cloud security monitoring. Security Orchestration, Automation, and Response (SOAR) platforms, such as Demisto or Splunk Phantom, automate routine security tasks, incident response workflows, and playbooks. Automation in cloud security monitoring enables organizations to rapidly respond to security incidents, execute predefined response actions, and orchestrate complex incident response processes.

Log management and analysis tools are essential components of cloud security monitoring, providing the ability to collect, store, and analyze log data from various cloud services and applications. Tools like ELK Stack (Elasticsearch, Logstash, Kibana) or Sumo Logic offer centralized log management capabilities. These tools facilitate the aggregation of log data, enable powerful search and analysis functionalities, and support the correlation of events across different log sources.

Cloud Access Security Brokers (CASBs) are specialized tools designed to monitor and secure the use of cloud services. CASBs, such as Netskope or Bitglass, provide visibility into shadow IT, enforce data loss prevention policies, and monitor user activities across multiple cloud applications. These tools act as intermediaries between users and cloud services, allowing organizations to extend their security policies to the cloud and ensure compliance with regulatory requirements.

Encryption and data loss prevention (DLP) tools are instrumental in securing sensitive data in the cloud and monitoring for potential data breaches. Cloud encryption solutions, such as Symantec Cloud Data Protection or Microsoft Azure Information Protection, enable organizations to encrypt data at rest and in transit, safeguarding it from unauthorized access. DLP tools monitor data flows, detect sensitive information, and enforce policies to prevent the inadvertent or malicious exposure of sensitive data.

Threat hunting, a proactive approach to security monitoring, involves actively searching for signs of malicious activities or potential security threats within an organization's environment. Threat hunting tools, such as Carbon Black or Crowdstrike Falcon X, provide security teams with advanced querying and analytics capabilities to proactively seek out indicators of compromise and identify potential security threats before they escalate.

Integration with Security Information Sharing Platforms (SISP) and Information Sharing and Analysis Centers (ISAC) is a strategy that allows organizations to benefit from collective threat intelligence and share information about security incidents with the broader cybersecurity community. Platforms like the Automated Indicator Sharing (AIS) system enable organizations to contribute and receive threat intelligence, enhancing their ability to detect and respond to emerging threats collaboratively.

As organizations embrace multi-cloud or hybrid cloud architectures, unified security management platforms become increasingly relevant. Cloud Security Posture Management (CSPM) tools, such as Prisma Cloud or CloudCheckr, provide a centralized view of security postures across multiple cloud platforms. These tools help organizations ensure consistent security configurations, monitor compliance with security policies, and detect misconfigurations that could expose cloud resources to security risks.

User and entity behavior analytics (UEBA) tools contribute to cloud security monitoring by focusing on the analysis of user behaviors and identifying deviations from normal patterns. UEBA solutions, such as Exabeam or Splunk User Behavior Analytics, use machine learning algorithms to detect anomalous activities that may indicate insider threats or compromised accounts. These tools enhance the ability to detect subtle and sophisticated security incidents that may go unnoticed by traditional rule-based monitoring.

In conclusion, the landscape of cloud security monitoring is diverse and evolving, with organizations leveraging a combination of specialized tools and strategies to address the unique challenges posed by cloud environments. From Cloud SIEM solutions for centralized event management to CASBs for securing cloud services, and from automated response with SOAR platforms to proactive threat hunting, organizations must adopt a holistic and adaptive approach to effectively monitor and respond to security threats in the cloud. As the threat landscape continues to evolve, the integration of these tools and strategies into a cohesive and proactive security posture becomes essential for organizations seeking to harness the benefits of cloud computing while mitigating associated security risks.

Ensuring Compliance in Cloud Environments

Ensuring compliance in cloud environments is a multifaceted challenge that requires a comprehensive approach to address the complex interplay of technological, regulatory, and organizational factors. At its core, compliance in the cloud revolves around aligning digital practices with established frameworks and regulations to safeguard data integrity, privacy, and security. One of the primary considerations in achieving compliance is understanding the diverse regulatory landscape that spans industries and geographies. This involves a meticulous examination of data protection laws, industry-specific regulations, and international standards, such as GDPR, HIPAA, or ISO 27001, that govern the handling of sensitive information. Moreover, organizations must meticulously map their cloud infrastructure, applications, and workflows to these regulatory requirements, ensuring that each component adheres to the stipulated guidelines.

An integral aspect of compliance in the cloud is the shared responsibility model, a paradigm where both cloud service providers and customers bear distinct responsibilities for security and compliance. Cloud service providers typically manage the security of the cloud infrastructure itself, including the physical data centers, networking, and hypervisors, while customers are responsible for securing their data, applications, and configurations within the cloud. This division necessitates a clear delineation of roles and responsibilities, often outlined in service level agreements (SLAs) and contracts, to ensure a cohesive and secure compliance framework.

To implement effective compliance strategies, organizations must adopt a risk-based approach that involves identifying, assessing, and prioritizing potential threats and vulnerabilities. Conducting regular risk assessments allows for the proactive identification of areas where compliance might be at risk, enabling organizations to implement mitigating controls and measures. This risk-based approach is particularly crucial in dynamic cloud environments where the threat landscape evolves rapidly. It requires continuous monitoring and evaluation to adapt compliance measures in response to emerging risks, technological advancements, and changes in regulatory requirements.

Furthermore, encryption and data governance play pivotal roles in securing sensitive information and maintaining compliance in cloud environments. Employing encryption mechanisms ensures that data is protected both in transit and at rest, safeguarding it from unauthorized access and potential breaches. Robust data governance practices, encompassing data classification, access controls, and auditing, are indispensable in maintaining compliance by defining and enforcing policies governing data usage, storage, and retention.

A cornerstone of compliance in cloud environments is the implementation of robust identity and access management (IAM) practices. Organizations must establish stringent controls over user access, authentication mechanisms, and authorization processes to prevent unauthorized access and ensure that only authorized personnel can interact with sensitive data and resources. This involves implementing strong authentication protocols, multi-factor authentication, and regularly reviewing and updating access permissions based on changing roles and responsibilities within the organization.

Continuous monitoring and auditing are imperative components of a comprehensive compliance strategy in the cloud. Real-time monitoring allows organizations to detect and respond promptly to security incidents, anomalies, and deviations from established compliance standards. Auditing processes, including regular internal and external audits, validate the effectiveness of security controls and ensure ongoing adherence to regulatory requirements. These activities provide organizations with a holistic view of their compliance posture, enabling them to address any gaps or shortcomings promptly.

As cloud environments inherently foster collaboration and resource sharing, third-party risk management becomes a critical element in ensuring compliance. Organizations must meticulously vet and monitor the security practices of their cloud service providers and other third-party entities, as their security posture directly impacts the overall compliance of the shared environment. This involves conducting due diligence on the security measures implemented by third parties, verifying their compliance with relevant regulations, and establishing contractual agreements that explicitly outline the security and compliance expectations.

Education and training are integral components of a successful compliance strategy in cloud environments. Organizations must invest in educating their workforce about the specific compliance requirements applicable to their industry and geographic location. This includes raising awareness about data protection principles, security best practices, and the proper use of cloud services. Regular training sessions and awareness programs empower employees to contribute actively to compliance efforts, reducing the likelihood of human errors and inadvertent violations.

Finally, organizations must adopt a proactive and adaptive approach to compliance in the cloud. This involves staying abreast of emerging technologies, evolving regulatory landscapes, and industry trends. Regularly updating policies, procedures, and security controls to align with the latest standards and best practices is crucial for maintaining a resilient and compliant posture. Additionally, fostering a culture of continuous improvement and accountability within the organization enhances the ability to adapt to changing compliance requirements and effectively mitigate new and evolving risks.

In conclusion, ensuring compliance in cloud environments is a multifaceted undertaking that demands a holistic and dynamic approach. By navigating the intricate interplay of regulatory frameworks, adopting a risk-based strategy, implementing robust security controls, and fostering a culture of compliance, organizations can navigate the complexities of the cloud landscape while safeguarding sensitive information and meeting regulatory obligations. Ultimately, the journey toward compliance in the cloud is an ongoing process that requires diligence, adaptability, and collaboration across all facets of an organization.

Chapter 6: Biometric Bastions: The Future of Identity Authentication

6.1 Evolution of Identity Authentication

The evolution of identity authentication represents a dynamic trajectory influenced by technological advancements, societal changes, and the ever-growing complexities of the digital landscape. Beginning with rudimentary forms of authentication, such as simple passwords and basic access controls, the early stages were characterized by a nascent understanding of digital security. As the digital realm expanded, so did the threats, prompting the need for more robust and sophisticated authentication mechanisms.

The paradigm shift towards multifactor authentication (MFA) marked a significant milestone in the evolution of identity authentication. Recognizing the vulnerabilities associated with single-factor methods, MFA introduced an additional layer of security by combining multiple authentication factors. This typically involves a combination of something the user knows (e.g., password), something the user has (e.g., a token or smart card), and something the user is (e.g., biometric data like fingerprints or facial recognition). MFA not only enhances security but also addresses the limitations of traditional authentication methods, providing a more resilient defense against unauthorized access.

Biometric authentication emerged as a transformative force, introducing a novel dimension to identity verification. Leveraging unique physiological or behavioral attributes, such as fingerprints, iris scans, or voice recognition, biometrics offered a more personalized and inherently secure method of authentication. The adoption of biometric technology has been fueled by its ability to provide a seamless user experience while significantly reducing the risk of identity theft and unauthorized access. However, the widespread deployment of biometrics has also raised concerns about privacy, data protection, and the potential for biometric data misuse.

The evolution of identity authentication has been intricately tied to the rise of mobile technology. The ubiquity of smartphones and the increasing reliance on mobile devices for various digital activities prompted the development of mobile authentication methods. Mobile-based authentication often leverages a combination of biometrics, device characteristics, and contextual information to verify a user's identity. The inherent portability of mobile devices has not only redefined user expectations for authentication convenience but has also introduced new challenges related to securing mobile platforms and managing the diverse array of devices.

The advent of contextual and behavioral authentication represents a paradigm shift from traditional static methods. Recognizing that user behavior and context can serve as valuable indicators of identity, this approach analyzes patterns such as device usage, location, and typical activity to establish a baseline for normal behavior. Deviations from this baseline may trigger additional authentication measures, providing a dynamic and adaptive security layer that responds to evolving threats and user activities. Contextual authentication aligns with the modern ethos of user-centric security, seeking to balance security with usability.

Blockchain technology has also left an indelible mark on the landscape of identity authentication. Decentralized identity solutions, enabled by blockchain, offer a novel approach where users have greater control over their identity information. The use of distributed ledgers for identity management enhances security by reducing the reliance on centralized databases vulnerable to single points of failure and cyberattacks. Blockchain-based identity authentication also holds the promise of reducing identity fraud by providing a tamper-resistant and transparent record of identity-related transactions.

As the digital ecosystem expands and interconnects, the concept of continuous and risk-based authentication has gained prominence. Rather than relying on discrete authentication events, continuous authentication continuously evaluates user behavior and assesses risk throughout a session. Adaptive authentication models dynamically adjust the level of security based on the perceived risk, allowing for a more nuanced and responsive approach to identity verification. This shift towards continuous authentication reflects the understanding that static, one-size-fits-all authentication models are increasingly inadequate in the face of sophisticated and evolving cyber threats.

Looking ahead, the integration of artificial intelligence (AI) and machine learning (ML) into identity authentication processes represents the next frontier. AI and ML technologies have the potential to analyze vast amounts of data, detect patterns, and adapt authentication models in real-time. This intelligent and adaptive approach can enhance the accuracy of identity verification while simultaneously improving the user experience by minimizing false positives. However, the widespread adoption of AI in authentication also brings challenges related to algorithmic bias, accountability, and the need for transparent and ethical use of these technologies.

In conclusion, the evolution of identity authentication is a dynamic journey shaped by the continual interplay of technological innovation, security imperatives, and user expectations. From rudimentary password-based systems to multifactor authentication, biometrics, mobile-centric approaches, contextual analysis, blockchain solutions, and the integration of AI, each phase represents a response to the evolving threat landscape and the imperative to balance security with usability. As the digital landscape continues to evolve, identity authentication will likely remain at the forefront of cybersecurity strategies, adapting to new challenges and opportunities in the quest for a secure and seamless digital future.

Traditional Authentication Methods and Their Limitations

Traditional authentication methods, such as passwords, have long been the bedrock of digital security, serving as the initial line of defense in safeguarding sensitive information. Passwords, however, exhibit inherent limitations that have become increasingly apparent in the face of evolving cyber threats. One of the primary drawbacks is the challenge of creating and remembering complex passwords. As organizations enforce stringent password policies to enhance security, users often resort to predictable patterns or reuse passwords across multiple accounts, creating vulnerabilities that malicious actors exploit through methods like credential stuffing attacks. The reliance on static passwords also neglects the dynamic nature of the cyber threat landscape, where stolen credentials can be misused long after they are compromised, leading to unauthorized access and data breaches.

Moreover, the human factor introduces significant vulnerabilities into traditional authentication methods. Social engineering attacks, where attackers manipulate individuals into divulging sensitive information, prey on the inherent trust placed in users. Phishing, a prevalent form of social engineering, involves deceptive tactics to trick individuals into revealing their usernames, passwords, or other confidential information. As the sophistication of phishing attacks continues to grow, even the most robust password policies can be circumvented through manipulation of human behavior, underscoring the limitations of relying solely on user-generated secrets for authentication.

Single-factor authentication, epitomized by the use of passwords alone, represents another limitation. The fundamental premise of single-factor authentication is grounded in "something the user knows." However, this narrow reliance on a single means of verification proves insufficient in mitigating the diverse array of threats in the digital landscape. Once an attacker gains access to the single factor, whether through theft, brute force, or social engineering, the entire security posture is compromised. This limitation is particularly critical as organizations increasingly embrace cloud services and remote access, necessitating a more robust and layered approach to authentication.

The static nature of traditional authentication methods poses a significant challenge in the context of a dynamic and interconnected digital environment. In an era where users access applications and services from various devices and locations, the rigidity of traditional authentication fails to adapt to the fluidity of user behavior. For instance, if a user typically accesses an application from a specific device and location, traditional authentication systems may not detect anomalous behavior, allowing unauthorized access to go unnoticed until after the fact. This static nature compromises the ability to identify and respond to security incidents in real-time, emphasizing the need for more dynamic and context-aware authentication methods.

Traditional authentication methods are also plagued by the predicament of secure key exchange and storage. Transmitting and storing passwords securely is a perennial challenge. Passwords, even if hashed, are susceptible to various attacks, including dictionary attacks and rainbow table attacks. Additionally, the centralization of user credentials in databases creates attractive targets for cybercriminals aiming to exploit vulnerabilities and gain unauthorized access. The compromise of a central repository of passwords can have far-reaching consequences, potentially leading to widespread unauthorized access and data breaches. This vulnerability underscores the need for alternative methods that distribute authentication credentials and reduce the impact of a single point of failure.

Furthermore, the rise of sophisticated cyber attacks and advanced persistent threats (APTs) has rendered traditional authentication methods susceptible to compromise. Techniques such as keylogging, where attackers clandestinely record keystrokes, enable adversaries to capture passwords as users enter them. Similarly, man-in-the-middle attacks intercept communication between users and systems, allowing attackers to eavesdrop on authentication exchanges. These methods can render even the most complex passwords useless, highlighting the limitations of traditional authentication in the face of adversaries employing sophisticated tactics and technologies.

The proliferation of interconnected systems and the advent of the Internet of Things (IoT) exacerbate the challenges associated with traditional authentication methods. As devices become integral components of everyday life, from smart home appliances to wearable technology, the sheer volume and diversity of endpoints complicate authentication. Traditional methods struggle to accommodate the unique characteristics and constraints of IoT devices, leading to potential security gaps and vulnerabilities. The limitations of traditional authentication become particularly pronounced in scenarios where the traditional username-password paradigm is impractical or insufficient to secure the diverse array of IoT devices and their interactions.

In conclusion, traditional authentication methods, epitomized by passwords and single-factor approaches, exhibit inherent limitations that hinder their effectiveness in the contemporary digital landscape. Challenges related to password complexity, human vulnerabilities, single points of failure, static nature, and susceptibility to advanced cyber threats underscore the need for a paradigm shift in authentication strategies. As organizations grapple with the imperative of securing digital assets and user identities, the exploration of multifactor authentication, biometrics, adaptive approaches, and emerging technologies becomes pivotal to overcome the shortcomings of traditional methods and usher in a new era of robust and adaptive digital authentication.

Introduction to Biometric Authentication

Biometric authentication, a sophisticated method of identity verification, relies on unique biological or behavioral characteristics to grant access to secure systems or facilities. The primary goal is to enhance security by authenticating individuals based on traits that are inherently personal and difficult to forge. Biometric modalities encompass a diverse range of physiological and behavioral attributes, including fingerprints, iris patterns, facial features, voiceprints, and even the distinct way individuals type or walk. Fingerprint recognition, one of the earliest and most widely adopted biometric technologies, relies on the unique ridge patterns and minutiae points present on an individual's fingertips. Iris recognition, on the other hand, analyzes the intricate patterns within the iris to create a distinctive template for each person.

Facial recognition, a rapidly evolving biometric method, utilizes advanced algorithms to map and analyze facial features, such as the distance between eyes or the shape of the nose, to establish a unique identity. Voice recognition, another behavioral biometric, examines vocal characteristics like pitch, tone, and rhythm to create a vocal signature unique to each individual. Keystroke dynamics and gait analysis, less common but equally intriguing, assess the unique typing patterns or walking styles of individuals, respectively. The diverse array of biometric modalities allows for flexibility in implementation, catering to various security needs and environmental constraints.

The adoption of biometric authentication is fueled by its potential to overcome limitations associated with traditional methods like passwords or PINs. Unlike static credentials that can be forgotten, shared, or stolen, biometric traits are inherently tied to the individual, reducing the likelihood of unauthorized access. The integration of biometrics into security systems has become increasingly prevalent in various sectors, including finance, healthcare, government, and personal devices. Financial institutions, for instance, leverage biometric authentication to secure online transactions, providing an additional layer of protection against fraudulent activities.

The healthcare sector benefits from biometrics by ensuring secure access to sensitive patient information and preventing unauthorized entry into restricted areas. Governments deploy biometric systems for border control, law enforcement, and citizen identification, streamlining processes and enhancing national security. In personal devices, such as smartphones and laptops, biometric authentication has become commonplace, with fingerprint and facial recognition features replacing traditional passwords for enhanced user convenience and security.

Despite its widespread adoption, biometric authentication is not without challenges and concerns. Privacy issues arise as the collection and storage of sensitive biometric data raise questions about individuals' control over their personal information. Biometric templates, the mathematical representations of biometric traits, must be securely stored and encrypted to prevent unauthorized access or misuse. Additionally, the risk of spoofing, where attackers attempt to mimic biometric traits to gain unauthorized access, necessitates continuous advancements in biometric technology to stay ahead of evolving security threats.

The usability of biometric systems is a critical consideration, as user acceptance plays a pivotal role in the successful implementation of these technologies. Factors such as accuracy, speed, and ease of use influence the overall user experience. Biometric systems must strike a balance between security and user convenience to encourage widespread adoption. Moreover, the interoperability of biometric solutions with existing infrastructure and technologies is vital for seamless integration into diverse environments.

In conclusion, biometric authentication represents a transformative approach to identity verification, leveraging the uniqueness of biological and behavioral traits to enhance security across various sectors. The evolution of biometric technologies, from fingerprints to facial recognition and beyond, underscores the continuous quest for more reliable and convenient authentication methods. As biometrics become increasingly integrated into daily life, addressing privacy concerns, ensuring data security, and optimizing user experience will be essential for unlocking the full potential of this innovative and powerful authentication paradigm.

6.2 Types of Biometric Authentication

Biometric authentication encompasses a diverse array of identification methods, each leveraging unique biological or behavioral characteristics to verify an individual's identity. Fingerprint recognition, a widely recognized and adopted biometric modality, relies on the distinct ridge patterns and minutiae points on an individual's fingertips. The analysis of these unique features creates a fingerprint template that serves as a digital representation for authentication purposes. Iris recognition, another prominent biometric type, focuses on the intricate patterns within the iris of the eye. The distinctiveness of these patterns allows for accurate identification, and iris recognition is known for its high level of accuracy and security.

Facial recognition, a rapidly evolving biometric technology, captures and analyzes facial features to create a unique facial template. Advanced algorithms consider factors such as the distance between eyes, the shape of the nose, and other facial landmarks to establish an individual's identity. Voice recognition, a behavioral biometric, relies on the distinct characteristics of an individual's voice, including pitch, tone, and rhythm. This modality is often employed in telephone-based authentication systems and has applications in secure voice-controlled systems.

Hand geometry recognition is based on the physical dimensions and proportions of an individual's hand, including the length and width of fingers and the shape of the palm. This modality is commonly used in physical access control systems where individuals need to place their hand on a reader for identification. Retina recognition, similar to iris recognition, examines the unique patterns within the retina at the back of the eye. Retina scans are known for their accuracy, but the technology requires close proximity to the scanning device.

Signature dynamics, a behavioral biometric, analyzes the unique way individuals sign their names. The pressure applied, stroke sequence, and other signature-related attributes contribute to the creation of a unique signature template. Gait analysis, another behavioral biometric, focuses on the distinctive way individuals walk. This modality is less common but can be utilized for continuous authentication in surveillance or access control systems.

DNA biometrics, a relatively recent and advanced form of biometric identification, examines the unique genetic code of individuals. While highly accurate, DNA biometrics are primarily used in forensic applications due to the complexity and invasiveness of the sampling process. Keystroke dynamics, a behavioral biometric related to typing patterns, assesses the unique rhythm and timing with which individuals type on keyboards. This modality is often used for user authentication in computer systems.

In conclusion, the various types of biometric authentication offer a spectrum of options for identity verification, each with its strengths and considerations. Fingerprint, iris, facial, and voice recognition dominate the landscape, providing a balance between accuracy and user convenience. Hand geometry, retina, signature dynamics, gait analysis, DNA, and keystroke dynamics contribute to the diversity of biometric modalities, catering to specific use cases and security requirements. As technology continues to advance, the exploration of new biometric methods and the refinement of existing ones will shape the future of authentication systems, enhancing security and user experience across different domains.

Fingerprint Recognition, Facial Recognition, Iris Scanning, etc.

Fingerprint recognition, a cornerstone of biometric authentication, involves the analysis of unique ridge patterns and minutiae points present on an individual's fingertips. This method relies on capturing an image of the fingerprint, extracting key features, and creating a digital template for comparison during subsequent authentication attempts. Renowned for its accuracy and widespread adoption, fingerprint recognition is commonly employed in access control systems, mobile devices, and law enforcement applications. Its ease of use and non-intrusive nature make it a preferred choice for personal identification.

Facial recognition, a rapidly evolving biometric technology, revolves around capturing and analyzing facial features to establish a person's identity. Advanced algorithms map distinctive facial landmarks, such as the distance between eyes, the shape of the nose, and other unique characteristics. This creates a facial template used for matching and identification purposes. Facial recognition finds applications in various sectors, from unlocking smartphones to surveillance and border control. While praised for its convenience, the technology raises concerns about privacy and potential misuse, necessitating careful consideration of ethical and legal implications.

Iris scanning, another prominent biometric modality, focuses on the intricate patterns within the iris of the eye. The iris, with its unique texture and characteristics, serves as a reliable identifier. Iris recognition systems employ specialized cameras to capture high-resolution images, and sophisticated algorithms analyze the distinct patterns for authentication. Known for its high level of accuracy and resistance to false positives, iris scanning is employed in secure environments, such as government facilities and high-security access points. However, challenges include the need for close proximity to the scanning device and potential discomfort for individuals with certain eye conditions.

Hand geometry recognition relies on the physical dimensions and proportions of an individual's hand, including the length and width of fingers and the shape of the palm. This modality is commonly used in physical access control systems, where individuals place their hand on a reader for identification. Hand geometry recognition is appreciated for its simplicity, ease of use, and resistance to environmental factors such as dirt or minor injuries. While not as widely adopted as fingerprint or facial recognition, it finds applications in scenarios where a hands-on approach is feasible.

Retina recognition, akin to iris recognition, involves examining the unique patterns within the retina at the back of the eye. Retina scans capture the intricate blood vessel patterns, creating a template for identification. This method is known for its accuracy, as the retina's vascular patterns are highly individualistic. However, retina recognition requires close proximity to the scanning device, making it less suitable for certain applications. The technology is primarily used in environments where a high level of security is paramount, such as research facilities or classified areas.

In summary, fingerprint recognition, facial recognition, iris scanning, hand geometry recognition, and retina recognition represent a diverse set of biometric modalities, each with its strengths and considerations. These technologies play pivotal roles in enhancing security, streamlining access control, and improving user experience across various domains. As biometric systems continue to advance, addressing concerns related to privacy, security, and user acceptance remains crucial for widespread and responsible implementation in diverse applications.

Advantages and Challenges of Biometric Technologies

Biometric technologies offer a plethora of advantages in identity verification and access control, revolutionizing the way individuals are authenticated across diverse applications. One of the primary benefits lies in the inherent uniqueness of biometric traits, be it fingerprints, facial features, iris patterns, or voiceprints. Unlike traditional authentication methods such as passwords or PINs, biometrics are tied directly to the individual, reducing the risk of unauthorized access resulting from forgotten, shared, or stolen credentials. This uniqueness enhances the security of sensitive systems, protecting them against identity fraud, unauthorized entry, and other security breaches.

The convenience and speed of biometric authentication contribute significantly to its widespread adoption. Users can authenticate themselves seamlessly by presenting a biometric trait, eliminating the need to remember complex passwords or carry physical tokens. This streamlined process not only enhances user experience but also reduces the likelihood of user-related security vulnerabilities, such as weak passwords or credentials left unattended. In applications like mobile devices, where user convenience is paramount, biometric authentication methods like fingerprint and facial recognition have become integral features, striking a balance between security and usability.

Biometric technologies also play a crucial role in enhancing operational efficiency. In various sectors such as healthcare, finance, and government, biometrics streamline processes by providing secure and quick identity verification. For example, in healthcare, biometric authentication ensures that only authorized personnel access sensitive patient records, contributing to compliance with privacy regulations and safeguarding patient confidentiality. Similarly, in financial institutions, biometrics help secure online transactions, reducing the risk of fraudulent activities and providing a robust layer of protection for both users and organizations.

Moreover, the deployment of biometric technologies in law enforcement has proven invaluable in solving crimes and identifying individuals with a high degree of accuracy. Fingerprint recognition, facial recognition, and other biometric methods aid in forensic investigations, matching suspects to crime scenes or verifying identities. This has led to a significant improvement in the efficiency of criminal justice systems worldwide, expediting investigations and contributing to public safety.

Despite these advantages, biometric technologies are not without challenges and concerns. Privacy issues are at the forefront, as the collection and storage of sensitive biometric data raise questions about individuals' control over their personal information. Biometric templates, which are the mathematical representations of biometric traits, must be stored securely and encrypted to prevent unauthorized access or misuse. The risk of data breaches leading to the compromise of biometric information underscores the need for stringent security measures and regulations to safeguard individuals' privacy.

Another challenge is the potential for biometric systems to be spoofed or deceived. Techniques such as fingerprint replication or facial image manipulation can be employed by attackers to trick biometric systems into granting unauthorized access. Continuous advancements in biometric technology, including the incorporation of liveness detection mechanisms, are necessary to stay ahead of evolving security threats and maintain the integrity of these systems. Striking a balance between user convenience and security is crucial to ensure that biometric technologies are widely accepted and utilized.

Usability concerns also arise in certain scenarios, as not all individuals may be comfortable with or capable of providing certain biometric traits. Disabilities, injuries, or medical conditions may affect the usability of specific biometric methods. For instance, individuals with certain eye conditions may find iris scanning uncomfortable, and those with hand injuries may face challenges with fingerprint recognition. Addressing these usability concerns is essential for ensuring inclusivity and preventing discrimination in the deployment of biometric technologies.

Interoperability is another challenge, especially when integrating biometric systems with existing infrastructure and technologies. Ensuring that biometric solutions can seamlessly work with diverse systems and platforms is essential for widespread adoption and compatibility across different applications. Additionally, standardization efforts are crucial to create a cohesive framework for the development and implementation of biometric technologies, fostering interoperability and facilitating their integration into various domains.

In conclusion, the advantages of biometric technologies, including enhanced security, convenience, operational efficiency, and their role in law enforcement, have propelled their widespread adoption across diverse applications. However, challenges such as privacy concerns, the risk of spoofing, usability issues, and interoperability challenges underscore the need for a comprehensive and responsible approach to the development, deployment, and regulation of biometric systems. Continuous innovation, stringent security measures, and ethical considerations are essential to unlock the full potential of biometric technologies while addressing the associated challenges in a rapidly evolving landscape.

Advantages and Challenges of Biometric Technologies

Biometric technologies, heralded for their transformative impact on identity verification and access control, bring forth a multitude of advantages and challenges that shape their adoption across diverse applications. Among the primary advantages is the inherent uniqueness of biometric traits, whether fingerprints, facial features, iris patterns, or voiceprints. This uniqueness serves as a robust foundation for secure authentication, as opposed to traditional methods like passwords or PINs that are susceptible to being forgotten, shared, or stolen. By directly tying authentication to individual physiological or behavioral characteristics, biometrics significantly mitigate the risk of unauthorized access, offering a more foolproof means of safeguarding sensitive systems and information.

The seamless integration of biometric authentication into everyday processes is another compelling advantage. In a world where user experience is paramount, biometrics provide a swift and convenient means of identity verification. Users can effortlessly authenticate themselves by presenting a biometric trait, eliminating the need for memorizing complex passwords or carrying physical tokens. This not only enhances the overall user experience but also mitigates vulnerabilities associated with user-related security lapses, such as weak passwords or credentials left unattended. Biometric authentication methods, particularly fingerprint and facial recognition, have become integral features in applications like mobile devices, striking a harmonious balance between security and usability.

Operational efficiency receives a substantial boost through the deployment of biometric technologies. In sectors such as healthcare, finance, and government, biometrics streamline processes by offering a secure and expeditious means of identity verification. In healthcare, for instance, biometric authentication ensures that only authorized personnel access sensitive patient records, contributing to compliance with privacy regulations and fortifying patient confidentiality. Similarly, in the financial sector, biometrics bolster the security of online transactions, reducing the risk of fraudulent activities and providing a resilient layer of protection for both users and organizations.

Law enforcement has witnessed transformative benefits with the integration of biometric technologies. Fingerprint recognition, facial recognition, and other biometric methods play a pivotal role in forensic investigations, aiding in the identification of suspects with a remarkably high degree of accuracy. This has significantly enhanced the efficiency of criminal justice systems worldwide, expediting investigations and contributing to public safety. The ability to link individuals to specific crime scenes or verify identities through biometrics has become an indispensable tool in solving crimes and maintaining societal security.

However, the promising landscape of biometric technologies is not devoid of challenges and concerns, with privacy issues at the forefront. The collection and storage of sensitive biometric data raise fundamental questions about individuals' control over their personal information. Biometric templates, which encapsulate the mathematical representations of biometric traits, demand secure storage and robust encryption to prevent unauthorized access or potential misuse. The ever-present risk of data breaches and the compromise of biometric information necessitate stringent security measures and comprehensive regulations to safeguard individuals' privacy rights.

A persistent challenge in the realm of biometrics is the potential for systems to be deceived or spoofed. Adversarial techniques, including fingerprint replication or facial image manipulation, can be employed to trick biometric systems into granting unauthorized access. Continuous advancements in biometric technology, incorporating features like liveness detection mechanisms, are imperative to stay ahead of evolving security threats and maintain the trustworthiness of these systems. Striking the delicate balance between user convenience and security is critical to ensure that biometric technologies are not only effective but also widely accepted and embraced by diverse user groups.

Usability concerns surface in specific scenarios where individuals may be uncomfortable providing certain biometric traits. Disabilities, injuries, or medical conditions can impact the practicality of certain biometric methods. For example, individuals with certain eye conditions may find iris scanning uncomfortable, and those with hand injuries may face challenges with fingerprint recognition. Addressing these usability concerns is crucial for ensuring inclusivity and preventing discrimination in the deployment of biometric technologies. Furthermore, ethical considerations become paramount, requiring careful evaluation of the societal implications and potential biases associated with the use of biometric data.

Interoperability emerges as a significant challenge when integrating biometric systems with existing infrastructure and technologies. Ensuring seamless compatibility across diverse systems and platforms is essential for widespread adoption and effective utilization of biometric solutions. Standardization efforts play a pivotal role in creating a cohesive framework for the development and implementation of biometric technologies, fostering interoperability and facilitating their integration into various domains.

In conclusion, the advantages of biometric technologies, ranging from heightened security and operational efficiency to user convenience and law enforcement applications, underscore their transformative potential. However, the challenges, including privacy concerns, the risk of spoofing, usability issues, and interoperability challenges, necessitate a comprehensive and responsible approach to their development, deployment, and regulation. Continuous innovation, stringent security measures, ethical considerations, and collaborative efforts are essential to unlock the full potential of biometric technologies while navigating the intricate landscape of advantages and challenges in a rapidly evolving technological ecosystem.

6.3 Implementing Biometric Authentication

Implementing biometric authentication involves the deployment of a sophisticated security mechanism that leverages unique physiological or behavioral characteristics of individuals for identity verification. At the forefront of this technology is the recognition and analysis of features such as fingerprints, iris patterns, voiceprints, and facial structures, among others. One of the key advantages of biometric authentication lies in its ability to provide a highly secure and convenient method of verifying user identity, surpassing traditional methods like passwords or PINs. The process typically begins with the enrollment phase, where an individual's biometric data is captured and stored securely in a database. This data is then used for comparison during the authentication phase.

Fingerprint recognition, a widely adopted biometric method, relies on the unique ridges and valleys of an individual's fingerprint. Advanced algorithms analyze minutiae points to create a distinctive fingerprint template. During authentication, the user places their finger on a sensor, and the system compares the captured fingerprint with the stored template, granting access upon a successful match. Iris recognition, another robust biometric method, involves capturing the intricate patterns within the iris of the eye. This technology relies on the fact that the iris is highly unique and stable over time. By using infrared light to create a detailed iris image, the system can match it against the stored template for authentication.

Voice recognition, a behavioral biometric, analyzes the unique characteristics of an individual's voice, including pitch, tone, and cadence. During enrollment, the system records the user's voice and extracts distinct features to create a voiceprint. Subsequently, during authentication, the user speaks a passphrase, and the system compares the captured voice with the stored voiceprint. Facial recognition, perhaps one of the most widely recognized biometric methods, maps and analyzes facial features, such as the distance between eyes, nose shape, and jawline. Deep learning algorithms have significantly improved facial recognition accuracy, allowing for reliable identification even in varying lighting conditions or facial expressions.

Biometric authentication, however, is not without its challenges. Privacy concerns have been a prominent issue, as the collection and storage of biometric data raise questions about the potential misuse or unauthorized access. Robust security measures, such as encryption and secure storage protocols, are imperative to address these concerns. Additionally, the accuracy of biometric systems is contingent on the quality of data capture and the sophistication of the algorithms employed. Factors such as environmental conditions, device quality, and the individual's physical condition can impact the reliability of biometric authentication.

The implementation of biometric authentication extends beyond individual devices to encompass a variety of applications and industries. In the realm of mobile devices, fingerprint and facial recognition have become standard features for unlocking smartphones and authorizing digital payments. Financial institutions deploy biometric authentication to enhance the security of online banking and transaction processes. Governments leverage biometrics for border control, national identification systems, and law enforcement purposes. The healthcare sector utilizes biometrics to secure patient records and restrict access to sensitive medical information.

In enterprise environments, biometric authentication plays a crucial role in bolstering cybersecurity measures. Biometric access control systems regulate entry to secure facilities, providing a seamless and secure alternative to traditional access cards or PIN codes. This not only enhances security but also mitigates the risk of unauthorized access due to lost or stolen credentials. Moreover, the use of biometrics in time and attendance systems ensures accurate tracking of employee work hours, reducing the potential for time fraud.

Despite the advantages, organizations must carefully consider the ethical implications and legal frameworks associated with biometric authentication. Striking a balance between enhanced security and individual privacy is paramount. Compliance with data protection regulations, such as the General Data Protection Regulation (GDPR), is essential to safeguard user rights and ensure responsible use of biometric data. Transparent communication regarding the collection, storage, and processing of biometric information is crucial to fostering trust among users.

As technology evolves, the future of biometric authentication holds promise for even more advanced methods and widespread integration. Continuous research and development aim to overcome existing challenges, such as susceptibility to spoofing or presentation attacks, by incorporating multi-modal biometrics and liveness detection. Multi-modal biometrics combine multiple biometric methods to enhance accuracy and reliability, creating a more robust authentication process. Liveness detection, on the other hand, involves verifying that the biometric being presented is from a live and present individual, preventing the use of static images or recordings for unauthorized access.

In conclusion, implementing biometric authentication represents a significant stride towards enhancing security and user convenience in various domains. The deployment of fingerprint, iris, voice, and facial recognition technologies has become pervasive in securing devices, applications, and critical infrastructure. While the challenges of privacy, accuracy, and ethical considerations persist, responsible implementation and adherence to regulatory frameworks can mitigate potential risks. As technology continues to advance, the future of biometric authentication holds the promise of even more sophisticated methods, ensuring a secure and seamless user experience in the digital age.

Integration with Devices and Applications

Integration with devices and applications is a critical aspect of modern technology ecosystems, facilitating seamless communication and collaboration between different hardware and software components. This process is fundamental in creating a cohesive and interconnected digital experience for users across a diverse range of devices and applications. Device integration involves the harmonious interaction of various hardware, such as smartphones, tablets, wearables, and IoT (Internet of Things) devices. Meanwhile, application integration focuses on the interoperability of software applications, ensuring they can communicate, share data, and work together efficiently.

At the heart of device integration is the concept of interoperability, where different devices can communicate and share information without complications. This interoperability is often achieved through standardized communication protocols and interfaces, enabling devices from different manufacturers to work together seamlessly. For example, the integration of smartphones with smart home devices allows users to control lighting, thermostats, and security systems from a single mobile app, creating a unified and user-friendly experience.

The proliferation of IoT devices further underscores the importance of device integration. IoT encompasses a wide array of connected devices, from smart refrigerators and thermostats to industrial sensors and wearable health trackers. Effective integration of these devices enables users to monitor and control them remotely, collect and analyze data for informed decision-making, and automate processes for increased efficiency. This interconnected web of devices, often referred to as the "Internet of Things," relies on robust integration frameworks to ensure the seamless flow of information.

Application integration, on the other hand, addresses the challenge of making diverse software applications work together cohesively. In the enterprise context, organizations deploy a variety of applications for functions such as customer relationship management (CRM), enterprise resource planning (ERP), and communication tools. Integrating these applications allows for streamlined workflows, real-time data sharing, and improved overall efficiency. Middleware solutions and application programming interfaces (APIs) play a pivotal role in enabling this integration, acting as bridges between different software systems.

Cloud computing has significantly influenced application integration by providing scalable and flexible platforms for hosting and accessing applications. Cloud-based integration solutions allow organizations to connect on-premises applications with cloud-based services, facilitating a hybrid IT environment. This flexibility is crucial for businesses seeking to adapt to changing requirements and leverage the benefits of cloud services without sacrificing the functionality of existing on-premises applications.

Mobile application integration is another prominent aspect, given the ubiquity of smartphones and tablets. Users expect a seamless experience across different applications, whether they are accessing social media, messaging platforms, or productivity tools. Integration allows applications to share data, such as user preferences and authentication credentials, providing a more cohesive user experience. Furthermore, the integration of mobile applications with backend systems enables real-time synchronization of data, ensuring that users have access to the latest information regardless of the device they are using.

The rise of APIs has become a cornerstone of application integration. APIs serve as the building blocks that allow different software systems to communicate and share data in a standardized and secure manner. They enable developers to create connections between applications, granting them access to specific functionalities or data sets. RESTful APIs, in particular, have gained widespread adoption due to their simplicity, scalability, and compatibility with web-based architectures. API-driven development has become a paradigm for building flexible and interoperable software solutions.

As organizations strive to create a seamless user experience, user interface (UI) and user experience (UX) design play integral roles in device and application integration. Consistent design principles and user interfaces across devices and applications contribute to a cohesive and intuitive user experience. Users should be able to transition between devices and applications seamlessly, with a consistent look and feel that reduces friction and enhances usability.

Security considerations are paramount in the integration of devices and applications. As the interconnectedness of digital systems grows, the attack surface for malicious actors also expands. Secure data transmission, encryption, and robust authentication mechanisms are essential components of a comprehensive security strategy. Organizations must implement measures to safeguard user data and protect against potential vulnerabilities arising from the integration of diverse devices and applications.

The advent of edge computing has added a new dimension to device and application integration. Edge computing involves processing data closer to the source of generation rather than relying solely on centralized cloud servers. This approach reduces latency and enhances real-time processing capabilities, making it particularly relevant for applications that require immediate responses, such as IoT devices in industrial settings or autonomous vehicles. Effectively integrating edge computing with traditional cloud-based systems requires careful consideration of data flow, processing capabilities, and security protocols.

In the context of artificial intelligence (AI) and machine learning (ML), integration becomes crucial for harnessing the full potential of these technologies. AI and ML algorithms often require large datasets for training and continuous learning. Integration with diverse data sources, such as databases, sensors, and external APIs, is necessary to feed these algorithms with relevant and up-to-date information. The integration of AI and ML capabilities into applications can enhance automation, decision-making processes, and the overall intelligence of digital systems.

In conclusion, the seamless integration of devices and applications is a cornerstone of the interconnected digital landscape. It involves not only the physical connection of diverse hardware but also the harmonious collaboration of software applications through standardized interfaces and communication protocols. From smartphones and IoT devices to enterprise applications and cloud services, effective integration enhances user experiences, improves operational efficiency, and unlocks the full potential of emerging technologies. As the digital ecosystem continues to evolve, the ability to integrate devices and applications will remain a key determinant of success in providing innovative and user-centric solutions.

Addressing Privacy and Ethical Considerations

Addressing privacy and ethical considerations is a paramount concern in the rapidly advancing landscape of technology, where the collection, storage, and utilization of personal data have become integral components of digital systems. Privacy, defined as the right to keep one's personal information and activities confidential, is essential in maintaining individual autonomy and trust in digital interactions. Ethical considerations, on the other hand, encompass the moral principles guiding the responsible development and use of technology, ensuring that innovation aligns with societal values and respects the rights of individuals.

In the realm of privacy, the pervasive nature of data collection raises concerns about the potential misuse or unauthorized access to sensitive information. As organizations and technologies gather vast amounts of personal data, ranging from biometric information to online behavior patterns, safeguarding privacy becomes a complex challenge. Privacy by design, an approach that integrates privacy considerations into the entire development process, is a crucial paradigm. This involves implementing robust security measures, data anonymization techniques, and clear user consent mechanisms from the inception of a technology or system.

One of the fundamental aspects of addressing privacy concerns is ensuring transparency and providing individuals with clear information about how their data will be collected, used, and shared. Privacy policies, often presented in lengthy and complex terms of service agreements, need to be made more accessible and comprehensible to the average user. Educating users about the importance of privacy and their rights in the digital realm is equally crucial, fostering a more informed and empowered user base.

The enactment of comprehensive data protection regulations, such as the General Data Protection Regulation (GDPR) in the European Union, signifies a significant step towards safeguarding individual privacy rights. GDPR establishes principles of data minimization, purpose limitation, and the right to erasure, giving individuals more control over their personal data. However, the global nature of digital interactions necessitates a broader, international approach to privacy regulation, as data often transcends geographical boundaries.

Furthermore, the advent of emerging technologies like artificial intelligence (AI) and machine learning introduces new dimensions to privacy considerations. These technologies often rely on vast datasets for training and continuous improvement, raising questions about the ethical sourcing and usage of such data. Striking a balance between the benefits of AI and the protection of individual privacy requires careful consideration of algorithms, bias mitigation strategies, and the responsible handling of sensitive information.

Ethical considerations extend beyond privacy to encompass a broader set of principles guiding the development and deployment of technology. The ethical implications of technology are particularly evident in areas like facial recognition, where concerns about surveillance, profiling, and potential misuse have prompted calls for regulatory intervention. Ethical frameworks for technology development should prioritize fairness, accountability, and transparency, ensuring that algorithms and systems are devoid of discriminatory biases and can be audited for accountability.

Another ethical dimension involves the responsible use of emerging technologies in fields like biotechnology, genomics, and surveillance. Genetic data, for instance, poses unique ethical challenges regarding consent, data ownership, and the potential for discrimination based on genetic information. The ethical development and use of biometric technologies, such as facial recognition or DNA analysis, require careful consideration of the societal implications and potential unintended consequences.

In the context of artificial intelligence, ethical concerns revolve around issues like algorithmic bias, explainability, and the societal impact of automated decision-making. Addressing bias in AI algorithms is a critical step in ensuring fair and equitable outcomes, especially in applications like hiring, finance, and criminal justice. Efforts to enhance the explainability of AI systems contribute to building trust and understanding, allowing individuals to comprehend the reasoning behind algorithmic decisions.

The ethical considerations surrounding autonomous systems, such as self-driving cars or drones, involve complex questions of accountability and decision-making in unforeseen circumstances. Establishing clear ethical guidelines for the development and deployment of autonomous technologies is essential to navigate the challenges of ensuring public safety while avoiding unintended consequences.

Moreover, the ethical responsibility of technology companies extends to the impact of their products on society at large. This includes addressing issues of misinformation, online harassment, and the societal implications of addictive design patterns in digital platforms. Social media platforms, in particular, face scrutiny for their role in shaping public discourse, amplifying echo chambers, and influencing political outcomes. Ethical considerations demand that technology companies prioritize the well-being of users and society over profit motives.

Incorporating diversity and inclusion in the design and development process is a crucial ethical consideration. Ensuring representation from diverse backgrounds helps mitigate biases in technology and ensures that products and services cater to a wide range of users. The lack of diversity in the tech industry has been identified as a contributing factor to biased algorithms and the perpetuation of discriminatory practices.

The ethical development of technology also involves a commitment to sustainability and environmental responsibility. The increasing demand for digital services and the energy consumption of data centers contribute to environmental concerns. Ethical technology development requires efforts to minimize the ecological footprint of digital infrastructure, explore renewable energy sources, and adopt practices that prioritize long-term environmental sustainability.

An overarching ethical principle in technology is the concept of "do no harm." This principle, inspired by medical ethics, emphasizes the need for technologists, developers, and organizations to anticipate and prevent potential harm that their creations might inflict on individuals, communities, and the environment. Responsible innovation involves continuous reflection on the societal impact of technology and a commitment to mitigating negative consequences.

In conclusion, addressing privacy and ethical considerations in the development and deployment of technology is essential for fostering a digital landscape that respects individual rights, promotes fairness, and prioritizes the well-being of society. Privacy protections, transparent practices, and adherence to ethical principles should be integral components of technological advancements. As technology continues to shape the future, a proactive and principled approach to privacy and ethics is crucial to ensure that innovation aligns with human values and contributes positively to the well-being of individuals and society as a whole.

6.4 Multi-Factor Authentication (MFA)

Multi-Factor Authentication (MFA) represents a pivotal advancement in the realm of cybersecurity, introducing an additional layer of defense beyond traditional username and password combinations. In the face of escalating cyber threats and the increasing sophistication of malicious actors, MFA stands as a robust safeguard, fortifying the authentication process by requiring users to provide multiple forms of identification. The primary motivation behind MFA lies in mitigating the vulnerabilities associated with relying solely on passwords, which can be susceptible to theft, brute-force attacks, or phishing schemes. By incorporating multiple factors for user verification, MFA significantly enhances the security posture of digital systems and access points.

The foundational concept of MFA revolves around the utilization of three distinct authentication factors: something the user knows, something the user has, and something the user is. The first factor, often the traditional password or PIN, represents knowledge-based authentication. Despite being susceptible to compromises, it remains an integral component of MFA, forming the initial layer of defense. The second factor involves something the user possesses, such as a physical token, smart card, or a one-time passcode generated by a mobile app. This possession-based authentication introduces an additional hurdle for unauthorized access, requiring not only knowledge of the password but also possession of a tangible item.

The third factor delves into biometric authentication, utilizing unique physiological or behavioral characteristics inherent to individuals. Biometric data, ranging from fingerprints and iris patterns to voiceprints and facial recognition, adds a layer of identity verification based on intrinsic attributes. This factor relies on the principle that biometric markers are inherently more difficult to replicate or compromise, enhancing the overall security of the authentication process. Integrating biometrics into MFA not only bolsters security but also contributes to a more user-friendly and seamless experience, eliminating the need to remember complex passwords or carry physical tokens.

MFA implementations can take various forms, adapting to the specific requirements and preferences of different systems and users. One prevalent approach involves two-factor authentication (2FA), where users are required to provide two of the three aforementioned factors for access. For instance, a user might enter a password (something they know) and then receive a one-time passcode on their mobile device (something they have) for additional verification. This combination significantly raises the bar for unauthorized access, particularly in scenarios where one factor alone might be compromised.

Another variant is three-factor authentication (3FA), where all three factors—knowledge-based, possession-based, and biometric—are employed for user verification. While 3FA offers an even higher level of security, it may be reserved for sensitive applications or industries where the utmost protection is paramount. Striking the right balance between security and usability is a key consideration in MFA implementation, as overly complex authentication processes might deter users or introduce usability challenges.

The widespread adoption of MFA is evident across various domains, from consumer-facing applications and online services to enterprise environments and critical infrastructure. Popular online platforms, recognizing the imperative of securing user accounts, have integrated MFA options into their authentication workflows. Users can opt for methods such as receiving authentication codes via SMS, using authenticator apps, or relying on biometric features like fingerprint recognition. The flexibility in MFA implementation accommodates the diverse preferences and technological capabilities of users and organizations.

In enterprise settings, MFA has become a cornerstone of cybersecurity strategies, particularly in securing access to sensitive information, networks, and critical systems. Beyond the traditional username-password paradigm, employees are often required to authenticate using additional factors, reinforcing the organization's defenses against unauthorized access and potential data breaches. This becomes especially crucial in the context of remote work and the increasing prevalence of cloud-based services, where the traditional security perimeter is less defined.

Financial institutions, recognizing the heightened risks associated with online transactions and account access, have embraced MFA to safeguard customer accounts. Authentication methods such as one-time passcodes, smart card verification, and biometric recognition add layers of protection to financial transactions, reducing the likelihood of fraudulent activities. The financial sector's adoption of MFA aligns with regulatory mandates and industry best practices aimed at enhancing the overall resilience of the sector against cyber threats.

While MFA represents a formidable defense against unauthorized access, its implementation is not without challenges. Usability concerns, potential for user resistance, and the need for seamless integration into existing workflows are aspects that organizations must carefully navigate. Striking a balance between robust security measures and a user-friendly experience is crucial for the widespread adoption and effectiveness of MFA.

Moreover, the dynamic landscape of cyber threats necessitates continuous innovation in MFA technologies. Adaptive authentication, for instance, leverages contextual information such as user location, device characteristics, and behavioral patterns to dynamically adjust the authentication requirements. This approach adds an extra layer of intelligence, enabling systems to adapt to varying risk levels and providing a more nuanced and responsive security framework.

As technology evolves, the future of MFA holds promise for even more sophisticated and user-friendly implementations. The integration of artificial intelligence (AI) and machine learning (ML) into MFA systems aims to enhance threat detection capabilities, identifying anomalies and potential security breaches in real time. Behavioral biometrics, which analyze user behavior patterns, typing dynamics, and mouse movements, represent an emerging frontier in

MFA, offering continuous authentication without relying solely on static credentials.

In conclusion, Multi-Factor Authentication stands as a cornerstone in the ongoing battle against cyber threats, offering a robust defense mechanism by requiring users to authenticate through multiple factors. From traditional passwords and possession-based methods to advanced biometric authentication, MFA provides a versatile and scalable approach to enhancing the security of digital systems. Its adoption across various sectors reflects a growing recognition of the imperative to fortify authentication processes in the face of evolving cyber threats. As technology continues to advance, MFA will likely play an even more pivotal role in securing the digital landscape, offering a dynamic and adaptive defense against unauthorized access and potential data breaches.

Combining Biometrics with Other Authentication Factors

Combining biometrics with other authentication factors represents a multifaceted approach to enhancing the security and reliability of authentication processes in digital systems. Biometrics, relying on unique physiological or behavioral characteristics of individuals, offers a robust form of identity verification. However, recognizing the need for layered security, the integration of biometrics with other authentication factors creates a more resilient defense against unauthorized access and potential threats.

At the core of this integration lies the recognition that a single authentication factor may have vulnerabilities, and combining multiple factors mitigates these weaknesses. The three primary authentication factors—something the user knows (knowledge-based), something the user has (possession-based), and something the user is (biometric)—can be combined in various configurations to create a multi-dimensional security framework.

The combination of biometrics with knowledge-based authentication, typically represented by passwords or PINs, offers a two-factor authentication (2FA) approach. Users are required to provide both something they know (password) and something they are (biometric) for access. This method significantly fortifies security, as even if a password is compromised, unauthorized access is still thwarted by the biometric factor. This approach is particularly prevalent in consumer-facing applications, where additional security layers are necessary to protect user accounts and sensitive information.

Integrating biometrics with possession-based authentication involves combining something the user has, such as a smart card or mobile device, with biometric verification. For example, a user might possess a smart card and also need to undergo fingerprint recognition for access. This approach adds an extra layer of complexity for potential attackers, as they would need both the physical possession and biometric characteristics of the authorized user.

In enterprise environments, combining biometrics with possession-based authentication is common for securing access to sensitive information and critical systems. Employees may use a smart card or a mobile authentication app, paired with fingerprint or facial recognition, to gain entry. This dual-layered approach safeguards against scenarios where physical tokens may be lost or stolen, while still ensuring that unauthorized individuals cannot exploit the biometric factor alone.

Three-factor authentication (3FA) involves combining all three authentication factors: something the user knows (password), something the user has (possession-based, like a token or smart card), and something the user is (biometric). This comprehensive approach creates a highly secure environment, especially in contexts where the utmost protection is essential. For instance, securing access to highly sensitive government facilities or critical infrastructure may necessitate the implementation of 3FA.

Biometrics also finds synergy with contextual authentication, where additional factors like user location, device characteristics, and behavioral patterns are considered. This adaptive authentication method tailors security requirements based on the specific context of the authentication attempt. For instance, if a user attempts to access a system from an unfamiliar location or device, the system may request additional biometric verification to ensure the legitimacy of the access attempt.

The combination of biometrics with one-time passcodes (OTPs) or time-based tokens introduces dynamic elements into the authentication process. Users may receive a time-sensitive code on their mobile device or via email, in addition to undergoing biometric verification. This time-sensitive element adds an extra layer of security, as the code becomes invalid after a short duration, reducing the risk of unauthorized access even if the biometric factor is compromised.

In financial transactions, the integration of biometrics with transaction-specific details enhances security. For example, a user making an online purchase may need to authenticate not only with their fingerprint but also by confirming transaction details displayed on the screen. This multifaceted approach ensures that the user not only possesses the correct biometric features but is also actively involved in the transaction verification process.

The adoption of biometrics in conjunction with other authentication factors is evident in various sectors, including healthcare, where securing access to patient records and sensitive medical information is paramount. In this context, healthcare providers may implement a combination of passwords, smart cards, and biometrics to ensure that only authorized personnel can access and update patient data. This layered approach safeguards patient privacy and complies with data protection regulations.

The widespread use of mobile devices has facilitated the integration of biometrics with mobile authentication methods. Smartphones equipped with fingerprint scanners, facial recognition technology, or even iris scanners allow users to authenticate with their unique biometric features. Combining these biometric methods with device possession adds an additional layer of security, as the authorized user must physically possess the authenticated mobile device.

However, the integration of biometrics with other authentication factors is not without challenges. Usability concerns, particularly in scenarios where users must navigate multiple layers of authentication, may impact the overall user experience. Striking a balance between security and user convenience is crucial to encourage widespread adoption. Additionally, considerations related to privacy and data protection become more intricate with the collection and storage of multiple authentication factors, necessitating robust security measures and compliance with relevant regulations.

As technology advances, the future of combining biometrics with other authentication factors holds promise for even more sophisticated and seamless implementations. The integration of artificial intelligence (AI) and machine learning (ML) into authentication systems aims to enhance the adaptability and responsiveness of security measures. Continuous monitoring of user behavior, coupled with biometric verification, can contribute to a more dynamic and context-aware authentication process.

In conclusion, the combination of biometrics with other authentication factors represents a strategic approach to fortifying digital security. Whether in consumer applications, enterprise environments, or critical infrastructure, the integration of something the user knows, has, and is creates a multi-layered defense against unauthorized access. As technology evolves, refining the integration of biometrics with adaptive and dynamic authentication methods will be essential in maintaining a delicate balance between security and user experience in the ever-evolving landscape of cybersecurity.

Enhancing Security Through MFA

Enhancing security through Multi-Factor Authentication (MFA) is a pivotal strategy in the relentless battle against escalating cyber threats and vulnerabilities in the digital landscape. MFA represents a paradigm shift from the traditional reliance on single-factor authentication, typically comprised of usernames and passwords, to a more robust and layered approach. The core principle of MFA lies in the requirement for users to provide multiple forms of identification, significantly bolstering the overall security posture of digital systems and access points.

The fundamental motivation behind MFA is to address the inherent weaknesses associated with relying solely on passwords for user authentication. Passwords are susceptible to various vulnerabilities, including brute-force attacks, credential stuffing, and phishing schemes that trick users into revealing their login credentials. By introducing additional layers of authentication, MFA mitigates these risks, making it significantly more challenging for malicious actors to gain unauthorized access to sensitive information, accounts, or systems.

The three primary authentication factors employed in MFA—something the user knows, something the user has, and something the user is—offer a multifaceted defense against potential security breaches. The first factor, knowledge-based authentication, typically involves passwords or personal identification numbers (PINs). While passwords remain a crucial element in the authentication process, MFA introduces additional layers that go beyond what users know, recognizing the need for a more sophisticated security framework.

The second factor, possession-based authentication, adds an extra layer by requiring users to possess a physical item or device for access. This could include smart cards, security tokens, or mobile devices. The possession-based factor ensures that even if an attacker gains knowledge of a user's password, they would still need a tangible item to complete the authentication process. This deters unauthorized access and enhances security, particularly in environments where sensitive data or critical systems are at stake.

Biometric authentication constitutes the third factor and involves utilizing unique physiological or behavioral characteristics of individuals. Biometrics, such as fingerprints, iris patterns, voiceprints, and facial recognition, offer a highly secure and convenient means of verifying user identity. By incorporating biometrics into the authentication process, MFA leverages attributes that are inherently difficult to replicate or compromise. This factor not only enhances security but also contributes to a more user-friendly and seamless authentication experience.

One of the significant advantages of MFA is its adaptability to various implementations and configurations, accommodating the diverse needs and preferences of users and organizations. Two-factor authentication (2FA), a prevalent form of MFA, typically combines knowledge-based and possession-based factors. For example, a user may enter a password (knowledge-based) and receive a one-time passcode on their mobile device (possession-based) for additional verification. This combination significantly raises the bar for unauthorized access, as both factors must be successfully validated.

Three-factor authentication (3FA) takes MFA a step further by incorporating all three authentication factors: knowledge-based, possession-based, and biometric. While 3FA offers an even higher level of security, it may be selectively implemented in scenarios where the utmost protection is imperative, such as securing access to critical infrastructure or highly sensitive information.

The adoption of MFA is evident across a spectrum of applications, industries, and sectors. Popular online platforms, recognizing the importance of securing user accounts, have integrated MFA options into their authentication workflows. Users can opt for methods such as receiving authentication codes via SMS, using authenticator apps, or relying on biometric features like fingerprint recognition. The flexibility in MFA implementation accommodates the diverse preferences and technological capabilities of users and organizations.

In enterprise environments, MFA has become a cornerstone of cybersecurity strategies, particularly in securing access to sensitive information, networks, and critical systems. Beyond the traditional username-password paradigm, employees are often required to authenticate using additional factors, reinforcing the organization's defenses against unauthorized access and potential data breaches. This becomes especially crucial in the context of remote work and the increasing prevalence of cloud-based services, where the traditional security perimeter is less defined.

Financial institutions, recognizing the heightened risks associated with online transactions and account access, have embraced MFA to safeguard customer accounts. Authentication methods such as one-time passcodes, smart card verification, and biometric recognition add layers of protection to financial transactions, reducing the likelihood of fraudulent activities. The financial sector's adoption of MFA aligns with regulatory mandates and industry best practices aimed at enhancing the overall resilience of the sector against cyber threats.

The integration of MFA in healthcare is pivotal for securing access to patient records and sensitive medical information. In this context, healthcare providers may implement a combination of passwords, smart cards, and biometrics to ensure that only authorized personnel can access and update patient data. This layered approach safeguards patient privacy and complies with data protection regulations.

The seamless integration of biometrics with MFA provides an added layer of sophistication to security measures. Biometric authentication methods, such as fingerprint recognition or facial scanning, enhance the reliability of the user verification process. The uniqueness and complexity of biometric markers add a level of security that is challenging to replicate, making it an invaluable component of MFA implementations.

MFA's effectiveness in enhancing security is particularly evident in scenarios where user identities need to be verified remotely. Remote authentication, facilitated by MFA, ensures that individuals accessing systems or services from different locations are subject to multi-layered verification. This is crucial for organizations embracing remote work and distributed teams, where securing remote access becomes a top priority.

The adoption of MFA, however, is not without its challenges. Usability concerns, potential for user resistance, and the need for seamless integration into existing workflows are aspects that organizations must carefully navigate. Striking a balance between robust security measures and a user-friendly experience is crucial for the widespread adoption and effectiveness of MFA.

Moreover, the dynamic landscape of cyber threats necessitates continuous innovation in MFA technologies. Adaptive authentication, for instance, leverages contextual information such as user location, device characteristics, and behavioral patterns to dynamically adjust the authentication requirements. This approach adds an extra layer of intelligence, enabling systems to adapt to varying risk levels and providing a more nuanced and responsive security framework.

As technology evolves, the future of MFA holds promise for even more sophisticated and user-friendly implementations. The integration of artificial intelligence (AI) and machine learning (ML) into MFA systems aims to enhance threat detection capabilities, identifying anomalies and potential security breaches in real time. Behavioral biometrics, which analyze user behavior patterns, typing dynamics, and mouse movements, represent an emerging frontier in

MFA, offering continuous authentication without relying solely on static credentials.

In conclusion, Multi-Factor Authentication stands as a pivotal strategy in fortifying digital security. By combining knowledge-based, possession-based, and biometric authentication factors, MFA creates a multi-layered defense against unauthorized access and potential data breaches. Its versatility and adaptability make it a crucial component of cybersecurity frameworks across various sectors. As technology continues to advance, refining MFA implementations and embracing innovative approaches will be essential to stay ahead of evolving cyber threats and ensure a secure digital environment.

Chapter 7: Insider Threats: Defending Against the Enemy Within

7.1 Understanding Insider Threats

Insider threats, a growing concern in the realm of cybersecurity, refer to the risks posed by individuals within an organization who exploit their privileged access to compromise the confidentiality, integrity, or availability of sensitive information. These threats can emanate from current or former employees, contractors, or business associates who, intentionally or unintentionally, engage in activities that jeopardize the organization's security posture. Understanding the dynamics of insider threats necessitates an exploration of various dimensions, ranging from the psychological factors driving malicious intent to the technological vulnerabilities that may be exploited. The motivations behind insider threats are multifaceted and can include disgruntlement, financial gain, ideological beliefs, or even unintentional negligence.

Psychological factors play a pivotal role in shaping insider threats. Employees may succumb to personal pressures, such as financial difficulties, and become susceptible to bribery or coercion. Disgruntled employees, harboring resentment towards their organization for reasons ranging from perceived injustices to dissatisfaction with work conditions, may act out in ways that compromise security. Additionally, individuals with ideological motivations, driven by political, religious, or social beliefs, may view their organization as a target or conduit for advancing their agenda. Understanding these psychological triggers is crucial for organizations seeking to implement effective preventive measures.

Moreover, the intentional nature of some insider threats highlights the significance of organizational culture and employee morale. A positive and inclusive workplace culture can foster a sense of loyalty and commitment among employees, reducing the likelihood of malicious intent. Conversely, a toxic environment may contribute to discontentment and increase the risk of insider threats. Therefore, organizations must prioritize creating a positive workplace atmosphere that values employee well-being, professional growth, and open communication.

Technical vulnerabilities also play a substantial role in enabling insider threats. Privileged access, granted to employees to perform their duties, can become a double-edged sword if not adequately monitored and controlled. Insiders may exploit their legitimate access to compromise systems, exfiltrate sensitive data, or disrupt operations. Inadequate access controls, weak authentication mechanisms, and insufficient monitoring can exacerbate the risks associated with insider threats. As technology evolves, organizations must continually reassess and fortify their cybersecurity infrastructure to stay ahead of potential threats.

Insider threats can manifest in various forms, each requiring tailored mitigation strategies. Malicious insiders may engage in activities such as data theft, sabotage, or the introduction of malware. In contrast, unintentional insiders may inadvertently compromise security through actions like falling victim to phishing attacks, neglecting cybersecurity best practices, or mishandling sensitive information. Organizations must adopt a comprehensive approach that combines technical safeguards, employee training, and vigilant monitoring to address both intentional and unintentional insider threats.

Detection and mitigation of insider threats involve the deployment of advanced technologies capable of monitoring user behavior, analyzing network traffic, and identifying anomalous patterns indicative of potential threats. User behavior analytics (UBA) and data loss prevention (DLP) systems are integral components of an effective insider threat detection strategy. These tools employ machine learning algorithms to establish baseline behavior for users and promptly alert security teams to deviations that may signify malicious intent. Regularly conducting thorough risk assessments and vulnerability analyses can further enhance an organization's ability to proactively identify and address potential insider threats.

Employee awareness and training constitute another critical element in combating insider threats. Educating employees about cybersecurity best practices, the importance of safeguarding sensitive information, and the consequences of negligent behavior can empower them to become active participants in the organization's security efforts. Regularly updated training programs can also familiarize employees with emerging threats, ensuring that they remain vigilant in the face of evolving cybersecurity landscapes.

Additionally, organizations must establish robust incident response plans specifically tailored to address insider threats. Timely detection is futile without an efficient response mechanism in place. Incident response plans should outline clear procedures for investigating suspected insider incidents, containing the impact, and implementing remediation measures. This includes not only technical aspects but also legal and human resources considerations to ensure a comprehensive and coordinated response.

Insider threats also extend beyond the traditional boundaries of an organization, as third-party vendors, contractors, and partners may inadvertently introduce risks. Collaborative efforts between organizations and their external partners are essential to ensure a unified approach to cybersecurity. Implementing strict access controls, conducting regular security audits, and establishing clear communication channels for reporting and addressing potential issues can mitigate the risks associated with third-party involvement.

Legal and regulatory compliance play a crucial role in addressing insider threats. Organizations must navigate a complex landscape of laws and regulations governing data protection, privacy, and cybersecurity. Failure to comply with these regulations not only exposes organizations to legal consequences but also undermines their ability to maintain the trust of customers and stakeholders. Developing a thorough understanding of applicable laws and implementing robust compliance frameworks is essential for mitigating legal risks associated with insider threats.

In conclusion, the multifaceted nature of insider threats necessitates a holistic and proactive approach to cybersecurity. Organizations must recognize the interplay between psychological factors, technical vulnerabilities, and human behavior to effectively safeguard against both intentional and unintentional insider threats. By fostering a positive workplace culture, implementing advanced technologies, prioritizing employee training, and complying with legal and regulatory requirements, organizations can significantly enhance their resilience to insider threats and protect the integrity, confidentiality, and availability of sensitive information. The evolving nature of cybersecurity challenges requires continuous adaptation and innovation to stay ahead of emerging threats and safeguard the digital assets that underpin modern organizations.

Differentiating Between Malicious and Non-Malicious Insiders

The differentiation between malicious and non-malicious insiders is a critical aspect of understanding and addressing insider threats within organizations. Malicious insiders pose intentional risks, driven by various motivations, while non-malicious insiders, often unwittingly, contribute to security vulnerabilities through negligence or ignorance. Malicious insiders typically act with the intent to cause harm, whether for personal gain, revenge, ideological reasons, or other malicious purposes. On the contrary, non-malicious insiders may compromise security inadvertently, lacking malicious intent but nonetheless presenting risks. The key to effectively managing insider threats lies in comprehending the distinct characteristics, behaviors, and motivations that differentiate these two categories.

Malicious insiders often exhibit behavioral red flags that, if detected, can serve as indicators of their intent. These indicators may include sudden changes in behavior, expressions of dissatisfaction with the organization, or unusual patterns of accessing sensitive information. Financial motivations, such as debts or financial troubles, can drive employees to exploit their access for personal gain. Additionally, disgruntled employees may seek revenge for perceived injustices, leading them to engage in activities that compromise organizational security. Ideological motivations, driven by political, religious, or social beliefs, can also prompt individuals to become malicious insiders, using their access to further their agenda. Understanding these psychological drivers is crucial for profiling potential malicious insiders and implementing proactive measures to mitigate the associated risks.

Non-malicious insiders, on the other hand, may compromise security inadvertently due to a lack of awareness, training, or understanding of cybersecurity best practices. Human error is a significant factor in this category, encompassing actions such as falling victim to phishing attacks, inadvertently disclosing sensitive information, or neglecting to follow established security protocols. These individuals do not harbor malicious intent but can inadvertently become conduits for cyber threats. The unintentional insider threat is often a result of insufficient cybersecurity education and awareness, emphasizing the need for organizations to invest in comprehensive training programs to equip employees with the knowledge and skills to recognize and mitigate potential risks.

The motivations behind malicious insider threats are diverse and can manifest in various forms. Financial gain is a common motivator, with insiders exploiting their access to sensitive information for personal profit through activities such as insider trading or selling proprietary data. Revenge is another powerful motivator, with employees seeking retribution for perceived grievances by intentionally causing harm to the organization. Ideological motivations may lead insiders to view their organization as a target for advancing their political, religious, or social beliefs, prompting actions that compromise security. Recognizing these motivations is pivotal for anticipating and addressing malicious insider threats before they escalate.

Non-malicious insiders, while lacking intentional harmful motives, can inadvertently contribute to security incidents through negligence or carelessness. Unintentional insider threats encompass a broad spectrum of actions, including the mishandling of sensitive information, failure to follow established security protocols, or unwittingly clicking on malicious links in phishing emails. These individuals may not be aware of the potential consequences of their actions, highlighting the importance of robust cybersecurity education and awareness programs to mitigate the risks associated with non-malicious insider threats.

The technological landscape plays a significant role in differentiating between malicious and non-malicious insiders. Malicious insiders often possess a deep understanding of the organization's systems and networks, enabling them to exploit technical vulnerabilities deliberately. They may use their insider knowledge to circumvent security controls, escalate privileges, or introduce malware. Non-malicious insiders, in contrast, may lack the technical sophistication to intentionally compromise security. Their actions are more likely to result from unintentional lapses in judgment, such as opening phishing emails or inadvertently exposing sensitive information, rather than deliberate efforts to exploit technical vulnerabilities.

Detection and mitigation strategies must be tailored to address the specific characteristics of both malicious and non-malicious insiders. Malicious insider threats often require advanced monitoring solutions, such as user behavior analytics (UBA) and data loss prevention (DLP) systems, capable of identifying anomalous patterns indicative of intentional wrongdoing. These technologies analyze user behavior, network traffic, and data access patterns to identify deviations from established norms, triggering alerts for further investigation. Behavioral analysis becomes a crucial component in identifying the subtle signs of malicious intent that may be present in the actions of insiders.

For non-malicious insiders, the emphasis shifts towards education, training, and the implementation of preventive measures. Organizations must prioritize comprehensive cybersecurity training programs that empower employees with the knowledge and skills to recognize and avoid common security pitfalls. This includes training on identifying phishing attempts, understanding the importance of strong password practices, and adhering to established security protocols. Additionally, implementing robust access controls, least privilege principles, and data classification policies can help mitigate the unintentional risks posed by non-malicious insiders.

Incident response plans also play a critical role in differentiating and addressing both types of insider threats. A well-defined incident response plan should outline clear procedures for investigating suspected insider incidents, regardless of whether the threat is malicious or non-malicious. Incident response teams must be equipped to handle the complexities associated with intentional insider attacks, including legal considerations, evidence collection, and potential collaboration with law enforcement agencies. Simultaneously, response plans should include mechanisms for addressing incidents stemming from unintentional insider actions, emphasizing remediation and education to prevent future occurrences.

Legal and regulatory considerations further differentiate malicious and non-malicious insider threats. Malicious insider activities may lead to legal consequences, with potential charges ranging from theft of trade secrets to violations of insider trading laws. Organizations must navigate the legal landscape to ensure compliance with applicable regulations and collaborate with legal authorities to address malicious insider incidents appropriately. Non-malicious insider incidents, while lacking intentional wrongdoing, may still have legal implications, especially in industries governed by strict data protection and privacy regulations. Understanding the legal ramifications of both types of insider threats is crucial for developing comprehensive response strategies that account for potential legal consequences.

In conclusion, the differentiation between malicious and non-malicious insiders is essential for developing effective strategies to address the diverse nature of insider threats. Recognizing the psychological motivations, behavioral indicators, and technological nuances associated with malicious insiders allows organizations to implement targeted detection and mitigation measures. Simultaneously, addressing the unintentional risks posed by non-malicious insiders requires a focus on education, training, and preventive measures to reduce the likelihood of human error. A holistic approach that combines technological solutions, employee awareness programs, and robust incident response planning is crucial for organizations seeking to navigate the complex landscape of insider threats and safeguard their sensitive information from both intentional and unintentional compromises.

Insider Threat Indicators and Warning Signs

Detecting insider threats necessitates a nuanced understanding of various indicators and warning signs that may manifest across behavioral, technological, and organizational dimensions. Behavioral indicators often serve as the first line of defense in identifying potential insider threats. Sudden and unexplained changes in an employee's behavior, such as increased irritability, withdrawal from colleagues, or expressions of discontentment, can be red flags signaling potential malicious intent. Similarly, employees exhibiting unusual patterns of accessing sensitive information, especially outside their regular duties, may warrant closer scrutiny. Monitoring for excessive data downloads, multiple login attempts, or unauthorized access to restricted areas can reveal potential insider threats.

Technological indicators play a crucial role in identifying anomalous activities associated with insider threats. Unusual network traffic, unexpected data transfers, or unauthorized use of privileged credentials may indicate malicious intent. Anomalies in login times, especially after normal business hours, may raise concerns about unauthorized access. Monitoring for patterns of data access that deviate from established norms can help identify insiders attempting to exfiltrate sensitive information. Leveraging technologies such as user behavior analytics (UBA) and data loss prevention (DLP) systems becomes instrumental in proactively identifying insider threat indicators within the technological landscape.

Communication patterns can also offer valuable insights into potential insider threats. Monitoring internal communications, especially those involving sensitive topics, can help identify employees who may be planning or engaging in malicious activities. Unusual patterns of communication, such as increased communication with external entities or the use of encrypted communication channels, may warrant investigation. Analyzing email content, attachments, and communication frequency can provide clues about potential insider threats, particularly those involving the exfiltration of sensitive information.

Beyond the technological and behavioral aspects, organizational indicators can shed light on potential insider threats. Employees facing financial difficulties or experiencing personal crises may be susceptible to external pressures, making them more likely to engage in malicious activities for financial gain. Instances of repeated policy violations, especially those related to data handling and information security, can serve as warning signs of potential insider threats. Organizations should also be attentive to disgruntled employees expressing dissatisfaction with the organization, as they may pose a higher risk of engaging in malicious activities.

The role of privileged access requires special attention when identifying insider threat indicators. Employees with privileged access, such as system administrators or those handling sensitive information, may possess the means to exploit security vulnerabilities intentionally. Monitoring privileged user activities, especially any unusual or unauthorized changes to system configurations, can help identify potential insider threats. The misuse of elevated privileges, such as unauthorized access to confidential data or the manipulation of critical systems, may be indicative of malicious intent.

Social engineering tactics, often employed by malicious insiders, can manifest as warning signs within an organization. Employees targeted by phishing emails, social manipulation, or coercion may inadvertently become conduits for insider threats. Monitoring for unusual requests for sensitive information, unauthorized changes to account credentials, or employees divulging sensitive information without proper verification can help identify potential insider threats stemming from social engineering tactics.

Employee offboarding processes also present an opportunity to identify insider threat indicators. Employees departing the organization may pose a heightened risk during the transition period. Monitoring the activities of departing employees, especially their interactions with sensitive information and systems, can help detect potential insider threats before they materialize. Timely revocation of access rights and comprehensive exit interviews can provide insights into the employee's state of mind and potential motivations for insider threats.

Insider threat indicators may also surface in the context of external relationships and third-party collaborations. Organizations with extensive partnerships or collaborations must be vigilant about the activities of individuals with access to sensitive information. Monitoring for unusual data transfers, unauthorized access by external entities, or anomalies in third-party behavior can help identify potential insider threats originating from external sources.

The integration of artificial intelligence and machine learning technologies further enhances the ability to identify insider threat indicators. These technologies can analyze vast datasets, including user behavior, network traffic, and communication patterns, to identify subtle deviations from established norms. Machine learning algorithms can adapt and evolve, learning from historical data to improve the accuracy of insider threat detection. Implementing advanced analytics tools can significantly enhance an organization's ability to proactively identify and respond to insider threats.

Continuous monitoring and proactive threat hunting become essential components of an effective insider threat detection strategy. Rather than relying solely on automated systems, organizations should empower security teams to actively search for indicators of potential insider threats. This may involve analyzing logs, conducting periodic security audits, and collaborating across departments to gather insights into employee behavior and activities. The human element remains invaluable in discerning nuanced patterns that automated systems might overlook.

Collaboration between different organizational departments, including human resources, IT, and security, is crucial for identifying and responding to insider threat indicators. Human resources can play a pivotal role in identifying employees facing personal or professional challenges that may increase their susceptibility to insider threats. Sharing this information with IT and security teams allows for a holistic assessment of potential risks and the implementation of targeted mitigation strategies.

Educating employees about insider threat indicators and the importance of reporting suspicious activities is a fundamental aspect of a comprehensive insider threat prevention program. Creating a culture of awareness and vigilance encourages employees to play an active role in identifying and reporting potential insider threats. Establishing clear channels for reporting, coupled with protection against retaliation for whistleblowers, fosters an environment where employees feel empowered to contribute to the organization's security.

In conclusion, recognizing insider threat indicators and warning signs requires a multifaceted approach that encompasses behavioral, technological, and organizational dimensions. By understanding the nuanced patterns associated with potential insider threats, organizations can implement proactive detection measures and develop effective response strategies. Leveraging advanced technologies, fostering collaboration across departments, and cultivating a culture of awareness are all integral components of a comprehensive insider threat detection and prevention program. As the cybersecurity landscape continues to evolve, organizations must remain adaptive and proactive in addressing the dynamic nature of insider threats to safeguard their sensitive information and maintain the integrity of their digital environments.

7.2 Insider Threat Mitigation Strategies

Mitigating insider threats is a multifaceted challenge that demands a comprehensive and strategic approach encompassing technological, organizational, and human-centric measures. Technological mitigation strategies form a cornerstone of an effective insider threat prevention program. Implementing robust access controls is crucial, utilizing the principle of least privilege to ensure employees only have access to the information and systems necessary for their roles. Regularly monitoring and auditing privileged user activities can help detect and prevent misuse of elevated access rights. Deploying data loss prevention (DLP) systems allows organizations to monitor, detect, and block the unauthorized transfer of sensitive information, providing a critical layer of defense against insider threats.

User behavior analytics (UBA) plays a pivotal role in technological mitigation by leveraging machine learning algorithms to analyze patterns of user activity. UBA systems establish baseline behavior for users and promptly identify deviations that may indicate potential insider threats. These advanced analytics tools can detect anomalous activities, such as unauthorized access or unusual data transfers, contributing to the early detection of insider threats. Additionally, implementing endpoint security solutions, including intrusion detection and prevention systems, helps safeguard individual devices against malicious activities initiated by insiders.

In conjunction with technological measures, organizational mitigation strategies are essential to create a holistic defense against insider threats. Establishing a positive and inclusive workplace culture fosters employee loyalty and reduces the likelihood of malicious intent. Organizations should prioritize open communication channels, employee well-being programs, and professional development opportunities to cultivate a positive work environment. Additionally, organizations must define and communicate clear security policies, ensuring that employees understand the importance of safeguarding sensitive information and the consequences of insider threats.

Employee training and awareness programs form a critical component of organizational mitigation strategies. Educating employees about cybersecurity best practices, the importance of data protection, and the risks associated with insider threats empowers them to be active participants in the organization's security efforts. Training should cover topics such as recognizing phishing attempts, securing passwords, and reporting suspicious activities. By building a security-conscious workforce, organizations enhance their resilience against both intentional and unintentional insider threats.

Incident response planning is integral to organizational mitigation strategies, providing a structured and coordinated approach to addressing insider threats when they occur. Organizations must develop and regularly update incident response plans that outline clear procedures for investigating, containing, and mitigating insider incidents. Collaboration between IT, security, legal, and human resources departments is essential to ensure a comprehensive and timely response. Conducting regular tabletop exercises allows organizations to test the effectiveness of their incident response plans and identify areas for improvement.

Human resources policies and procedures play a critical role in organizational mitigation against insider threats. Implementing thorough background checks during the hiring process can help identify potential red flags and mitigate the risk of bringing malicious actors into the organization. Clear onboarding and offboarding processes ensure that employees are granted appropriate access during their tenure and that access is promptly revoked upon departure. Human resources departments also play a key role in addressing employee grievances and conflicts proactively, reducing the likelihood of disgruntled employees turning into insider threats.

Legal and regulatory compliance is an integral aspect of organizational mitigation strategies. Organizations must stay abreast of relevant laws and regulations governing data protection, privacy, and cybersecurity. Compliance frameworks should be implemented and regularly audited to ensure adherence to legal requirements. Understanding the legal consequences of insider threats and having mechanisms in place to collaborate with law enforcement agencies, if necessary, is crucial for mitigating the potential impact of insider incidents.

External collaboration and information sharing form an emerging dimension of organizational mitigation strategies. Organizations can benefit from sharing threat intelligence with industry peers, government agencies, and cybersecurity communities. Collaborative efforts help create a collective defense against insider threats by leveraging shared insights, best practices, and lessons learned. Information sharing platforms and industry partnerships contribute to a more resilient cybersecurity ecosystem.

In addition to technological and organizational measures, addressing the human element is essential for comprehensive insider threat mitigation. Employee monitoring, when conducted transparently and within legal boundaries, can serve as a deterrent to potential malicious insiders. Establishing clear policies regarding acceptable use of company resources, monitoring practices, and consequences for policy violations helps set expectations for employees and reinforces the organization's commitment to security.

Whistleblower protection is a crucial component of human-centric mitigation strategies. Creating a culture where employees feel comfortable reporting suspicious activities without fear of retaliation encourages early detection of insider threats. Establishing confidential reporting channels and educating employees about the whistleblower protection program contribute to building trust and cooperation within the organization.

Behavioral analysis and profiling are emerging as innovative approaches to insider threat mitigation. By monitoring and analyzing employee behavior over time, organizations can identify patterns indicative of potential insider threats. Machine learning algorithms can assist in identifying deviations from established behavioral norms, enabling proactive intervention before malicious intent is realized. This approach aligns with the concept of continuous monitoring, where organizations maintain vigilance over employee behavior throughout their tenure.

In conclusion, insider threat mitigation requires a synergistic blend of technological, organizational, and human-centric strategies. Technologically, robust access controls, user behavior analytics, and endpoint security solutions form the foundation of defense against insider threats. Organizational measures include fostering a positive workplace culture, implementing comprehensive training programs, and developing effective incident response plans. Human-centric strategies involve proactive human resources policies, legal and regulatory compliance, external collaboration, and innovative approaches such as behavioral analysis. By adopting a holistic and adaptive approach, organizations can effectively mitigate the risks associated with insider threats and safeguard their sensitive information and digital assets. As the threat landscape evolves, ongoing refinement and innovation in mitigation strategies remain essential for maintaining a resilient cybersecurity posture.

Role-Based Access Control

Role-Based Access Control (RBAC) stands as a foundational principle in the realm of information security, providing a systematic and efficient approach to managing access to digital resources within an organization. At its core, RBAC is a method of access control that ties system permissions and privileges to the roles individuals hold within an organization. The concept of roles becomes pivotal, as it streamlines the often complex task of granting and revoking access rights based on job responsibilities and hierarchical positions. RBAC is designed to enhance security, streamline administrative processes, and ensure that individuals have access only to the resources necessary for their specific roles.

In the RBAC model, each user is assigned one or more roles, and each role is associated with specific permissions or access rights. These permissions dictate what actions a user with a particular role can perform within the information system. This role-to-permission mapping simplifies access management by allowing administrators to focus on defining roles and their associated permissions, rather than managing permissions for each user individually. The granularity of access control is thus abstracted, leading to a more scalable and maintainable security infrastructure.

The RBAC model is structured around three primary components: users, roles, and permissions. Users are individuals who interact with the information system, roles represent sets of responsibilities or job functions, and permissions specify the actions or operations that users with a particular role are allowed to perform. The RBAC model also introduces the concept of an assignment, where a user is associated with one or more roles, establishing a clear link between the user's responsibilities and the permissions they possess.

One of the key advantages of RBAC is its ability to enhance the principle of least privilege. By assigning users the minimum set of permissions required to perform their job functions, RBAC reduces the risk of unauthorized access and potential security breaches. This aligns with the overarching goal of information security to limit access to sensitive data and critical systems, mitigating the impact of insider threats and external attacks.

The RBAC model is flexible and adaptable, allowing organizations to tailor access control policies to their specific needs. As organizational structures evolve, roles can be easily adjusted to accommodate changes in responsibilities or staffing. This adaptability streamlines the management of access control policies, ensuring that they remain aligned with the dynamic nature of modern organizations.

RBAC can be implemented at various levels within an organization, including the operating system, databases, applications, and network resources. This versatility enables organizations to enforce consistent access control policies across diverse technological environments. For example, in an enterprise setting, RBAC may be applied to control access to file systems, databases, and proprietary software applications.

RBAC also simplifies the onboarding and offboarding processes for employees. When a new employee joins an organization, administrators can assign the relevant roles based on the employee's job function, granting them the necessary permissions from the outset. Conversely, when an employee departs or changes roles, access rights can be swiftly adjusted by modifying their role assignments. This not only enhances security by reducing the window of opportunity for unauthorized access but also streamlines administrative tasks, improving overall operational efficiency.

In large organizations with complex hierarchical structures, RBAC helps maintain a clear and manageable access control framework. Different departments and business units may have unique access requirements, and RBAC provides a structured approach to defining roles that align with these specific needs. This modularity ensures that access control policies remain coherent and scalable, even as the organization expands or undergoes structural changes.

RBAC also facilitates the audit and compliance processes by providing a transparent view of who has access to what resources. Auditors can easily review role assignments and permissions to ensure that access control policies adhere to regulatory requirements and internal security standards. This transparency not only aids in regulatory compliance but also supports internal governance initiatives by promoting accountability and oversight.

However, RBAC is not without its challenges. The successful implementation of RBAC requires careful planning and ongoing maintenance. The process of defining roles and their associated permissions demands a thorough understanding of the organization's structure, business processes, and data sensitivity. Regular audits and reviews are essential to ensure that role assignments align with the evolving needs of the organization and that unnecessary or outdated roles are promptly addressed.

Furthermore, RBAC may face challenges in scenarios where users have dynamic or ad-hoc responsibilities that do not neatly align with predefined roles. In such cases, organizations may need to complement RBAC with additional access control mechanisms, such as attribute-based access control (ABAC), to accommodate more granular and flexible control over access permissions.

RBAC's evolution has led to the development of extended models, such as Hierarchical RBAC (HRBAC) and Constrained RBAC (CRBAC), which introduce additional complexities to address specific organizational requirements. HRBAC incorporates the hierarchical relationships that exist within an organization, allowing for more nuanced role assignments based on reporting structures. CRBAC introduces constraints on role activations, deactivations, and role transitions, adding a layer of control to further refine access policies.

In conclusion, Role-Based Access Control serves as a cornerstone in modern information security by providing a structured and scalable approach to access management. By aligning access permissions with job functions through the assignment of roles, RBAC enhances security, streamlines administrative tasks, and supports regulatory compliance. While challenges exist, careful planning and ongoing maintenance can help organizations harness the full potential of RBAC to create a robust and adaptable access control framework. As technology and organizational landscapes continue to evolve, RBAC remains a valuable tool for organizations seeking to balance the dual objectives of enhancing security and facilitating operational efficiency in an ever-changing digital landscape.

User Activity Monitoring and Analysis

User Activity Monitoring and Analysis (UAMA) constitutes a critical component of modern cybersecurity strategies, offering organizations insights into the actions and behaviors of individuals interacting with their information systems. This proactive approach to security involves the continuous observation, logging, and analysis of user activities to detect anomalous behavior, potential security incidents, and insider threats. UAMA encompasses a spectrum of techniques and technologies aimed at capturing, processing, and interpreting user actions, providing organizations with a comprehensive understanding of their digital environments. The primary goals of UAMA include enhancing security, mitigating risks, ensuring compliance, and facilitating incident response through the analysis of user behavior across various platforms, applications, and networked resources.

The foundational premise of UAMA is to monitor and analyze user actions within an organization's information systems. This includes tracking logins, file accesses, data transfers, application usage, and other activities conducted by users across endpoints and networked devices. By aggregating this data, security teams gain visibility into the normal patterns of user behavior, enabling the identification of deviations that may indicate security incidents or potential insider threats. The continuous nature of UAMA ensures that security personnel can promptly respond to emerging threats, reducing the window of opportunity for malicious actors.

Monitoring user activities allows organizations to implement the principle of least privilege effectively. By understanding the specific actions users typically perform in the course of their duties, administrators can tailor access permissions to the minimum necessary for each role. UAMA aids in identifying unnecessary or suspicious activities, allowing organizations to refine access controls and reduce the risk of unauthorized access to sensitive data or critical systems. This alignment with the principle of least privilege enhances overall security posture and helps mitigate the impact of insider threats.

In the context of insider threats, UAMA plays a crucial role in identifying unusual or malicious behavior exhibited by employees or other trusted individuals with access to organizational resources.

Behavioral analytics, a subset of UAMA, involves the application of machine learning algorithms to detect patterns indicative of potential threats. These algorithms learn from historical user behavior data, allowing them to identify deviations that may signify unauthorized access, data exfiltration, or other malicious activities. UAMA, therefore, serves as a proactive mechanism for detecting insider threats before they escalate.

User Activity Monitoring and Analysis is not limited to identifying malicious activities alone; it also assists organizations in addressing unintentional insider threats resulting from human error. By monitoring user actions, organizations can detect and mitigate inadvertent data breaches, accidental deletions of critical files, or other actions that may compromise data integrity or system availability. This dual functionality of UAMA aligns with the broader goal of creating a comprehensive security strategy that addresses both intentional and unintentional threats.

The implementation of UAMA involves the deployment of monitoring tools and technologies across an organization's IT infrastructure. These tools collect and aggregate user activity data from various sources, such as logs, network traffic, and endpoint devices. Advanced UAMA solutions leverage real-time monitoring capabilities, enabling security teams to receive immediate alerts when anomalous behavior is detected. Additionally, the analysis of historical user activity data allows organizations to identify patterns that may indicate long-term, subtle threats rather than immediate risks.

Endpoint monitoring is a crucial aspect of UAMA, as endpoints serve as entry points for user interactions with organizational systems. Monitoring endpoint activities involves tracking file accesses, application usage, and system configurations. Anomalous patterns, such as unauthorized software installations or changes to critical system settings, can be indicative of security incidents or potential threats. Endpoint monitoring also aids in quickly identifying and isolating compromised devices to prevent further damage.

Network-based UAMA involves the analysis of network traffic to detect suspicious or unauthorized activities. This includes monitoring data transfers, communication patterns, and connections to external servers. Unusual outbound traffic or connections to known malicious domains may indicate data exfiltration or the presence of malware. Network-based UAMA is particularly effective in identifying threats that may not manifest at the endpoint level, providing a holistic view of user activities across the organization.

The integration of UAMA with Security Information and Event Management (SIEM) systems enhances its capabilities by correlating user activity data with other security events and contextual information. SIEM platforms consolidate data from diverse sources, allowing security teams to correlate user activities with system events, security alerts, and threat intelligence. This correlation enables a more comprehensive analysis of security incidents and facilitates a timely and informed response.

Privacy considerations are paramount in the implementation of UAMA, as monitoring user activities inherently involves collecting and analyzing potentially sensitive information. Organizations must strike a balance between monitoring for security purposes and respecting user privacy. Transparent communication about monitoring practices, obtaining user consent where applicable, and implementing measures to anonymize or encrypt sensitive data contribute to building trust and maintaining a respectful approach to user privacy.

The regulatory landscape also influences the deployment of UAMA, as various data protection and privacy laws impose requirements on how organizations handle user information. Ensuring compliance with regulations such as the General Data Protection Regulation (GDPR) in the European Union or the Health Insurance

Portability and Accountability Act (HIPAA) in the United States is essential. Organizations must implement UAMA in a manner that aligns with legal requirements, including data retention policies, access controls, and reporting mechanisms.

UAMA is not a one-size-fits-all solution; its effectiveness depends on the context, the organization's specific security needs, and the nature of its digital environment. Organizations must tailor their UAMA strategies to align with their risk profile, industry regulations, and the evolving threat landscape. Regular assessments and adjustments to UAMA policies and technologies are essential to maintaining effectiveness in the face of changing security challenges.

In conclusion, User Activity Monitoring and Analysis is a cornerstone of modern cybersecurity strategies, providing organizations with the tools and insights needed to proactively manage and mitigate security risks. By continuously monitoring and analyzing user actions, organizations can enhance security, detect insider threats, and address both intentional and unintentional risks. The deployment of UAMA technologies, integration with SIEM systems, and adherence to privacy and regulatory considerations contribute to building a robust and adaptive security posture. As organizations navigate the complexities of the digital landscape, UAMA remains an invaluable tool for maintaining visibility into user activities and safeguarding against evolving cybersecurity threats.

7.3 Building a Culture of Trust and Security

Building a culture of trust and security within an organization represents a fundamental and multifaceted approach to fostering an environment where individuals feel confident in the protection of sensitive information and are committed to upholding cybersecurity best practices. At the core of this cultural endeavor is the establishment of trust, both among employees and between employees and the organization. Trust is a foundation that underpins effective collaboration, innovation, and the overall well-being of the workplace.

However, trust is intimately linked with security, as a breach of information can erode trust and compromise the very fabric of organizational culture. Therefore, the development of a culture that intertwines trust and security is a strategic imperative for organizations seeking to navigate the complex landscape of modern cybersecurity threats.

Central to building a culture of trust and security is leadership's commitment to championing these values and integrating them into the organization's core values and mission. Leadership sets the tone for the entire organization, and when leaders prioritize trust and security, it signals to employees that these aspects are not only important but integral to the organization's success. Leadership commitment translates into the allocation of resources, the implementation of security policies, and the demonstration of adherence to best practices, creating a foundation for trust to flourish.

Communication plays a pivotal role in cultivating a culture of trust and security. Transparent and open communication about cybersecurity policies, the rationale behind security measures, and the importance of individual contributions to the overall security posture fosters an environment where employees feel informed and engaged. Regular communication channels, such as newsletters, town hall meetings, and training sessions, serve as platforms to reinforce the organization's commitment to security and build awareness about evolving cyber threats.

Empowering employees through education and training is a cornerstone of a trust-centric security culture. Cybersecurity awareness programs provide employees with the knowledge and skills to recognize potential threats, understand their role in maintaining security, and respond effectively to security incidents. By investing in ongoing training initiatives, organizations enable employees to make informed decisions and contribute actively to the organization's defense against cyber threats. This empowerment not only enhances the organization's overall security posture but also builds a sense of collective responsibility.

The development of a positive workplace culture is intertwined with the promotion of trust and security. Organizations that prioritize employee well-being, work-life balance, and a supportive atmosphere create a foundation for trust to thrive. When employees feel valued, supported, and encouraged, they are more likely to adopt security best practices willingly. Conversely, a toxic or stressful work environment can lead to lapses in judgment, increased susceptibility to social engineering attacks, and overall diminished security awareness.

Recognizing and acknowledging the contributions of employees to the organization's security efforts reinforces a positive culture. When individuals who actively engage in security practices are acknowledged, whether through formal recognition programs, incentives, or simple expressions of gratitude, it reinforces the value of their efforts. This positive reinforcement not only motivates the individuals involved but also sets an example for others to follow, creating a culture where security is seen as a shared responsibility.

The integration of security considerations into the fabric of daily operations contributes to the normalization of security practices. When security is seamlessly woven into the workflow and decision-making processes, it becomes ingrained in the organization's DNA. This integration includes considerations such as secure coding practices in software development, privacy by design in product and service offerings, and proactive risk assessments in project planning. By making security an integral part of organizational processes, the organization demonstrates a commitment to long-term resilience against cyber threats.

Trust in technology and systems is a critical aspect of building a culture of trust and security. Organizations must invest in robust and resilient cybersecurity infrastructure that instills confidence in employees. This includes secure network configurations, up-to-date software, encryption mechanisms, and multi-factor authentication. When employees trust that the systems they rely on are secure, it positively influences their overall perception of the organization's commitment to cybersecurity.

Collaboration between security teams and other departments is pivotal in building a culture of trust and security. When security is perceived as a collaborative effort rather than an impediment, it fosters a sense of unity and shared responsibility. Security teams should work closely with IT, human resources, legal, and other departments to align security policies with organizational objectives. Involving employees from various departments in the decision-making process regarding security measures enhances their sense of ownership and fosters a culture where security is not seen as a hindrance but as an integral part of achieving common goals.

Building a culture of trust and security also involves addressing the human element of cybersecurity. Employees should be encouraged to report security incidents, potential threats, or even their own mistakes without fear of punitive measures. Establishing a blame-free reporting culture encourages open communication and ensures that security incidents are promptly addressed. This approach recognizes that humans are fallible, and the emphasis should be on learning and improvement rather than punishment.

An effective incident response plan is a critical component of a trust-centric security culture. When employees are confident that the organization has a well-defined and practiced plan for responding to security incidents, it instills trust in the organization's ability to manage and mitigate the impact of a breach. Regular testing and simulation exercises ensure that the incident response plan remains effective and that employees are familiar with their roles and responsibilities during a security incident.

Legal and ethical considerations play a vital role in building a culture of trust and security. Organizations must adhere to applicable data protection and privacy laws, ensuring that employees' personal information is handled responsibly and ethically. Respecting privacy rights builds trust among employees and stakeholders, reinforcing the organization's commitment to ethical business practices.

The concept of continuous improvement is inherent in building a culture of trust and security. Organizations should regularly assess their security posture, update policies and procedures, and adapt to evolving cyber threats. Continuous monitoring and evaluation enable organizations to identify areas for improvement, address vulnerabilities, and stay ahead of emerging threats. This commitment to ongoing improvement reinforces the organization's dedication to maintaining a resilient and trustworthy security posture.

In conclusion, building a culture of trust and security is a holistic and dynamic process that requires commitment, communication, education, and collaboration. By fostering an environment where trust is prioritized, and security is integrated into the organization's values and operations, organizations can create a resilient defense against cyber threats. This culture not only enhances the organization's overall security posture but also contributes to a positive workplace environment where individuals feel empowered, informed, and invested in the collective effort to safeguard sensitive information and digital assets. As organizations navigate the evolving landscape of cybersecurity challenges, building a culture of trust and security remains an essential and ongoing endeavor.

Balancing Security Measures with Employee Trust

Balancing security measures with employee trust represents a delicate equilibrium in the realm of organizational cybersecurity, requiring a nuanced approach to safeguarding sensitive information while fostering a workplace culture built on trust and collaboration. In an era where cyber threats continually evolve, organizations grapple with the challenge of implementing robust security measures without undermining the trust and autonomy of their workforce. Striking this balance necessitates a comprehensive understanding of the interplay between security protocols, employee expectations, and the overall organizational culture.

Security measures are often implemented to protect against a myriad of cyber threats, ranging from external attacks to insider risks. These measures include access controls, encryption, multi-factor authentication, and monitoring systems that aim to fortify the organization's defenses and mitigate potential vulnerabilities. While these security protocols are essential for safeguarding sensitive data and maintaining regulatory compliance, their impact on employee trust and autonomy requires careful consideration. Heavy-handed security measures can inadvertently create an atmosphere of surveillance and erode the sense of autonomy among employees, potentially fostering a culture of suspicion and resistance.

Transparent communication is a cornerstone of balancing security measures with employee trust. Organizations must articulate the necessity of specific security protocols, helping employees understand the rationale behind these measures and how they contribute to the overall protection of sensitive information. Clear and open communication builds awareness and trust, assuring employees that security measures are not arbitrary impositions but strategic initiatives designed to safeguard their work and the organization as a whole. Transparent communication fosters a sense of collaboration and shared responsibility, aligning employees with the organization's security objectives.

Education and awareness programs play a pivotal role in achieving a harmonious balance between security measures and employee trust. Providing comprehensive training on cybersecurity best practices, the evolving threat landscape, and the potential consequences of security lapses empowers employees to become active participants in the organization's security efforts. Education initiatives should emphasize the importance of security measures in protecting not only organizational assets but also individual privacy and the confidentiality of sensitive information. By fostering a culture of awareness, organizations can mitigate resistance to security measures and promote a shared commitment to a secure workplace.

Striking the right balance also involves tailoring security measures to align with the organization's unique culture and the nature of its work. Recognizing that one-size-fits-all approaches may not be effective, organizations should implement security measures that are proportional to the level of sensitivity associated with different roles and responsibilities. For instance, employees in research and development may require more stringent security measures than those in administrative roles. Customizing security protocols demonstrates an understanding of the diverse needs within the organization, enhancing the likelihood of acceptance and cooperation from employees.

The concept of trust is inherently linked to transparency, and organizations must navigate the challenge of maintaining transparency while implementing necessary security measures. Transparent policies regarding data collection, monitoring practices, and the storage of personal information build trust by keeping employees informed about how their data is handled. Privacy considerations are paramount, and organizations should be explicit about the boundaries of data usage, assuring employees that security measures are designed to protect, not exploit, their personal information. Establishing clear lines of communication regarding the organization's commitment to privacy reinforces trust in the security framework.

Employee involvement in the decision-making process surrounding security measures is a key element in building trust. Seeking input from employees on matters related to security policies and protocols demonstrates a commitment to inclusivity and recognizes that employees are valuable stakeholders in the organization's security ecosystem. Involving employees in discussions about security measures allows organizations to consider the human perspective, identify potential concerns, and tailor solutions that address both security needs and employee expectations. This collaborative approach fosters a sense of ownership and shared responsibility, reinforcing the organization's commitment to a security culture that respects employee input.

While security measures are often perceived as restrictive, organizations can implement user-friendly technologies and practices to minimize the impact on employee workflows. Embracing user-centric design principles ensures that security solutions are integrated seamlessly into existing processes, minimizing disruption and frustration. Technologies such as single sign-on, biometric authentication, and secure collaboration tools contribute to a positive user experience while upholding security standards. By prioritizing usability, organizations can mitigate resistance to security measures and enhance overall employee satisfaction.

Balancing security measures with employee trust requires a thoughtful approach to monitoring and surveillance. Excessive monitoring can lead to a perception of distrust and an invasion of privacy. Organizations must strike a balance between monitoring essential for security purposes and respecting employees' right to privacy. Implementing transparent monitoring policies, clearly defining the scope and purpose of monitoring, and ensuring that surveillance aligns with legal and ethical standards are critical components of maintaining trust. Additionally, organizations should communicate clearly about the circumstances under which monitoring may be necessary, such as investigating security incidents or ensuring compliance with regulatory requirements.

In the event of security incidents or breaches, organizations must adopt a transparent and accountable approach to maintaining trust.

Rapid and clear communication about the incident, its impact, and the steps being taken to address it demonstrates accountability and fosters trust among employees. Providing guidance on how employees can contribute to the organization's response efforts, such as reporting suspicious activities promptly, creates a collaborative atmosphere during challenging times. Acknowledging the organization's responsibility for cybersecurity and openly discussing lessons learned from incidents contribute to a culture of continuous improvement and resilience.

The role of leadership is pivotal in balancing security measures with employee trust. Leaders must exemplify a commitment to security, both in words and actions, to set the tone for the entire organization. Leaders should prioritize transparent communication, actively engage with employees on security matters, and demonstrate the importance of security through their own adherence to protocols. When leaders actively participate in security awareness programs, it reinforces the message that security is a shared responsibility. Additionally, leaders should be approachable, encouraging employees to voice concerns or seek clarification on security-related issues, fostering an environment of trust and open communication.

Legal and ethical considerations are paramount when implementing security measures that may impact employee trust. Organizations must comply with relevant data protection and privacy laws, ensuring that security practices align with legal requirements. Transparent communication about data handling practices, consent mechanisms, and the rights of individuals regarding their personal information is crucial. Ethical considerations extend to the responsible use of surveillance technologies, data storage practices, and the ethical treatment of employees in the context of security measures. By adhering to legal and ethical standards, organizations build trust by demonstrating a commitment to protecting both the organization and individual rights.

Regular assessments and feedback mechanisms provide organizations with insights into the effectiveness of security measures and their impact on employee trust. Soliciting feedback from employees regarding their experiences with security protocols, addressing concerns, and making adjustments based on feedback contribute to an adaptive and responsive security culture. Periodic security assessments and audits allow organizations to evaluate the efficacy of existing measures, identify areas for improvement, and demonstrate a commitment to continuous enhancement of the security posture.

In conclusion, balancing security measures with employee trust requires a holistic and strategic approach that integrates transparency, communication, education, collaboration, and user-centric design. By fostering a culture where trust and security are mutually reinforcing, organizations can navigate the complexities of the modern cybersecurity landscape while maintaining a positive and productive workplace environment. Striking this delicate balance is an ongoing endeavor that requires organizational commitment, adaptability, and a deep understanding of the symbiotic relationship between security measures and employee trust. As organizations evolve in response to emerging threats, technological advancements, and changing workplace dynamics, the pursuit of this equilibrium remains integral to sustaining a resilient and trusted cybersecurity posture.

Educating Employees on Insider Threat Risks

Educating employees on insider threat risks is an essential and multifaceted endeavor that forms a critical component of any organization's cybersecurity strategy. The term "insider threat" encompasses a range of risks arising from the actions or negligence of individuals within an organization, including employees, contractors, or business partners. Effectively addressing these risks requires a comprehensive educational approach that enhances employee awareness, instills a sense of responsibility, and fosters a culture of cybersecurity consciousness.

Central to employee education on insider threat risks is the cultivation of awareness regarding the diverse forms that insider threats can take. Employees should be informed about unintentional threats stemming from human error, such as inadvertent data breaches, accidental exposure of sensitive information, or the mishandling of company assets. Simultaneously, awareness efforts must address intentional threats arising from malicious intent, including insider attacks, corporate espionage, or disgruntled employees seeking to harm the organization. By providing a nuanced understanding of the various manifestations of insider threats, employees are better equipped to recognize potential risks within their work environments.

Communication plays a pivotal role in educating employees about insider threat risks. Clear and accessible communication channels should be established to convey information about the consequences of insider threats, both for the organization and for individual employees. Real-world examples and case studies can illustrate the impact of insider threats, emphasizing the financial, reputational, and legal ramifications. Open dialogue fosters a sense of shared responsibility, encouraging employees to actively participate in the organization's efforts to mitigate insider threat risks.

Training programs are a cornerstone of employee education on insider threats, providing structured learning opportunities to impart knowledge and skills. These programs should cover a spectrum of topics, including the identification of suspicious behavior, recognizing phishing attempts, securing sensitive information, and reporting incidents promptly. Interactive and scenario-based training exercises can simulate real-world situations, allowing employees to apply their knowledge in a practical context. By emphasizing the role of each employee in the collective defense against insider threats, training programs empower individuals to be vigilant and proactive in safeguarding organizational assets.

Employee education should encompass an understanding of the motivations behind insider threats, addressing both external factors and internal grievances. Individuals may succumb to external pressures, such as financial incentives from external entities seeking sensitive information. Internally, grievances related to job dissatisfaction, disputes, or perceived injustices may drive employees to engage in malicious activities. By delving into the psychology behind insider threats, organizations can foster empathy, encourage open communication, and implement preventive measures to address potential concerns before they escalate.

In the context of insider threat education, emphasis should be placed on the importance of reporting suspicious activities without fear of reprisal. Establishing confidential reporting channels, whistleblower protection programs, and a culture that values and encourages reporting contributes to early detection and intervention. Employees should feel assured that their observations will be taken seriously, investigated thoroughly, and that their cooperation is integral to the organization's security efforts. This collaborative approach builds trust between employees and the organization, facilitating a more resilient defense against insider threats.

The integration of insider threat education into the onboarding process for new employees is crucial in establishing a strong foundation of cybersecurity awareness. During orientation, employees should receive comprehensive training on the organization's security policies, acceptable use of company resources, and the potential risks associated with insider threats. Providing new hires with a clear understanding of their role in maintaining security from the outset contributes to a security-conscious culture and reduces the likelihood of inadvertent insider threats.

Continuous and adaptive learning mechanisms ensure that employees stay abreast of evolving insider threat risks. Regularly scheduled training sessions, updates on emerging threat vectors, and refresher courses contribute to a dynamic and informed workforce. Incorporating gamification elements into training modules can enhance engagement and retention of key concepts. The goal is to create a culture where cybersecurity education is an ongoing and integral part of professional development, reinforcing the organization's commitment to a proactive defense against insider threats.

Human resources departments play a pivotal role in aligning insider threat education with personnel management practices. Thorough background checks during the hiring process help identify potential red flags and mitigate the risk of bringing malicious actors into the organization. Clear policies and procedures for onboarding and offboarding employees ensure that access privileges are granted and revoked appropriately. Proactive conflict resolution and employee assistance programs contribute to addressing interpersonal issues before they escalate into insider threats. The collaboration between human resources and cybersecurity teams is essential to creating a holistic approach to insider threat mitigation.

Case studies and real-world examples of insider threat incidents, whether within the organization or in similar industry contexts, can serve as powerful educational tools. Analyzing past incidents provides valuable insights into the tactics, techniques, and procedures employed by malicious insiders. This knowledge helps employees recognize potential warning signs and understand the consequences of certain behaviors. Case studies also underscore the importance of a proactive and vigilant approach to insider threat mitigation, reinforcing the organization's commitment to learning from past experiences.

Technological literacy is a critical component of insider threat education, particularly in the era of rapidly evolving digital landscapes. Employees should be educated on the use of secure communication tools, the importance of regular software updates, and the risks associated with unauthorized software installations. Understanding the security features of company-issued devices, the implications of bring-your-own-device (BYOD) policies, and the role of encryption in protecting sensitive information empowers employees to make informed decisions in their daily work.

Simulated phishing exercises represent a practical and effective method of educating employees on the tactics employed by external actors seeking to exploit insider threats. These exercises involve sending simulated phishing emails to employees and monitoring their responses. The results provide valuable insights into areas that may require additional education and help employees develop a heightened awareness of phishing techniques. These exercises should be conducted regularly to reinforce the importance of skepticism and cautious behavior in the face of potential threats.

Leadership commitment to insider threat education is integral to its success. When organizational leaders prioritize and actively participate in cybersecurity education initiatives, it signals the importance of these efforts throughout the entire hierarchy. Leadership should model exemplary behavior by adhering to security protocols, participating in training programs, and fostering a culture where cybersecurity is ingrained in the organizational ethos. By demonstrating a commitment to ongoing education, leaders inspire employees to prioritize security as an integral part of their professional responsibilities.

Legal and regulatory compliance considerations should be woven into insider threat education programs. Employees must be informed about the legal implications of engaging in malicious activities, violating data protection laws, or breaching confidentiality agreements. Understanding the consequences of insider threats from a legal standpoint reinforces the severity of such actions and contributes to a culture of compliance. Organizations should provide employees with resources to seek legal guidance if they have concerns about potential insider threat activities.

In conclusion, educating employees on insider threat risks is a dynamic and multifaceted undertaking that requires a holistic approach encompassing communication, training, collaboration, and ongoing learning. By fostering awareness, providing targeted training, and creating a culture that values cybersecurity, organizations can empower employees to actively contribute to the prevention and mitigation of insider threats. The integration of insider threat education into various aspects of the employee lifecycle, coupled with a commitment to transparency and continuous improvement, contributes to building a resilient defense against the complex and ever-evolving landscape of insider threat risks. As organizations navigate the challenges of the digital era, a well-informed and security-conscious workforce remains a cornerstone of effective insider threat mitigation.

7.4 Case Studies and Lessons Learned

Case studies and lessons learned serve as invaluable resources in the realm of cybersecurity, providing organizations with insights into real-world incidents, the impact of security strategies, and the dynamics of evolving threat landscapes. Examining specific cases offers a nuanced understanding of the complexities surrounding cybersecurity challenges and allows organizations to derive actionable lessons to fortify their defenses. These case studies often illuminate the interconnected nature of technical, human, and procedural aspects of security incidents, offering a holistic perspective that goes beyond mere technical details.

One illustrative case involves the 2013 Target data breach, a watershed moment that highlighted the potential consequences of third-party vulnerabilities and the interconnected nature of supply chain risks. In this incident, cybercriminals exploited a weakness in Target's HVAC vendor's system, gaining unauthorized access to Target's network. The attackers then navigated through the network, ultimately compromising the credit card information of millions of customers. This case underscores the importance of robust third-party risk management, emphasizing that the security posture of interconnected entities can impact each other significantly. The lesson learned is that organizations must comprehensively assess and monitor the security practices of their third-party partners to mitigate potential vulnerabilities in the supply chain.

Another compelling case is the WannaCry ransomware attack of 2017, which wreaked havoc globally by exploiting a vulnerability in Microsoft Windows. The attack propagated rapidly, affecting organizations ranging from healthcare institutions to government agencies. One crucial lesson from this incident is the imperative of timely and thorough patch management. The exploited vulnerability had a available patch, but many affected organizations had not applied it. This case underscores the critical role of proactive security hygiene, including timely patching and system updates, in mitigating the risk of widespread and damaging cyberattacks.

The Equifax data breach of 2017 represents a case study that underscores the significance of vulnerability management and incident response. In this incident, attackers exploited a known vulnerability in the Apache Struts web application framework to gain unauthorized access to sensitive personal information of over 147 million individuals. The breach exposed systemic weaknesses in Equifax's vulnerability management practices and raised questions about the organization's incident response readiness. The lesson learned is that organizations must prioritize vulnerability remediation and continuously enhance their incident response capabilities to minimize the impact of security incidents and protect sensitive data.

The NotPetya ransomware attack in 2017 targeted organizations globally, causing widespread disruption and financial losses. NotPetya propagated through a compromised software update mechanism, affecting organizations that used a tax accounting software widely used in Ukraine. The attack underscored the need for robust supply chain security and the potential dangers of a compromised software update process. The lesson learned is that organizations should scrutinize and secure their software supply chain, including validating the integrity of software updates and maintaining contingency plans for responding to supply chain compromises.

The SolarWinds supply chain attack, discovered in late 2020, represents a sophisticated and highly impactful case study. Cyber adversaries compromised the software supply chain of SolarWinds, a widely used IT management and monitoring tool provider, injecting malicious code into software updates. This led to the compromise of numerous organizations, including government agencies and major corporations, through a trusted and widely used software vendor. The incident highlighted the challenges associated with detecting and responding to supply chain attacks, emphasizing the need for enhanced visibility, threat intelligence sharing, and continuous monitoring of the software supply chain.

The lessons learned from these cases extend beyond technical considerations to encompass the importance of organizational resilience, crisis management, and communication strategies. In each case, effective communication and transparency played a crucial role in mitigating reputational damage and rebuilding trust with stakeholders. Organizations must recognize that cybersecurity incidents are not solely technical challenges; they also involve communication and coordination across various internal and external stakeholders.

Moreover, the cases emphasize the necessity of a proactive and adaptive cybersecurity strategy that integrates threat intelligence, continuous monitoring, and incident response planning. Cyber threats are dynamic and persistent, requiring organizations to stay ahead of evolving tactics and techniques employed by malicious actors. Regular threat intelligence sharing and collaboration with industry peers contribute to a collective defense against emerging threats, enabling organizations to learn from the experiences of others and enhance their cybersecurity postures.

The case studies also underscore the importance of cultural aspects in cybersecurity. Building a security-conscious culture within an organization involves not only technological measures but also fostering awareness, responsibility, and accountability among employees. Cybersecurity is a shared responsibility, and organizations must invest in educating and empowering their workforce to recognize and respond to potential threats. Human factors, including social engineering and insider threats, consistently feature prominently in cybersecurity incidents, emphasizing the need for a comprehensive approach that addresses both technical and human elements.

In conclusion, case studies and lessons learned from notable cybersecurity incidents offer organizations a wealth of insights to inform and refine their security strategies. These real-world examples underscore the interconnected nature of cybersecurity challenges, emphasizing the need for a holistic and adaptive approach. By examining these cases, organizations can extract valuable lessons related to supply chain security, vulnerability management, incident response, communication strategies, and the cultural aspects of cybersecurity. The continuous evolution of cyber threats requires organizations to remain vigilant, proactive, and collaborative in their efforts to safeguard their digital assets and maintain the trust of stakeholders in an ever-changing landscape of cybersecurity risks.

Real-world Examples of Insider Threats

Real-world examples of insider threats underscore the multifaceted nature of cybersecurity risks originating from within an organization, emphasizing the challenges organizations face in mitigating intentional or unintentional actions that can compromise sensitive information. One notable case involves Edward Snowden, a former National Security Agency (NSA) contractor who, in 2013, leaked classified documents revealing the extent of global surveillance programs conducted by intelligence agencies. Snowden's insider threat underscored the potential damage that a trusted individual with privileged access can inflict on national security and highlighted the need for robust access controls and monitoring mechanisms.

In the corporate sphere, the case of Chelsea Manning, a U.S. Army intelligence analyst, exemplifies the insider threat risks associated with individuals entrusted with access to sensitive information. In 2010, Manning leaked classified military documents to WikiLeaks, exposing diplomatic cables and sensitive intelligence reports. Manning's actions shed light on the challenges organizations face in managing the insider threat posed by personnel with legitimate access to sensitive data. The incident prompted a reevaluation of security protocols, access controls, and the need for enhanced monitoring to detect and respond to anomalous behavior.

The case of Harold Martin, a former NSA contractor, offers another perspective on insider threats within intelligence agencies. In 2016, Martin was arrested for stealing a vast amount of classified information over a period of two decades. This case highlighted the prolonged and surreptitious nature of insider threats, emphasizing the importance of continuous monitoring and behavioral analytics to detect abnormal patterns of access and data exfiltration. Martin's actions underscored the need for organizations to go beyond perimeter security and implement robust measures for monitoring internal activities.

Insider threats are not limited to government agencies; they also impact industries like finance. The case of Sergey Aleynikov, a former Goldman Sachs programmer, exemplifies the potential financial ramifications of insider threats. In 2009, Aleynikov was arrested for stealing proprietary trading code from Goldman Sachs with the intent of using it in his new job. This case highlights the risk of intellectual property theft and corporate espionage by insiders seeking to gain a competitive advantage. It underscores the importance of protecting sensitive business assets and the need for organizations to implement stringent data protection measures.

In the healthcare sector, the case of a former employee at the University of Pittsburgh Medical Center (UPMC) exemplifies the insider threat risks associated with healthcare data. In 2014, a UPMC employee accessed and stole sensitive patient information, which was later used for filing fraudulent tax returns. This incident underscored the unique challenges faced by healthcare organizations in safeguarding patient data and the potential for insider threats to compromise sensitive medical information. It emphasizes the need for healthcare institutions to prioritize both technical safeguards and employee education to mitigate the risk of insider threats.

The case of Reality Winner, a former NSA contractor, provides insights into the intersection of insider threats and the leaking of classified information to the media. In 2017, Winner was arrested for leaking an intelligence report related to Russian interference in the U.S. election. This case highlights the challenges organizations face in preventing the unauthorized disclosure of sensitive information by insiders with access to classified materials. It emphasizes the importance of implementing measures to protect against both intentional and inadvertent leaks that can have far-reaching consequences.

Insider threats are not exclusive to high-profile cases; they can also manifest in smaller organizations. The case of a former IT administrator at a financial services firm serves as an example of an insider threat motivated by financial gain. In this instance, the employee exploited privileged access to manipulate financial records, embezzling funds over an extended period. This case underscores the importance of monitoring privileged access and implementing controls to detect and prevent financial fraud perpetrated by insiders.

The case of Jun Ying, a former Equifax executive, highlights the insider threat risks associated with stock trading based on non-public information. In 2018, Ying was charged with insider trading after allegedly using confidential information about the Equifax data breach to sell company stock before the breach was publicly disclosed. This case underscores the need for organizations to implement measures to prevent insider trading and ensure the ethical handling of non-public information to protect both the company's integrity and the financial markets.

The case of a former employee at Tesla exemplifies the insider threat risks associated with sabotage. In 2018, a Tesla employee sabotaged the company's manufacturing operations by making unauthorized changes to the production system and disclosing sensitive information to third parties. This case highlights the potential for insiders to intentionally disrupt operations, damage reputation, or steal intellectual property. It underscores the importance of robust access controls, employee monitoring, and incident response capabilities to address malicious insider actions.

Insider threats also extend to the realm of academia, as demonstrated by the case of a former researcher at Iowa State University. In 2020, the researcher was arrested for stealing proprietary seed technology and providing it to a Chinese company. This case underscores the risks associated with intellectual property theft in academic institutions and the need for universities to implement measures to protect research and innovation. It emphasizes the broader implications of insider threats, not only on organizations but also on national interests and economic competitiveness.

The case of a former IT contractor at the Australian Bureau of Meteorology serves as an example of an insider threat with potential nation-state involvement. In 2016, it was reported that a contractor had maliciously accessed sensitive systems, leading to concerns about the compromise of critical weather and national security data. This case highlights the geopolitical dimensions of insider threats and the need for organizations, especially those dealing with critical infrastructure, to be vigilant against both internal and external actors seeking unauthorized access.

In conclusion, real-world examples of insider threats provide a diverse and illuminating panorama of the risks organizations face from individuals with access to sensitive information. These cases underscore the importance of implementing a comprehensive insider threat mitigation strategy that encompasses technological controls, employee education, continuous monitoring, and incident response capabilities. The lessons learned from these cases emphasize the dynamic and evolving nature of insider threats, requiring organizations to remain vigilant and adaptive in their efforts to safeguard against both intentional and unintentional risks originating from within. As the cybersecurity landscape continues to evolve, the insights gleaned from these real-world examples contribute to a more informed and proactive approach to mitigating the multifaceted challenges posed by insider threats.

Extracting Key Lessons for Insider Threat Prevention

Extracting key lessons for insider threat prevention involves a comprehensive examination of real-world cases, industry best practices, and evolving cybersecurity strategies. One fundamental lesson centers on the critical role of robust access controls and privileged user management. Many insider threat incidents, such as the cases of Edward Snowden and Chelsea Manning, underscore the need for organizations to implement stringent access controls that limit users' ability to access sensitive information based on their roles and responsibilities. Restricting privileged access helps minimize the potential damage that insiders can inflict, whether intentionally or unintentionally. Implementing the principle of least privilege ensures that individuals only have access to the information necessary for their job functions, reducing the attack surface and mitigating the risk of unauthorized data access or exfiltration.

Continuous monitoring and behavioral analytics emerge as essential components of an effective insider threat prevention strategy. The dynamic and often subtle nature of insider threats, as evidenced in cases like the prolonged activities of Harold Martin, necessitates ongoing monitoring to detect anomalous behavior patterns. Behavioral analytics leverage machine learning and advanced algorithms to analyze user activities, identifying deviations from normal behavior that may indicate potential insider threats. By establishing baselines for typical user behavior and promptly detecting deviations, organizations can proactively respond to suspicious activities before they escalate. Continuous monitoring also facilitates the early detection of insider threats, contributing to a more agile and responsive cybersecurity posture.

Employee education and awareness play a pivotal role in preventing insider threats, as demonstrated by cases like that of Chelsea Manning. Organizations must invest in comprehensive training programs that educate employees about cybersecurity best practices, the potential consequences of insider threats, and the importance of responsible data handling. Training should encompass recognizing phishing attempts, understanding the risks associated with sharing sensitive information, and fostering a culture of security-consciousness. Emphasizing the shared responsibility of employees in maintaining the organization's security posture contributes to building a workforce that is vigilant, informed, and actively engaged in preventing insider threats.

In the realm of supply chain security, lessons from incidents like the SolarWinds supply chain attack highlight the importance of rigorous third-party risk management. Organizations often rely on external vendors and partners, making it crucial to assess and monitor the security practices of these entities. Integrating supply chain risk management into the overall cybersecurity strategy involves evaluating the security posture of third-party vendors, conducting regular assessments, and establishing contractual obligations regarding security standards. Organizations must recognize that the security of interconnected entities is interdependent, and a compromise in the supply chain can have cascading effects. Vigilance in supply chain security is essential to preventing insider threats that may originate from external sources.

The significance of proactive vulnerability management is evident in cases like the Equifax data breach. Organizations must prioritize identifying and remedying vulnerabilities promptly to prevent potential exploitation by malicious insiders or external actors. Regular assessments, patch management, and penetration testing contribute to a proactive vulnerability management strategy. This lesson underscores the need to go beyond reactive measures and adopt a preventive approach to minimize the risk of insider threats exploiting known vulnerabilities. By addressing weaknesses in a timely manner, organizations enhance their overall resilience and reduce the likelihood of insider threats leveraging compromised systems.

The intersection of insider threats and intellectual property theft is exemplified by cases like that of a former researcher at Iowa State University. Organizations, particularly in academia and research-intensive sectors, must prioritize protecting intellectual property and sensitive research data. Implementing measures such as data encryption, strict access controls, and employee education on the importance of safeguarding proprietary information helps mitigate the risk of insider threats seeking to exploit valuable assets. Recognizing the economic and strategic implications of intellectual property theft underscores the need for organizations to implement tailored strategies to protect innovation and proprietary knowledge.

Communication and transparency emerge as critical components of insider threat prevention, as seen in cases where effective communication mitigated reputational damage. Organizations must establish clear channels for reporting suspicious activities, create a culture that encourages whistleblowing, and provide employees with the confidence that their observations will be taken seriously. Transparent communication about the organization's commitment to security, the consequences of insider threats, and the importance of individual contributions builds trust and reinforces a shared responsibility for preventing insider threats. Transparent communication is a foundational element in crisis management, helping organizations navigate the aftermath of insider threat incidents and maintain the trust of stakeholders.

The integration of ethical considerations into insider threat prevention is evident in cases like the arrest of Jun Ying for insider trading based on non-public information about the Equifax data breach. Organizations must prioritize ethical behavior and ensure that employees understand the legal and moral implications of insider trading, unauthorized disclosure of sensitive information, and other unethical practices. This lesson extends to the responsible handling of non-public information, emphasizing the need for organizations to cultivate an ethical culture that aligns with legal standards and societal expectations. Ethical considerations are integral to preventing insider threats and maintaining the organization's integrity.

Lessons from insider threat incidents underscore the importance of legal and regulatory compliance in cybersecurity. Organizations must adhere to data protection laws, industry regulations, and privacy standards to avoid legal repercussions and safeguard sensitive information. The Equifax data breach, for instance, resulted in legal and regulatory consequences for the organization. Organizations should proactively assess and address compliance requirements, integrate legal considerations into their cybersecurity strategies, and prioritize the responsible handling of personal and sensitive data. Compliance with legal standards enhances the organization's resilience against insider threats and regulatory scrutiny.

The multifaceted nature of insider threat prevention necessitates the integration of technological solutions with human-centric strategies. While technical controls, such as access controls, monitoring systems, and encryption, form the foundation of insider threat prevention, organizations must recognize the human element. Insider threats often involve social engineering, manipulation, or exploitation of human vulnerabilities. Therefore, fostering a culture of security-consciousness, employee education, and a collective commitment to preventing insider threats is paramount. The human-centric approach recognizes that employees are both potential targets and the frontline defense against insider threats, emphasizing the need for a holistic and inclusive cybersecurity strategy.

In conclusion, extracting key lessons for insider threat prevention involves synthesizing insights from real-world cases and industry best practices. Robust access controls, continuous monitoring, employee education, supply chain vigilance, proactive vulnerability management, intellectual property protection, transparent communication, ethical considerations, legal compliance, and a human-centric approach collectively form a comprehensive insider threat prevention strategy. As organizations navigate the evolving landscape of cybersecurity risks, these lessons provide a roadmap for building resilience, fostering a security-conscious culture, and mitigating the diverse challenges posed by insider threats. The proactive integration of these lessons into organizational cybersecurity strategies contributes to a dynamic and adaptive approach that aligns with the intricacies of preventing insider threats in the digital age.

Chapter 8: Blockchain Armor: Safeguarding the Decentralized Frontiers

8.1 Introduction to Blockchain Technology

Blockchain technology, a revolutionary innovation that emerged with the advent of cryptocurrencies, represents a decentralized and distributed ledger system designed to provide transparency, security, and trust in digital transactions. At its core, a blockchain is a continuously growing chain of blocks, where each block contains a list of transactions. Unlike traditional centralized databases, which rely on a single authoritative entity for record-keeping, blockchain operates on a decentralized network of computers, often referred to as nodes, that collectively validate and record transactions. The concept of blockchain was introduced in 2008 by an individual or group using the pseudonym Satoshi Nakamoto, as the underlying technology for the groundbreaking cryptocurrency, Bitcoin.

The fundamental architecture of a blockchain consists of a chain of blocks, where each block contains a cryptographic hash of the previous block, a timestamp, and a list of transactions. The immutability of the blockchain arises from the cryptographic hash linking each block to its predecessor. Once a block is added to the chain, altering the information in any previous block would require changing all subsequent blocks, making tampering highly impractical and computationally infeasible. This inherent security feature contributes to the trustworthiness of the data recorded on the blockchain, making it resistant to manipulation or fraud.

The decentralized nature of blockchain technology is a key distinguishing feature. In a traditional centralized system, a single entity or authority manages and controls the database, making it susceptible to single points of failure, hacking, and manipulation. In contrast, a blockchain operates on a peer-to-peer network, where every participant (node) in the network has a copy of the entire blockchain. This decentralized consensus mechanism eliminates the need for a central authority, fostering a distributed and trustless environment where participants can transact directly with one another without intermediaries.

Blockchain employs consensus algorithms to validate and agree on the state of the ledger across the network. One common consensus mechanism is Proof of Work (PoW), which requires participants, known as miners, to solve complex mathematical problems to validate transactions and add new blocks to the chain. PoW, while secure, has faced criticism due to its energy-intensive nature. An alternative consensus mechanism is Proof of Stake (PoS), where participants, known as validators, are chosen to create new blocks based on the amount of cryptocurrency they hold and are willing to "stake" as collateral. PoS aims to reduce energy consumption and enhance scalability.

Smart contracts, another integral aspect of blockchain technology, are self-executing contracts with the terms of the agreement directly written into code. Smart contracts automatically execute and enforce the terms when predefined conditions are met, eliminating the need for intermediaries and streamlining complex business processes. Ethereum, a prominent blockchain platform, introduced the concept of smart contracts, expanding the applications of blockchain beyond simple transactions to include decentralized applications (DApps) and programmable functionalities.

Blockchain's impact extends beyond cryptocurrencies, finding applications in diverse industries such as finance, supply chain, healthcare, and governance. In the financial sector, blockchain enables faster and more secure cross-border transactions by eliminating intermediaries and reducing settlement times. Supply chain management benefits from blockchain's ability to provide an immutable and transparent record of the journey of products from manufacturers to consumers, enhancing traceability and reducing fraud. In healthcare, blockchain facilitates secure and interoperable sharing of patient data among healthcare providers while maintaining patient privacy. Governments are exploring the use of blockchain for transparent and secure voting systems, land registry management, and identity verification.

Challenges and considerations accompany the widespread adoption of blockchain technology. Scalability remains a critical issue, especially for public blockchains like Bitcoin and Ethereum, as they face limitations in transaction processing speed and network throughput. Privacy concerns arise from the pseudonymous nature of blockchain transactions, prompting the development of privacy-focused solutions such as zero-knowledge proofs. Additionally, regulatory frameworks and legal considerations continue to evolve as governments grapple with defining the status of cryptocurrencies, smart contracts, and blockchain-based assets.

In conclusion, blockchain technology represents a transformative force in the realm of digital transactions, introducing a decentralized, transparent, and secure approach to record-keeping. The concept of a distributed ledger, cryptography, consensus mechanisms, and smart contracts collectively form the foundation of blockchain's capabilities. As blockchain continues to evolve and find applications in various industries, addressing scalability, privacy, and regulatory challenges will be crucial for its sustained growth. The journey of blockchain from its inception as the underlying technology for cryptocurrencies to its current status as a catalyst for innovation across sectors exemplifies its potential to redefine the way we transact, collaborate, and establish trust in the digital age.

Decentralization and Distributed Ledger Concepts

Decentralization and distributed ledgers stand as foundational principles in the realm of modern computing, particularly within the context of blockchain technology. Decentralization, in its essence, refers to the distribution of authority, control, and decision-making across a network, mitigating the reliance on a central governing entity. This departure from centralized models, where a single authority holds dominion over critical functions, introduces a paradigm shift with far-reaching implications for security, transparency, and resilience. The genesis of decentralized systems can be traced to the recognition that reliance on a central authority poses vulnerabilities such as single points of failure, susceptibility to manipulation, and heightened security risks. Decentralization fosters a network where power is diffused among participants, creating a more resilient, transparent, and democratic framework.

At the core of decentralization is the idea of peer-to-peer (P2P) communication, a departure from the client-server model that characterizes many traditional systems. In a decentralized network, each participant, or node, has equal standing, and interactions occur directly between peers without the need for intermediaries. This peer-to-peer architecture not only enhances the efficiency of communication but also contributes to the robustness of the network by eliminating a single point of control that could be exploited or compromised. The advent of decentralized technologies, exemplified by blockchain, has propelled the exploration and implementation of decentralized systems across various domains, including finance, governance, supply chain management, and more.

Distributed ledgers represent a tangible manifestation of decentralization, embodying the idea of a shared, synchronized, and tamper-resistant record of information distributed across multiple nodes. Unlike centralized ledgers, which are maintained by a single entity, distributed ledgers exist as replicated copies across the nodes of a network. This redundancy not only ensures the availability of data even if some nodes fail but also fortifies the ledger against tampering or unauthorized modifications. The consensus mechanism, a key aspect of distributed ledgers, enables nodes to agree on the state of the ledger, ensuring that all participants share a common, verifiable version of the truth. This shared truth, immutable and transparent, forms the backbone of trust in decentralized systems.

Blockchain technology serves as a prominent instantiation of both decentralization and distributed ledgers. In a blockchain, data is structured into blocks, and each block contains a cryptographic hash of the previous block, forming a continuous chain of linked information. This chain of blocks, distributed across nodes, constitutes a decentralized and distributed ledger. The cryptographic linking of blocks through hashes ensures the integrity of the entire chain, making it computationally infeasible to alter any block without modifying all subsequent blocks. This tamper-resistant quality is a key attribute that underpins the trustworthiness of blockchain-based systems.

The consensus mechanism within a blockchain network is pivotal for maintaining agreement among participants regarding the state of the ledger. Proof of Work (PoW), the consensus mechanism introduced by Bitcoin, requires participants, known as miners, to solve complex mathematical problems to validate transactions and add new blocks to the chain. PoW ensures that participants expend computational resources, making it economically unfeasible to manipulate the ledger. However, the energy-intensive nature of PoW has spurred the development of alternative consensus mechanisms, such as Proof of Stake (PoS), where participants are chosen to create new blocks based on the amount of cryptocurrency they hold and are willing to "stake" as collateral. PoS aims to reduce energy consumption and enhance scalability.

The concept of a trustless system, a term often associated with decentralized architectures, refers to the ability of participants to transact and interact without the need for implicit trust in a central authority. Trust is instead established through cryptographic protocols, consensus mechanisms, and the transparency of the distributed ledger. Trustlessness empowers users by minimizing reliance on intermediaries and fostering a peer-to-peer environment where transactions are executed based on predefined rules and protocols. This concept has profound implications for sectors such as finance, where traditional intermediaries like banks and clearinghouses may be replaced by decentralized and trustless systems.

Smart contracts, a significant innovation enabled by blockchain, further exemplify the integration of decentralization and distributed ledgers. Smart contracts are self-executing contracts with the terms encoded in code. These contracts automatically execute when predefined conditions are met, eliminating the need for intermediaries and streamlining complex business processes. Ethereum, a blockchain platform that introduced smart contracts, expanded the capabilities of blockchain beyond simple transactions, allowing developers to create decentralized applications (DApps) with programmable functionalities. Smart contracts enhance the efficiency, transparency, and automation of processes, fostering a new paradigm for decentralized applications.

Decentralization and distributed ledgers extend their influence beyond the realm of cryptocurrencies and blockchain, finding applications in various industries. In finance, decentralized finance (DeFi) leverages blockchain to recreate traditional financial services without the need for intermediaries. Decentralized exchanges, lending platforms, and tokenized assets exemplify the transformative potential of decentralization in the financial sector. In supply chain management, distributed ledgers enhance transparency by providing an immutable and shared record of the journey of products from manufacturers to consumers. This transparency reduces fraud, ensures traceability, and enhances the overall efficiency of supply chain processes.

Healthcare stands as another sector where decentralization and distributed ledgers hold promise. Blockchain can facilitate the secure and interoperable sharing of patient data among healthcare providers, enabling a patient-centric model where individuals have greater control over their health information. This decentralized approach enhances data security and privacy while fostering collaboration among disparate healthcare entities. Additionally, decentralized identity solutions, leveraging blockchain, are explored as a means to provide individuals with greater control over their digital identities, reducing reliance on centralized identity providers.

Challenges and considerations accompany the adoption of decentralization and distributed ledgers. Scalability remains a persistent challenge, especially in public blockchain networks, as they face limitations in transaction processing speed and network throughput. Efforts to address scalability include the exploration of layer-two solutions, such as sidechains and state channels, and the development of more scalable consensus mechanisms. Privacy concerns also emerge, as the transparent nature of blockchain transactions can compromise user anonymity. Solutions like zero-knowledge proofs and privacy-focused blockchains aim to address these privacy considerations.

Legal and regulatory frameworks are still evolving in response to the decentralized nature of blockchain and cryptocurrencies. Governments grapple with defining the status of digital assets, determining taxation policies, and establishing frameworks for Initial Coin Offerings (ICOs) and tokenized securities. Striking a balance between fostering innovation and mitigating risks associated with fraud and illicit activities remains a complex challenge.

In conclusion, decentralization and distributed ledgers represent transformative concepts that redefine how information is stored, shared, and transacted in the digital age. From the foundational principles of peer-to-peer communication to the intricate mechanisms of blockchain consensus and smart contracts, these concepts empower individuals, enhance security, and foster innovation across diverse industries. The journey towards a more decentralized future involves addressing technical challenges, navigating regulatory landscapes, and continually refining the balance between trustlessness and accountability. As decentralization continues to shape the landscape of technology and business, its profound impact on transparency, efficiency, and inclusivity reverberates across sectors, heralding a new era of decentralized possibilities.

Blockchain in Cybersecurity: A Paradigm Shift

The intersection of blockchain technology and cybersecurity heralds a transformative paradigm shift, promising to reshape how organizations approach the daunting challenges of safeguarding digital assets and sensitive information in an increasingly interconnected world. At its core, blockchain introduces a decentralized and tamper-resistant framework that fundamentally alters the traditional landscape of cybersecurity. The immutable and transparent nature of blockchain's distributed ledger, coupled with cryptographic principles and consensus mechanisms, addresses longstanding issues of trust, transparency, and resilience in the face of evolving cyber threats.

One of the foundational contributions of blockchain to cybersecurity lies in its capacity to mitigate the risks associated with data tampering and unauthorized access. Traditional centralized databases, susceptible to single points of failure and vulnerable to cyberattacks, often serve as attractive targets for malicious actors seeking to manipulate or exfiltrate sensitive information. Blockchain, with its decentralized ledger architecture and cryptographic hashing, introduces a level of security that makes tampering with stored data exceptionally challenging. Each block in the blockchain contains a cryptographic hash of the previous block, creating a chain of interlinked, immutable records. Any attempt to alter information in a specific block would necessitate changing all subsequent blocks, rendering the entire chain resistant to unauthorized modifications.

The decentralized nature of blockchain further contributes to cybersecurity by eliminating the vulnerabilities associated with a central point of control. In traditional systems, a single breach or compromise can have cascading effects, potentially exposing vast amounts of sensitive data. Decentralization distributes the authority and control across a network of nodes, ensuring that there is no single target for cyber adversaries. This diffusion of control enhances the resilience of the system, making it inherently more resistant to attacks that exploit centralized vulnerabilities. As a result, blockchain serves as a powerful deterrent against large-scale data breaches and cyberattacks.

Smart contracts, a key feature enabled by blockchain technology, introduce a layer of programmability and automation to cybersecurity protocols. These self-executing contracts, with terms encoded in code, automatically execute predefined actions when specific conditions are met. In the realm of cybersecurity, smart contracts can be leveraged to automate incident response, threat detection, and access control. For instance, a smart contract could autonomously trigger responses to detected security incidents, execute predefined security measures, or manage access permissions based on dynamic threat intelligence. This programmable and automated aspect of smart contracts enhances the efficiency and responsiveness of cybersecurity protocols, reducing the human factor in the decision-making process and accelerating the overall incident response time.

Decentralized Identity Management (DID) emerges as a groundbreaking application of blockchain in addressing identity-related cybersecurity challenges. Traditional identity management systems often rely on centralized repositories of user data, making them lucrative targets for cybercriminals seeking to exploit or steal personal information. In a decentralized identity framework enabled by blockchain, individuals have greater control over their digital identities, and user data is stored in a secure and tamper-resistant manner. Users can selectively share specific attributes or credentials without revealing their entire identity, enhancing privacy and minimizing the risks associated with large-scale data breaches.

The concept of decentralized trust, a hallmark of blockchain, transforms the way trust is established and maintained in digital interactions. In the absence of a central authority, blockchain relies on cryptographic mechanisms and consensus algorithms to ensure the integrity and validity of transactions. This trustless environment fosters secure peer-to-peer transactions without the need for intermediaries, reducing the attack surface and vulnerabilities associated with centralized trust models. Blockchain's decentralized trust paradigm finds applications in various cybersecurity domains, from secure financial transactions to supply chain integrity and beyond.

Supply chain security stands out as an area where blockchain introduces a revolutionary approach to cybersecurity. The complexities of modern supply chains, involving numerous stakeholders and intricate networks, create vulnerabilities that can be exploited by malicious actors. Blockchain provides a transparent and traceable ledger that records every transaction and movement of goods along the supply chain. This enhanced visibility not only reduces the risk of fraud and counterfeiting but also enables rapid identification and response to security incidents. With blockchain, organizations can establish a verifiable and immutable record of the provenance and authenticity of products, bolstering the overall security and integrity of the supply chain.

The decentralized and transparent nature of blockchain also contributes to improving the cybersecurity posture of Internet of Things (IoT) ecosystems. The proliferation of connected devices in IoT introduces a myriad of security challenges, including device vulnerabilities, data integrity concerns, and the potential for unauthorized access. Blockchain's ability to establish a tamper-resistant and auditable record of IoT data transactions enhances the integrity and reliability of information generated by these devices. Furthermore, the use of smart contracts can automate the enforcement of security policies and access controls within IoT networks, reducing the risk of compromise and enhancing overall cybersecurity resilience.

Despite the promising advantages, the adoption of blockchain in cybersecurity is not without its challenges and considerations. Scalability remains a persistent issue, particularly in public blockchain networks, as the volume of transactions and data increases. Efforts to address scalability challenges involve exploring layer-two solutions, consensus algorithm enhancements, and advancements in blockchain interoperability. Additionally, the energy consumption associated with certain consensus mechanisms, such as Proof of Work (PoW), has sparked environmental concerns, prompting the exploration of more sustainable alternatives like Proof of Stake (PoS).

Legal and regulatory frameworks also play a crucial role in shaping the landscape of blockchain in cybersecurity. The nascent nature of blockchain technology has led to a dynamic and evolving regulatory environment. Governments and regulatory bodies are working to define the legal status of cryptocurrencies, smart contracts, and blockchain-based assets. Striking a balance between fostering innovation and mitigating risks associated with fraud and illicit activities remains a complex challenge for policymakers.

In conclusion, the integration of blockchain technology into cybersecurity represents a paradigm shift with far-reaching implications for how organizations protect their digital assets and sensitive information. The decentralized, tamper-resistant, and transparent nature of blockchain introduces a level of security and trust that challenges traditional cybersecurity models. From mitigating the risks of data tampering and unauthorized access to enabling programmable security measures through smart contracts, blockchain reshapes the cybersecurity landscape. As organizations continue to explore and implement blockchain solutions, addressing scalability, environmental concerns, and regulatory considerations will be pivotal in unlocking the full potential of blockchain as a transformative force in cybersecurity. The journey towards a decentralized and secure digital future is marked by innovation, collaboration, and a reimagining of established cybersecurity norms in the face of an ever-evolving threat landscape.

8.2 Securing Transactions with Blockchain

The realm of transactional security undergoes a profound transformation with the integration of blockchain technology, offering a paradigm shift in how organizations secure, validate, and authenticate digital transactions. At its core, blockchain introduces a decentralized, tamper-resistant ledger that fundamentally alters the traditional models of transaction security. In contrast to centralized systems vulnerable to single points of failure and susceptible to manipulation, blockchain distributes the authority and control across a network of nodes, creating a resilient and transparent environment that enhances the security of transactions across diverse sectors.

The immutability of the blockchain ledger serves as a cornerstone in securing transactions. Traditional centralized databases, often vulnerable to data tampering and unauthorized alterations, pale in comparison to the tamper-resistant nature of blockchain. Each transaction is encapsulated within a block, and the blocks are linked cryptographically, creating a chain where altering one block necessitates changing all subsequent blocks. This cryptographic linkage ensures that once a transaction is recorded on the blockchain, it becomes practically impossible to retroactively modify or delete. This feature establishes a level of trust and integrity in digital transactions that is unmatched by traditional centralized systems.

Smart contracts, a key innovation enabled by blockchain, play a pivotal role in automating and securing transactions. These self-executing contracts with predefined terms encoded in code automatically execute and enforce the terms when specific conditions are met. In the realm of transaction security, smart contracts provide a programmable layer that facilitates the automation of contractual agreements, reducing the need for intermediaries and enhancing the efficiency of transaction processes. By embedding security protocols directly into the code, smart contracts enable organizations to automate security measures, such as escrow services, conditional payments, and multi-signature authentication, streamlining complex transactional workflows.

Decentralized Identity Management (DID) emerges as a groundbreaking application of blockchain in securing user identities and enhancing transactional security. Traditional identity management systems, often centralized and vulnerable to breaches, store user data in a manner that makes it an attractive target for cybercriminals. Blockchain's decentralized identity framework empowers individuals with greater control over their digital identities, ensuring that user data is stored securely and tamper-resistant. Users can selectively share specific attributes or credentials without revealing their entire identity, minimizing the risks associated with identity theft and enhancing the security of online transactions.

Cryptocurrencies, the pioneering application of blockchain technology, exemplify a novel approach to securing financial transactions. Blockchain's decentralized architecture, cryptographic principles, and consensus mechanisms eliminate the need for intermediaries in financial transactions, reducing the attack surface and vulnerabilities associated with centralized financial systems. Cryptocurrencies, such as Bitcoin, utilize blockchain to secure and validate transactions through a process known as mining, where participants compete to solve complex mathematical problems to validate transactions and add them to the blockchain. This decentralized validation process ensures the integrity and security of financial transactions without relying on a central authority.

Supply chain security experiences a transformative impact with the integration of blockchain, as it provides an immutable and transparent ledger to secure the entire lifecycle of transactions within the supply chain. The complexity of modern supply chains, involving numerous stakeholders and intricate networks, creates vulnerabilities that can be exploited by malicious actors. Blockchain's transparent and traceable ledger records every transaction and movement of goods, reducing the risk of fraud, counterfeiting, and unauthorized alterations. This enhanced visibility enables organizations to secure transactions, establish the provenance and authenticity of products, and respond rapidly to security incidents, thus fortifying the overall security of the supply chain.

Internet of Things (IoT) ecosystems benefit from the security enhancements introduced by blockchain. The proliferation of connected devices in IoT introduces security challenges related to device vulnerabilities, data integrity, and the potential for unauthorized access. Blockchain's tamper-resistant and auditable ledger enhances the integrity and reliability of information generated by IoT devices. Each transaction recorded on the blockchain is securely encrypted and linked to previous transactions, creating a secure and transparent chain of information. Furthermore, the use of smart contracts within IoT networks automates the enforcement of security policies and access controls, reducing the risk of compromise and enhancing the overall cybersecurity resilience of IoT ecosystems.

The decentralized and transparent nature of blockchain also contributes to securing digital assets and intellectual property. In industries where the protection of digital assets is paramount, such as media and entertainment, blockchain provides a secure and transparent framework for managing rights, royalties, and licenses. The immutability of the blockchain ledger ensures the integrity of ownership records, protecting creators and stakeholders from unauthorized use or infringement. Smart contracts can automate royalty payments, ensuring that content creators receive fair compensation without the need for intermediaries.

Despite the promising advantages, the integration of blockchain in securing transactions is not without challenges. Scalability remains a persistent concern, particularly in public blockchain networks, as the volume of transactions increases. Efforts to address scalability challenges involve exploring layer-two solutions, consensus algorithm enhancements, and advancements in blockchain interoperability. Additionally, the energy consumption associated with certain consensus mechanisms, such as Proof of Work (PoW), has spurred environmental concerns, prompting the exploration of more sustainable alternatives like Proof of Stake (PoS).

Legal and regulatory considerations also play a crucial role in shaping the landscape of blockchain in securing transactions. The nascent nature of blockchain technology has led to a dynamic and evolving regulatory environment. Governments and regulatory bodies are working to define the legal status of cryptocurrencies, smart contracts, and blockchain-based assets. Striking a balance between fostering innovation and mitigating risks associated with fraud and illicit activities remains a complex challenge for policymakers.

In conclusion, the integration of blockchain technology in securing transactions represents a transformative leap forward in transactional security. The decentralized, tamper-resistant, and transparent nature of blockchain introduces a level of security and trust that challenges traditional models. From securing financial transactions through cryptocurrencies to enhancing the transparency and integrity of supply chain transactions, blockchain reshapes the landscape of transaction security. As organizations continue to explore and implement blockchain solutions, addressing scalability, environmental concerns, and regulatory considerations will be pivotal in unlocking the full potential of blockchain as a transformative force in securing transactions. The journey towards a decentralized and secure digital future is marked by innovation, collaboration, and a reimagining of established transactional security norms in the face of an ever-evolving threat landscape.

Cryptographic Techniques in Blockchain

The underpinning security of blockchain technology relies heavily on a suite of cryptographic techniques that ensure the integrity, confidentiality, and authenticity of digital transactions within a decentralized and tamper-resistant environment. At the heart of blockchain's cryptographic framework is the concept of public-key cryptography, also known as asymmetric cryptography. This foundational technique involves the use of paired keys – a public key, which is shared openly, and a private key, known only to the key owner. Public-key cryptography enables secure digital signatures, a fundamental component in validating the authenticity of transactions recorded on the blockchain.

Digital signatures, facilitated by public-key cryptography, play a pivotal role in ensuring the integrity and authenticity of transactions. When a user initiates a transaction, they use their private key to create a digital signature that uniquely represents the transaction data. This digital signature is then appended to the transaction and can be verified by anyone with access to the corresponding public key. The verification process confirms the origin and authenticity of the transaction, as only the rightful owner of the private key could have generated the correct digital signature. Digital signatures, therefore, serve as a cryptographic mechanism to prevent tampering and unauthorized alterations of transactions recorded on the blockchain.

Hash functions represent another critical cryptographic element in the blockchain landscape. Hash functions take an input (or message) and produce a fixed-size string of characters, often referred to as the hash value or hash digest. The deterministic nature of hash functions ensures that the same input will always produce the same hash value. In blockchain, hash functions contribute to the creation of blocks and the chaining of these blocks together. Each block contains a hash of the previous block's header, creating a cryptographically linked chain. The immutability of the blockchain arises from the fact that altering any transaction in a block would require recalculating the hash of that block and all subsequent blocks, making it computationally infeasible.

Cryptographic hash functions also find application in the creation of Merkle trees, an efficient data structure that organizes transactions within a block. In a Merkle tree, transactions are grouped in pairs, and the hash of each pair is then combined and hashed again until a single hash, known as the Merkle root, is obtained. This Merkle root is included in the block's header and serves as a concise representation of all the transactions within the block. Verifying the inclusion of a specific transaction in a block involves a comparatively efficient process of navigating the Merkle tree, contributing to the overall efficiency and security of the blockchain.

Public and private key cryptography, coupled with hash functions, forms the basis for secure and private communication within blockchain networks. When users want to communicate securely, they can employ a hybrid cryptographic approach that combines the strengths of both symmetric and asymmetric cryptography. In this scenario, a shared secret, often a symmetric key, is established between parties using public-key cryptography. Subsequent communication is then encrypted using the symmetric key, which is more computationally efficient than asymmetric encryption. This combination of cryptographic techniques ensures the confidentiality and privacy of messages exchanged among participants on the blockchain network.

Zero-knowledge proofs, a more advanced cryptographic technique, contribute to enhancing privacy and confidentiality within blockchain transactions. These proofs enable a party to prove the authenticity of certain information without revealing the actual information itself. For instance, a zero-knowledge proof can confirm that a user possesses a specific piece of information without disclosing the information itself. In the context of blockchain, zero-knowledge proofs find applications in privacy-focused cryptocurrencies, where users can prove ownership or validity of transactions without revealing the transaction details. This cryptographic technique adds an additional layer of privacy and confidentiality to blockchain transactions, particularly in scenarios where participants seek to protect sensitive information.

Homomorphic encryption represents another cryptographic innovation that holds potential for enhancing privacy within blockchain. This encryption scheme allows computations to be performed on encrypted data without decrypting it first. In a blockchain context, homomorphic encryption could enable secure and private computation of transactions while the data remains encrypted. This capability has implications for confidential smart contracts and privacy-focused applications, where sensitive information can be processed without exposing the raw data. However, homomorphic encryption faces challenges related to computational complexity and performance, requiring ongoing research and development to make it practical for widespread blockchain adoption.

Ring signatures and stealth addresses are cryptographic techniques that enhance transaction privacy in certain blockchain networks, particularly privacy-focused cryptocurrencies. Ring signatures allow a user to sign a message on behalf of a group, making it computationally infeasible to determine which specific individual within the group produced the signature. This ensures transaction unlinkability and enhances privacy by obscuring the true origin of a transaction. Stealth addresses, on the other hand, generate unique, one-time addresses for each transaction, making it difficult to establish a link between multiple transactions associated with a single user. These cryptographic techniques contribute to the privacy features of blockchain networks designed to prioritize anonymity and confidentiality.

The consensus mechanism, while not a traditional cryptographic technique, is a crucial component in securing transactions within a blockchain network. Proof of Work (PoW) and Proof of Stake (PoS) are two prominent consensus mechanisms that ensure agreement on the state of the blockchain across the network. PoW involves miners solving complex mathematical problems to validate transactions and add new blocks to the chain, while PoS selects validators based on the amount of cryptocurrency they hold and are willing to "stake" as collateral. These mechanisms secure the network by making it economically unfeasible for malicious actors to tamper with transactions or attempt double-spending attacks.

Despite the robust cryptographic techniques employed in blockchain, challenges and considerations persist. Quantum computing, with its potential to break widely-used cryptographic algorithms like RSA and ECC, poses a long-term threat to the security of blockchain networks. The development of quantum-resistant cryptographic algorithms is an active area of research to address this emerging challenge. Additionally, the usability and user experience of managing cryptographic keys, especially private keys, present challenges for mainstream adoption. Solutions and innovations in user-friendly key management are essential to facilitate broader participation in blockchain ecosystems.

In conclusion, the amalgamation of cryptographic techniques within blockchain forms the bedrock of its security architecture, ensuring the integrity, confidentiality, and authenticity of digital transactions in a decentralized environment. From public and private key cryptography to hash functions, zero-knowledge proofs, homomorphic encryption, and advanced privacy-focused techniques like ring signatures and stealth addresses, each cryptographic element plays a distinct role in fortifying the security of blockchain networks. As blockchain technology continues to evolve and find broader applications, the ongoing development of cryptographic innovations and the adaptation to emerging challenges will be crucial to maintaining the trust and security of decentralized transactions in the digital age.

Smart Contracts and Their Security Implications

Smart contracts, a pivotal innovation enabled by blockchain technology, represent self-executing agreements with the terms of the contract directly written into code. These programmable contracts automate and enforce the execution of predefined actions when specific conditions are met, eliminating the need for intermediaries and introducing a new paradigm in contract management and execution. The advent of smart contracts, popularized by platforms like Ethereum, has profound implications across various industries, ranging from finance and supply chain to healthcare and governance. However, the deployment and execution of smart contracts bring with them a unique set of security considerations and challenges.

The foundation of smart contract security lies in the underlying blockchain technology, which employs cryptographic techniques for transaction validation and consensus mechanisms to secure the network. Smart contracts are executed within a decentralized environment, typically on a blockchain, ensuring transparency, immutability, and tamper-resistant execution. However, the security of smart contracts is not only dependent on the robustness of the underlying blockchain but also on the solidity of the code written to define the contract's logic. Flaws and vulnerabilities in smart contract code can lead to unintended consequences, financial losses, and exploitation by malicious actors.

One of the key security considerations in smart contracts is the principle of code is law, emphasizing that the code written to execute a smart contract is the ultimate authority in determining the contract's behavior. While this principle aligns with the transparency and autonomy inherent in blockchain, it also means that any vulnerabilities or errors in the code can have real-world consequences. Security audits, code reviews, and rigorous testing are essential practices to identify and address vulnerabilities before deploying smart contracts on a blockchain network. The complexity of smart contract code and the potential for unforeseen interactions with other contracts or external systems amplify the importance of thorough security assessments.

One notable security challenge in smart contracts is the susceptibility to code vulnerabilities and exploits. Common vulnerabilities, such as reentrancy attacks, integer overflow/underflow, and unchecked external calls, can be exploited by attackers to manipulate the smart contract's behavior and compromise its intended functionality. For example, a reentrancy attack occurs when an external contract repeatedly calls back into the target contract before the original execution is completed, potentially allowing malicious actors to drain funds or manipulate state variables. Security best practices, including input validation, secure coding standards, and the use of standardized libraries, are crucial in mitigating these vulnerabilities.

The issue of gas limits in smart contracts adds another layer to their security considerations. Gas is the unit of computation in blockchain networks, and each smart contract execution consumes a specific amount of gas. If a smart contract requires more gas than the block gas limit allows, the execution may fail or be vulnerable to denial-of-service attacks. Developers must carefully optimize their smart contracts to stay within gas limits while ensuring that the contracts are functional and secure. Additionally, unexpected changes in gas costs, such as network congestion or upgrades, can impact the economic feasibility and security of smart contracts.

Oracles, external systems that provide real-world data to smart contracts, introduce a unique set of security challenges. Smart contracts often need external information, such as stock prices or weather conditions, to execute certain functions. However, the reliance on oracles poses a potential vulnerability, as malicious or compromised oracles can provide inaccurate or manipulated data to smart contracts. This can lead to unintended consequences, especially in financial contracts where accurate and timely data is critical. Mitigating this risk involves using reputable oracles, implementing multiple oracles for redundancy, and incorporating cryptographic techniques to verify the authenticity of oracle data.

The concept of upgradability in smart contracts, while providing flexibility and the ability to fix vulnerabilities, introduces security concerns related to the potential misuse of upgrade mechanisms. If not implemented carefully, upgradeability features can be exploited by malicious actors to introduce malicious code, compromise the integrity of the smart contract, or even take control of the entire contract. Security-conscious design principles, including transparent upgrade mechanisms, community governance, and ditability, are essential in balancing the benefits of upgradability with the potential risks.

Governance mechanisms within blockchain networks, which determine decision-making processes related to protocol upgrades and changes, play a crucial role in the security of smart contracts. Decentralized autonomous organizations (DAOs) and token-based governance models enable stakeholders to participate in decision-making. However, poorly designed governance structures or centralized control can lead to controversial hard forks, disputes, and potential vulnerabilities. Striking a balance between decentralization and effective governance is essential for ensuring the security and stability of smart contracts and the underlying blockchain ecosystem.

The phenomenon of flash loans, a unique financial instrument enabled by smart contracts, introduces both opportunities and security challenges. Flash loans allow users to borrow funds without collateral, provided the borrowed amount is returned within the same transaction. While this innovation facilitates complex financial strategies, it also presents the risk of manipulation and abuse. Malicious actors can exploit flash loans to manipulate prices, execute arbitrage attacks, or destabilize decentralized financial protocols. Ensuring the security of smart contracts in the context of flash loans requires careful consideration of risk mitigation measures, including circuit breakers, price oracles, and protocol upgrades.

The broader ecosystem of decentralized finance (DeFi) applications, built on smart contract platforms, introduces a myriad of security considerations. The interconnected nature of DeFi protocols, composability, and the rapid pace of innovation in the space amplify the potential impact of security vulnerabilities. Exploits in one protocol can have cascading effects on other interconnected protocols, leading to financial losses for users and systemic risks. Rigorous security audits, responsible disclosure practices, and collaboration within the blockchain community are crucial for identifying and addressing vulnerabilities in the evolving landscape of DeFi applications.

Despite the inherent security challenges, the continuous development of best practices, standards, and security tools contributes to improving the resilience of smart contracts. Formal verification, a technique that mathematically proves the correctness of smart contract code, is gaining traction as a means to enhance security. Platforms and tools that facilitate secure development practices, such as static analysis tools, automated testing frameworks, and secure coding libraries, play a vital role in reducing the likelihood of vulnerabilities in smart contracts.

In conclusion, the advent of smart contracts has ushered in a new era of programmable and automated agreements, revolutionizing various industries and decentralized applications. However, the security implications of smart contracts necessitate a vigilant and proactive approach to ensure the integrity, functionality, and resilience of these self-executing contracts. From code vulnerabilities and gas optimization to oracle risks, upgradability challenges, and the evolving landscape of decentralized finance, the security considerations in smart contracts are multifaceted. As the blockchain community continues to advance security practices, conduct thorough audits, and collaboratively address emerging challenges, smart contracts stand poised to become a cornerstone of decentralized, secure, and transparent digital ecosystems.

8.3 Decentralized Identity Management

Decentralized Identity Management:

Decentralized Identity Management (DID) emerges as a transformative paradigm in the digital landscape, redefining how individuals assert and control their identities across online platforms. In contrast to traditional identity management systems that rely on centralized authorities to verify and store user information, decentralized identity introduces a framework where individuals have greater control over their digital identities. At its core, DID leverages blockchain technology and cryptographic principles to create a secure and tamper-resistant ecosystem for managing, sharing, and verifying identity information.

The traditional model of identity management faces numerous challenges, ranging from privacy concerns and data breaches to the cumbersome processes of repeatedly verifying identity across different online services. Centralized identity systems, often operated by third-party entities, accumulate vast amounts of user data, making them attractive targets for cyberattacks and raising concerns about user privacy and consent. Decentralized identity seeks to address these challenges by shifting the control and ownership of identity information back to the individual.

Blockchain technology serves as the foundational infrastructure for decentralized identity solutions. By leveraging the decentralized and immutable nature of blockchain ledgers, DIDs create a secure and transparent environment for storing and managing identity-related data. Each individual on the network is assigned a unique identifier, typically in the form of a decentralized identifier (DID), which is linked to their cryptographic key pair. The private key, known only to the individual, enables them to control and access their identity information, while the public key facilitates secure interactions and verifications within the decentralized identity ecosystem.

One of the key advantages of decentralized identity is the concept of self-sovereign identity (SSI). SSI empowers individuals with full control over their identity information, allowing them to selectively share specific attributes or credentials without divulging unnecessary personal details. This granular control not only enhances privacy but also reduces the risk of identity theft and unauthorized access. Users can present verifiable credentials issued by trusted entities without relying on intermediaries, fostering a more direct and secure means of identity verification.

Verifiable credentials represent a fundamental component of decentralized identity ecosystems. These credentials, issued by trusted entities such as government agencies, educational institutions, or employers, are cryptographically signed statements that attest to specific attributes or qualifications of an individual. Verifiable credentials are stored in the individual's decentralized identity wallet, and the owner can selectively present them to different parties as needed. The cryptographic nature of these credentials ensures their integrity and authenticity, allowing relying parties to verify the information without the need for a central authority.

Decentralized identity systems often incorporate the concept of identity hubs, secure repositories where individuals store and manage their identity data. These hubs, typically encrypted and controlled by the individual's private key, provide a secure and convenient way to organize and share verifiable credentials. The use of identity hubs enhances the portability and interoperability of decentralized identity, enabling individuals to seamlessly use their identity across various services and applications.

Interoperability is a crucial aspect of decentralized identity, and various standards and protocols aim to facilitate the seamless exchange of identity information across different platforms. The Decentralized Identity Foundation (DIF) and the World Wide Web Consortium (W3C) play pivotal roles in developing standards such as the Decentralized Identifier (DID) specification and the Verifiable Credentials Data Model. These standards provide a common framework for the creation, issuance, and verification of decentralized identity components, fostering a more interoperable and collaborative ecosystem.

Decentralized identity is not only about individual control but also about establishing trust in a trustless environment. Trust anchors, entities that are widely recognized and trusted within the decentralized identity ecosystem, play a crucial role in facilitating trust and interoperability. These anchors may include government entities, financial institutions, or well-established organizations that issue verifiable credentials widely accepted across the ecosystem. The decentralized and transparent nature of blockchain ensures that trust anchors' credentials are verifiable and tamper-resistant, contributing to the overall trustworthiness of the decentralized identity ecosystem.

The application of decentralized identity extends beyond individual interactions to broader societal contexts, such as online communities, government services, and healthcare systems. In online communities, decentralized identity mitigates the risks of impersonation and identity fraud by providing a more reliable and verifiable means of user identification. Government services can benefit from the efficiency and security of decentralized identity in areas such as issuing digital passports, driver's licenses, and other official documents. In healthcare, decentralized identity facilitates secure and interoperable sharing of patient information, ensuring that individuals have control over their health data while maintaining the integrity of the records.

While the potential benefits of decentralized identity are substantial, challenges and considerations persist. User adoption remains a crucial factor, and efforts to educate individuals about the advantages of decentralized identity, as well as the importance of safeguarding their private keys, are essential. Usability and user experience must be prioritized to ensure that decentralized identity solutions are accessible and user-friendly, especially for individuals who may not be familiar with blockchain technology.

Security concerns, particularly the risk of losing access to one's identity due to a lost private key, necessitate robust recovery mechanisms and user-friendly key management solutions. The delicate balance between privacy and regulatory compliance is another challenge, as decentralized identity systems must align with evolving legal frameworks while preserving individual privacy rights. Additionally, the scalability and performance of decentralized identity solutions, especially in the context of mass adoption, require ongoing research and development to address technical limitations.

In conclusion, decentralized identity management stands at the forefront of a paradigm shift in how individuals assert and control their digital identities. By leveraging blockchain technology, cryptographic principles, and standards-driven interoperability, decentralized identity introduces a secure, user-centric, and privacy-enhancing approach to identity management. The journey towards mainstream adoption involves addressing challenges related to usability, security, and regulatory compliance while emphasizing the transformative potential of giving individuals greater control over their online identities. As decentralized identity continues to evolve, its impact extends beyond individual empowerment to redefine the dynamics of trust, privacy, and security in our increasingly digital and interconnected world.

Eliminating Single Points of Failure in Identity Systems

The quest for robust and resilient identity systems has led to a paradigm shift in the design and architecture of these systems, with a key focus on eliminating single points of failure. Traditional identity systems often rely on centralized repositories or authorities, creating vulnerabilities that can be exploited by malicious actors and jeopardizing the security and integrity of individuals' personal information. Recognizing the limitations of centralized models, contemporary identity systems leverage decentralized and distributed architectures to mitigate the risks associated with single points of failure and enhance the overall reliability and security of identity management.

Centralized identity systems, wherein a single authoritative entity holds and manages user information, pose significant risks in terms of security, privacy, and system reliability. A breach or compromise of the central repository could result in a massive data breach, exposing sensitive personal information of millions of individuals. The single point of failure in such systems not only makes them lucrative targets for cyberattacks but also introduces a systemic risk wherein the failure of a central authority can disrupt access to services for a large population. The decentralization of identity systems seeks to address these vulnerabilities by distributing control and authority across a network of nodes.

Decentralized identity systems, often built on blockchain technology, introduce a distributed ledger that records and manages identity-related transactions in a secure, tamper-resistant manner. Each participant in the network retains control over their identity information, stored in a decentralized and encrypted fashion. The elimination of a single central authority ensures that there is no one target for attackers to exploit, reducing the risk of large-scale data breaches and unauthorized access. Blockchain's consensus mechanisms further contribute to the security of decentralized identity systems, ensuring agreement on the state of the distributed ledger across the network.

In the context of eliminating single points of failure, the concept of self-sovereign identity (SSI) emerges as a fundamental principle. SSI empowers individuals with ownership and control over their identity information, enabling them to selectively share specific attributes or credentials without relying on intermediaries. The individual's identity resides in their control, stored in a decentralized identity wallet often secured by cryptographic keys. This model eliminates the reliance on a single centralized authority to verify and manage identity, shifting the paradigm towards a more resilient and user-centric approach.

Blockchain, as the underlying technology for many decentralized identity systems, introduces a novel approach to securing identity information. The decentralized ledger ensures that identity data is distributed across nodes in the network, making it resistant to tampering and unauthorized alterations. Each participant in the network has their copy of the ledger, creating redundancy and eliminating the vulnerability associated with a single point of failure. The cryptographic hashing and linking of blocks in the blockchain provide an immutable record of identity transactions, enhancing the integrity and transparency of the identity system.

Interoperability is a critical aspect of decentralized identity systems aiming to eliminate single points of failure. Different identity providers, applications, and services need to seamlessly interact and recognize identity information across the decentralized ecosystem. Standards such as the Decentralized Identifier (DID) specification and the Verifiable Credentials Data Model facilitate interoperability by providing a common framework for creating, issuing, and verifying decentralized identity components. This interoperability reduces reliance on a single provider or platform, further eliminating the risk associated with a central point of control.

The elimination of single points of failure in identity systems extends beyond technology to governance models. Decentralized identity often incorporates governance mechanisms that involve multiple stakeholders in decision-making processes related to protocol upgrades, changes, and dispute resolution. Decentralized Autonomous Organizations (DAOs) and token-based governance models distribute decision-making authority among participants, reducing the risk of centralized control and ensuring that the identity system evolves in a decentralized and resilient manner.

In the pursuit of eliminating single points of failure, the role of secure key management becomes paramount. In decentralized identity systems, individuals control cryptographic keys that authenticate and authorize their identity transactions. The loss or compromise of these keys can result in the loss of access to one's identity or, conversely, unauthorized access by malicious actors. Robust key management practices, including secure storage, backup mechanisms, and user-friendly recovery processes, are essential to ensure the security and resilience of decentralized identity systems.

The concept of decentralized identity hubs contributes to the elimination of single points of failure by providing individuals with a secure and user-friendly repository for managing their identity data. These hubs, often encrypted and controlled by the individual's private key, serve as secure storage for verifiable credentials and other identity-related information. The decentralized nature of these hubs, distributed across the network, ensures redundancy and availability, reducing the risk of a single point of failure affecting access to identity information.

The integration of zero-knowledge proofs in decentralized identity systems adds an additional layer of privacy and security. Zero-knowledge proofs allow individuals to prove the authenticity of certain information without revealing the actual information itself. In the context of identity, this means that a user can prove possession of specific attributes or credentials without disclosing the details, enhancing privacy and reducing the exposure of sensitive information. This cryptographic technique contributes to the overall security posture of decentralized identity systems, making them more resistant to identity theft and unauthorized access.

Despite the promising advancements in decentralized identity, challenges and considerations persist. Usability remains a crucial factor in ensuring widespread adoption, as individuals need user-friendly interfaces and experiences to interact seamlessly with decentralized identity systems. Education and awareness efforts are essential to convey the benefits of decentralized identity and guide users in securing their cryptographic keys effectively. Additionally, legal and regulatory frameworks must evolve to address the unique challenges and opportunities presented by decentralized identity, striking a balance between privacy, security, and compliance.

In conclusion, the journey towards eliminating single points of failure in identity systems represents a fundamental shift towards decentralized, user-centric, and resilient models. The adoption of blockchain technology, cryptographic principles, self-sovereign identity, and interoperable standards collectively contribute to the vision of a more secure and privacy-enhancing identity ecosystem. As decentralized identity systems continue to evolve, addressing technological, usability, and regulatory challenges will be pivotal in realizing the transformative potential of identity management that empowers individuals, enhances security, and eliminates the vulnerabilities associated with centralized points of control.

Privacy and Security Considerations in Decentralized Identity

The evolution of decentralized identity heralds a paradigm shift in how individuals manage and assert their online personas. In the decentralized identity landscape, paramount considerations revolve around preserving the privacy of users while ensuring robust security measures to safeguard against potential threats. Unlike traditional identity systems, which often rely on centralized authorities and repositories, decentralized identity systems leverage blockchain technology, cryptographic principles, and user-centric models to address privacy and security concerns. In this complex interplay, the design, implementation, and ongoing evolution of decentralized identity systems demand meticulous attention to both privacy and security aspects to build a trustworthy and resilient digital identity ecosystem.

Privacy is a cornerstone in the foundation of decentralized identity systems. Self-sovereign identity (SSI) principles underscore the importance of individuals having control over their personal information, allowing them to selectively share specific attributes or credentials without compromising unnecessary details. Decentralized identity empowers users to manage their identities independently, reducing the reliance on intermediaries and minimizing the exposure of sensitive information. The concept of minimal disclosure, a fundamental tenet of privacy in decentralized identity, ensures that individuals disclose only the necessary information for a given transaction or interaction, thereby mitigating the risks associated with unnecessary data exposure.

At the core of decentralized identity's privacy architecture is the use of decentralized identifiers (DIDs) and verifiable credentials. DIDs are unique identifiers linked to cryptographic key pairs, providing a foundation for users to assert control over their identity. Verifiable credentials, cryptographically signed statements issued by trusted entities, attest to specific attributes or qualifications of an individual. These credentials, stored in a decentralized identity wallet, enable users to present verified information without revealing the entirety of their personal details. This selective disclosure mechanism empowers users with fine-grained control over their privacy, allowing them to navigate digital interactions with greater confidence.

Blockchain, the underlying technology for many decentralized identity systems, introduces transparency and immutability to the storage and management of identity-related transactions. While these features enhance security, they also present privacy challenges. The public nature of blockchain transactions raises concerns about the exposure of identity-related data to potential observers. Efforts to address this challenge involve the use of privacy-preserving technologies such as zero-knowledge proofs, ring signatures, and homomorphic encryption. These cryptographic techniques allow individuals to interact with the blockchain without revealing sensitive information, preserving privacy while maintaining the integrity and security of the decentralized identity ecosystem.

Interoperability, a key goal in decentralized identity, brings forth both opportunities and privacy considerations. The seamless exchange of identity information across different platforms, services, and applications necessitates standardized protocols and formats. The Decentralized Identifier (DID) specification and the Verifiable Credentials Data Model are examples of standards aiming to enhance interoperability. However, the standardization of data formats raises questions about the potential for creating a standardized profile of users across different services. Striking a balance between interoperability and privacy requires ongoing collaboration within the decentralized identity community to ensure that individuals retain control over their information while enjoying the benefits of a connected and interoperable digital identity ecosystem.

The security considerations in decentralized identity intertwine with privacy to create a robust and trustworthy framework. The elimination of single points of failure, a fundamental security objective, is achieved through the decentralized and distributed nature of blockchain technology. Each participant in the decentralized identity network maintains a copy of the ledger, reducing the risk of a single point of compromise. The cryptographic hashing and linking of blocks in the blockchain ensure tamper-resistant record-keeping, enhancing the security of identity-related transactions. Decentralized identity architectures, thus, not only enhance privacy but also fortify the overall security posture by eliminating vulnerabilities associated with centralized control.

Secure key management emerges as a critical aspect of both privacy and security in decentralized identity. Cryptographic keys, often in the form of private and public key pairs, authenticate and authorize identity transactions. The secure generation, storage, and backup of these keys are paramount to prevent unauthorized access or the loss of access to one's identity. User-friendly key management practices, including secure hardware wallets, multi-signature authentication, and effective recovery mechanisms, contribute to a user-centric approach that prioritizes both security and usability.

The concept of identity hubs in decentralized identity architectures adds another layer to privacy and security considerations. Identity hubs, often encrypted and controlled by the individual's private key, serve as secure repositories for verifiable credentials and other identity-related information. These hubs provide a user-friendly and accessible means for individuals to manage and share their credentials. The decentralized and redundant nature of identity hubs contributes to both privacy and security by ensuring that individuals have reliable and resilient storage for their identity data, reducing the risk of a single point of failure.

The integration of zero-knowledge proofs into decentralized identity systems enhances privacy by allowing individuals to prove possession of specific information without revealing the actual information itself. This cryptographic technique ensures that transactions can be verified without exposing sensitive details, adding an additional layer of privacy to identity interactions. Zero-knowledge proofs contribute to the overall security of decentralized identity systems by reducing the attack surface and mitigating the risks associated with identity theft or malicious observation.

Governance mechanisms play a crucial role in both privacy and security considerations within decentralized identity ecosystems. Decentralized Autonomous Organizations (DAOs) and token-based governance models involve multiple stakeholders in decision-making processes related to protocol upgrades, changes, and dispute resolution. The transparency and inclusivity of these governance mechanisms contribute to the trustworthiness of the decentralized identity ecosystem. However, the governance structures themselves must balance openness with the need to address potential malicious actors and ensure the continued integrity and security of the decentralized identity network.

Challenges and considerations persist on the path to achieving the delicate balance between privacy and security in decentralized identity. Usability remains a key factor in ensuring that individuals can effectively manage their identities without compromising security or privacy. Education and awareness efforts are crucial to guide users in understanding the implications of decentralized identity and adopting secure practices. The evolving landscape of legal and regulatory frameworks adds complexity, requiring ongoing dialogue and collaboration between the decentralized identity community and regulatory bodies to create a harmonious and compliant environment.

In conclusion, the journey towards a privacy-enhancing and secure decentralized identity ecosystem represents a transformative endeavor. The intertwining considerations of privacy and security necessitate a holistic approach that leverages cryptographic principles, user-centric design, and collaborative governance. As decentralized identity systems continue to evolve, addressing the challenges of interoperability, usability, and regulatory compliance will be essential to realizing the vision of an inclusive, resilient, and privacy-preserving digital identity landscape.

8.4 Challenges and Future Trends

The landscape of decentralized identity is marked by both promise and complexity, as it navigates the challenges inherent in its evolution while charting a course towards future trends that promise to shape the digital identity paradigm. As decentralized identity systems strive to redefine how individuals manage their online personas, a multitude of challenges must be addressed to ensure widespread adoption and the realization of their transformative potential. Simultaneously, emerging trends offer glimpses into the future, hinting at the ways decentralized identity may further mature, adapt to evolving needs, and impact the broader digital ecosystem.

One of the persistent challenges in the decentralized identity space revolves around usability. As the technology underpinning decentralized identity, such as blockchain and cryptographic principles, is inherently complex, making these systems user-friendly is crucial for their adoption. Ensuring that individuals, regardless of technical expertise, can seamlessly manage their cryptographic keys, interact with decentralized identity wallets, and navigate the intricacies of selective disclosure and verification processes is essential. Usability challenges extend beyond technical aspects to encompass educational efforts, raising awareness about the benefits of decentralized identity, and guiding users in securing their digital identities effectively. Bridging the gap between the complexities of the technology and the accessibility of decentralized identity solutions remains a critical hurdle.

Privacy, while a fundamental principle in decentralized identity, also presents challenges that demand nuanced solutions. Striking the right balance between privacy and regulatory compliance is an ongoing consideration. The evolving landscape of data protection laws, such as the General Data Protection Regulation (GDPR), introduces complexities for decentralized identity systems that aim to empower individuals with control over their data. Navigating the intricacies of legal frameworks without compromising the privacy-enhancing features of decentralized identity requires collaboration between the decentralized identity community and regulatory bodies. Additionally, addressing the potential for standardized profiles across decentralized identity services and platforms is vital to maintaining user privacy in an interoperable ecosystem.

Scalability is another challenge that looms large in the decentralized identity space. As the user base and transaction volumes grow, ensuring that decentralized identity systems can handle the increased load becomes imperative. Scalability challenges extend beyond the performance of the underlying blockchain technology to include the interoperability of different decentralized identity solutions. Standards such as the Decentralized Identifier (DID) specification and the Verifiable Credentials Data Model aim to enhance interoperability, but the scalability of these standards across diverse applications and use cases remains an ongoing consideration. As decentralized identity moves towards mainstream adoption, the ability to scale efficiently without compromising security and performance is crucial.

Security considerations continue to be at the forefront of challenges in decentralized identity. While blockchain technology inherently provides robust security through decentralization and cryptographic principles, vulnerabilities can emerge in the implementation of decentralized identity systems. Secure key management practices, recovery mechanisms, and protection against evolving cyber threats are essential components of a resilient decentralized identity ecosystem. As the technology evolves, addressing potential vulnerabilities, conducting rigorous security audits, and collaborating on best practices become ongoing efforts to ensure the integrity and trustworthiness of decentralized identity solutions.

Interoperability, a key goal in the decentralized identity space, faces challenges related to diverse standards, protocols, and implementations. Achieving seamless exchange and recognition of identity information across different platforms, services, and applications requires ongoing collaboration within the decentralized identity community. The alignment of standards, the development of common frameworks, and the establishment of trust anchors that span across decentralized identity ecosystems are crucial for realizing the vision of a truly interoperable digital identity landscape. Overcoming interoperability challenges ensures that users can enjoy the benefits of decentralized identity across a spectrum of services without encountering barriers or fragmentation.

The evolving regulatory landscape introduces both challenges and opportunities for decentralized identity. While privacy-centric features align with the spirit of data protection regulations, reconciling the decentralized and often pseudonymous nature of blockchain transactions with the requirements of Know Your Customer (KYC) and Anti-Money Laundering (AML) regulations poses challenges. Collaborative efforts between the decentralized identity community, legal experts, and regulatory bodies are necessary to develop frameworks that ensure compliance without compromising the foundational principles of decentralized identity. Striking this delicate balance is pivotal for the broader acceptance of decentralized identity within regulatory frameworks.

Looking towards the future, several trends promise to shape the trajectory of decentralized identity. Self-sovereign identity (SSI), a foundational principle that empowers individuals with control over their digital identities, is expected to gain traction. The maturation of SSI models will likely involve the development of more user-friendly interfaces, improved key management solutions, and increased integration with mainstream applications and services. As users become more accustomed to the idea of controlling their digital identities, SSI has the potential to become a standard approach in the broader digital ecosystem.

The integration of decentralized identity with other emerging technologies, such as decentralized finance (DeFi) and the Internet of Things (IoT), represents a significant trend. Decentralized identity can enhance the security and trustworthiness of DeFi applications by providing verifiable credentials and reducing the reliance on centralized identity providers. In the realm of IoT, decentralized identity can play a crucial role in securing interactions between devices, ensuring data integrity, and enabling more efficient and secure device management. The intersection of decentralized identity with these technologies creates a synergy that amplifies the benefits of each, contributing to a more interconnected and secure digital landscape.

As the concept of decentralized identity gains momentum, the role of decentralized identifiers (DIDs) and verifiable credentials is expected to evolve. The standardization and widespread adoption of these components will likely lead to increased interoperability and a more cohesive decentralized identity ecosystem. DIDs may become the cornerstone of user-centric identity across various applications and services, and the concept of verifiable credentials may extend beyond personal attributes to encompass a broader range of qualifications and affiliations. This evolution aligns with the broader trend of moving towards a more user-centric, privacy-preserving, and secure digital identity landscape.

The exploration of advanced cryptographic techniques, such as homomorphic encryption and privacy-preserving protocols, is poised to enhance the privacy features of decentralized identity. These techniques allow for secure computation on encrypted data, enabling individuals to perform operations on their data without revealing the actual information. The integration of such cryptographic advancements can contribute to a more resilient and privacy-enhancing decentralized identity ecosystem, addressing concerns related to data exposure and transaction transparency.

Governance models within decentralized identity systems are expected to mature, ensuring that decision-making processes are transparent, inclusive, and align with the values of the community. Decentralized Autonomous Organizations (DAOs) and token-based governance mechanisms will likely play a pivotal role in shaping the direction of decentralized identity ecosystems. The evolution of governance models is intertwined with the broader trend of community-driven development and collaborative decision-making, fostering a sense of ownership and participation among stakeholders.

In conclusion, the challenges and future trends in decentralized identity form a dynamic landscape that reflects the ongoing maturation of this transformative technology. Overcoming challenges related to usability, privacy, scalability, security, and interoperability requires continuous collaboration and innovation within the decentralized identity community. As decentralized identity moves from a niche concept to a mainstream digital paradigm, the integration of user-centric models, advanced cryptographic techniques, and collaborative governance structures will be instrumental in shaping a digital identity landscape that is secure, privacy-preserving, and aligned with the evolving needs of individuals in our increasingly interconnected world.

Scalability and Performance Challenges

The pursuit of scalable and high-performance decentralized identity solutions represents a critical frontier in the ongoing evolution of digital identity systems. While the principles of decentralization, blockchain technology, and cryptographic security underpin the transformative potential of decentralized identity, the quest to accommodate a growing user base, handle increasing transaction volumes, and ensure swift response times presents a set of intricate challenges. The scalability and performance hurdles faced by decentralized identity systems demand nuanced solutions to strike a balance between user expectations, security imperatives, and the broader vision of an interoperable and resilient digital identity landscape.

At the heart of scalability challenges in decentralized identity lies the inherent tension between decentralization and the need for efficient transaction processing. Traditional identity systems often rely on centralized architectures that can handle large volumes of transactions with relative ease. However, the decentralized nature of blockchain-based identity solutions, while providing security benefits, introduces complexities in transaction throughput and confirmation times. Blockchain consensus mechanisms, such as Proof of Work (PoW) or Proof of Stake (PoS), designed to ensure trust and immutability, inherently impose constraints on the speed at which transactions can be processed and added to the distributed ledger.

The decentralized ledger, a cornerstone of many decentralized identity architectures, consists of a chain of blocks, each containing a limited number of transactions. This finite capacity per block introduces challenges in accommodating a high volume of identity-related transactions. As the user base grows and more interactions occur within the decentralized identity ecosystem, the demand for scalability becomes imperative. The tension between maintaining a decentralized and tamper-resistant ledger and the necessity for rapid transaction processing underscores the need for innovative solutions that address these seemingly conflicting requirements.

Interoperability, a key goal in decentralized identity, compounds scalability challenges. As users engage with diverse applications, services, and platforms, the decentralized identity ecosystem must seamlessly exchange and recognize identity information across this heterogeneous landscape. Standards such as the Decentralized Identifier (DID) specification and the Verifiable Credentials Data Model contribute to interoperability by providing common frameworks for creating, issuing, and verifying decentralized identity components. However, the integration and adoption of these standards across a multitude of use cases introduce additional layers of complexity in achieving scalable and interoperable decentralized identity solutions.

Smart contracts, self-executing agreements encoded on the blockchain, play a pivotal role in decentralized identity ecosystems. These contracts define the rules for identity transactions, credential issuance, and verification. However, the execution of smart contracts introduces scalability challenges, particularly in environments with high transaction volumes. The computation and validation overhead associated with smart contract execution can lead to congestion, slower transaction processing times, and increased fees. As decentralized identity systems expand to support a broader range of applications and use cases, optimizing the performance of smart contracts becomes paramount for ensuring a responsive and efficient ecosystem.

The evolution of decentralized identity must grapple with the delicate balance between on-chain and off-chain data. On-chain data refers to information directly recorded on the blockchain, contributing to the tamper-resistant and transparent nature of decentralized identity ledgers. However, the inclusion of large amounts of on-chain data can impede scalability due to increased storage requirements and longer transaction confirmation times. Off-chain solutions, such as second-layer scaling solutions or sidechains, offer a way to alleviate on-chain congestion by processing certain transactions away from the main blockchain. Striking the right balance between on-chain and off-chain data becomes a strategic consideration in optimizing the scalability and performance of decentralized identity systems.

The evolving landscape of consensus mechanisms further contributes to scalability challenges. While Proof of Work and Proof of Stake are well-established mechanisms, newer consensus models, such as Delegated Proof of Stake (DPoS) or Practical Byzantine Fault Tolerance (PBFT), aim to enhance scalability and throughput. However, each consensus mechanism comes with its trade-offs, impacting factors like decentralization, security, and the ability to scale. Navigating the choices among consensus mechanisms requires a nuanced understanding of the specific requirements and priorities of a decentralized identity ecosystem, considering both current and future scalability needs.

The issue of scalability extends beyond the technical aspects to encompass governance and decision-making within decentralized identity ecosystems. As these systems mature, governance models and decision-making processes must scale effectively to accommodate an expanding community of stakeholders. Decentralized Autonomous Organizations (DAOs) and token-based governance mechanisms play a crucial role in fostering community participation and inclusivity. However, ensuring that governance structures can adapt to the growing complexity and diversity of decentralized identity requires ongoing collaboration and iterative development.

Performance challenges in decentralized identity systems manifest not only in transaction processing but also in the latency of identity verification processes. Verifying credentials, especially in scenarios where quick and seamless identity verification is essential, demands a high-performance infrastructure. The time required for cryptographic operations, consensus mechanisms, and smart contract execution collectively contribute to the overall latency. Balancing the need for a robust and secure verification process with the imperative for swift response times poses a continuous challenge in optimizing the performance of decentralized identity ecosystems.

Addressing scalability and performance challenges requires a multi-faceted approach that incorporates technical innovations, governance enhancements, and collaborative efforts within the decentralized identity community. Sharding, a technique that partitions the blockchain into smaller, manageable segments, offers a potential solution to increase throughput and scalability. The development of layer-two scaling solutions, such as state channels or sidechains, provides avenues for processing certain transactions off-chain, reducing congestion on the main blockchain. Research into new consensus algorithms that prioritize scalability without compromising security continues to advance the state of the art in decentralized identity systems.

The pursuit of interoperability, critical for the seamless exchange of identity information across different platforms, involves aligning standards and fostering collaboration. The ongoing work on standards such as DIDs and Verifiable Credentials lays the groundwork for achieving a more interoperable decentralized identity ecosystem. The development of open-source frameworks, toolkits, and reference implementations contributes to the collective effort to create scalable and interoperable solutions. As decentralized identity continues to mature, the emphasis on education and awareness becomes paramount, ensuring that stakeholders across industries and domains understand the benefits and intricacies of decentralized identity.

Looking towards the future, emerging technologies hold promise in addressing scalability and performance challenges. The integration of advanced cryptographic techniques, such as zero-knowledge proofs and privacy-preserving protocols, not only enhances privacy but also contributes to more efficient and scalable identity transactions. Continued research and development in consensus mechanisms, particularly those designed for scalability, offer potential breakthroughs that can redefine the landscape of decentralized identity. The evolution of governance models towards more decentralized and inclusive decision-making processes is expected to align with the principles of decentralized identity and scale effectively as communities grow.

In conclusion, scalability and performance challenges in decentralized identity represent a frontier where technological innovation, community collaboration, and strategic decision-making converge. The ongoing efforts to address these challenges are crucial for unlocking the transformative potential of decentralized identity systems. As the digital landscape continues to evolve, the scalability and performance of decentralized identity will shape its acceptance, impact, and ability to redefine how individuals assert and control their identities in an interconnected and decentralized digital world.

Emerging Innovations in Blockchain Security

Blockchain technology, originally conceived as the underlying infrastructure for cryptocurrencies, has rapidly evolved into a transformative force across various industries, reshaping the landscape of data management, trust, and security. As blockchain adoption proliferates, so does the imperative to fortify the security measures surrounding this distributed ledger technology. Innovations in blockchain security are crucial to addressing the evolving threat landscape, ensuring the integrity and confidentiality of transactions, and fostering trust in decentralized systems. This exploration delves into the cutting-edge advancements that are shaping the future of blockchain security, encompassing cryptographic techniques, consensus mechanisms, privacy-enhancing technologies, and holistic approaches to secure decentralized ecosystems.

Cryptographic techniques form the bedrock of blockchain security, providing the means to secure transactions, protect user identities, and ensure the tamper-resistant nature of the distributed ledger.

In the realm of emerging cryptographic innovations, post-quantum cryptography has garnered significant attention. With the advent of quantum computers, traditional cryptographic algorithms like RSA and ECC face the risk of being broken. Post-quantum cryptography seeks to develop encryption methods that can withstand the computational power of quantum machines, thereby future-proofing blockchain systems against potential threats posed by quantum computing advancements. Research into lattice-based cryptography, hash-based cryptography, and other quantum-resistant techniques represents a pioneering effort to secure blockchain transactions in a quantum-empowered era.

Zero-knowledge proofs, a cryptographic technique that allows one party (the prover) to prove the authenticity of a statement to another party (the verifier) without revealing the actual information, have emerged as a powerful tool for enhancing privacy and confidentiality in blockchain transactions. Innovations within zero-knowledge proofs include zk-SNARKs (Zero-Knowledge Succinct Non-Interactive Arguments of Knowledge) and zk-STARKs (Zero-Knowledge Scalable Transparent ARguments of Knowledge), each offering distinct advantages in terms of efficiency, transparency, and scalability. These cryptographic advancements enable users to demonstrate the validity of transactions or smart contract execution without divulging sensitive information, thus striking a delicate balance between privacy and transparency in blockchain applications.

Consensus mechanisms, the protocols that enable nodes in a blockchain network to agree on the state of the ledger, play a pivotal role in blockchain security. The quest for scalability and energy efficiency has led to the exploration of novel consensus models. Proof of Stake (PoS) mechanisms, where validators are chosen to create new blocks based on the amount of cryptocurrency they hold and are willing to "stake" as collateral, aim to replace energy-intensive Proof of Work (PoW) models. Ethereum's transition to Ethereum

2.0, which embraces a PoS consensus, exemplifies this shift towards sustainability. Additionally, Delegated Proof of Stake (DPoS) and Practical Byzantine Fault Tolerance (PBFT) mechanisms contribute to the diversification of consensus approaches, each presenting unique advantages in terms of scalability, speed, and energy efficiency.

The integration of privacy-focused blockchains and privacy-preserving technologies marks a significant stride in blockchain security. Privacy coins, such as Monero and Zcash, utilize advanced cryptographic techniques to obfuscate transaction details, ensuring that transaction amounts and participant identities remain confidential. Innovations like ring signatures and confidential transactions enhance the privacy features of these blockchain networks, providing users with a heightened level of anonymity. Furthermore, advancements in privacy-focused smart contracts, exemplified by projects like Enigma and Secret Network, aim to extend privacy protections to decentralized applications (dApps), enabling secure and confidential execution of smart contracts without compromising the underlying transparency of the blockchain.

Interoperability, the seamless exchange of information and assets across different blockchain networks, is a burgeoning frontier in blockchain security. As the blockchain ecosystem expands with diverse networks catering to various use cases, achieving interoperability becomes paramount for fostering a cohesive and interconnected digital landscape. Innovations in interoperability protocols, such as Polkadot, Cosmos, and Aion, facilitate cross-chain communication and asset transfers. These frameworks introduce novel consensus mechanisms, such as Nominated Proof-of-Stake (NPoS) and Tendermint, to overcome the challenges of interoperability while maintaining the security and integrity of blockchain transactions across heterogeneous networks.

Holistic approaches to blockchain security encompass a spectrum of strategies that go beyond individual cryptographic or technical innovations. Threat intelligence and blockchain analytics platforms are emerging to provide real-time monitoring and analysis of blockchain transactions, helping identify suspicious activities and potential security breaches. Moreover, advancements in quantum-resistant key management solutions, such as quantum key distribution (QKD) and multi-party computation (MPC), offer robust methods for securing cryptographic keys against the threat of quantum attacks. These holistic security measures acknowledge the need for comprehensive solutions that address not only the cryptographic aspects but also the broader ecosystem surrounding blockchain technology.

Governance models within blockchain networks are experiencing innovations aimed at enhancing security, transparency, and decentralization. Decentralized Autonomous Organizations (DAOs) leverage blockchain's self-executing smart contracts to automate decision-making processes and governance. Innovations in token-based governance models introduce mechanisms where stakeholders can influence the development and evolution of blockchain protocols based on the number of tokens they hold. These governance innovations empower the community to actively participate in shaping the security policies and protocols governing blockchain networks, fostering a sense of ownership and collective responsibility.

Smart contract security, a critical aspect of decentralized applications (dApps) built on blockchain platforms, has witnessed innovative strides to mitigate vulnerabilities and enhance the resilience of these self-executing agreements. Formal verification techniques, leveraging mathematical methods to prove the correctness of smart contracts, offer a proactive approach to identifying and rectifying security flaws before deployment. Tools like MythX and automated bug bounty programs introduce advancements in smart contract auditing, helping developers identify potential vulnerabilities and security loopholes. Moreover, sandbox environments and simulation tools provide safe spaces for testing smart contracts, allowing developers to refine and fortify their code against potential exploits.

The convergence of blockchain technology with other emerging technologies, such as Artificial Intelligence (AI) and Internet of Things (IoT), presents a fertile ground for innovative security solutions. AI-driven threat detection and response systems leverage machine learning algorithms to analyze patterns and anomalies in blockchain transactions, offering proactive security measures against fraudulent activities. Integrating blockchain with IoT introduces secure and transparent methods for managing and verifying the integrity of data generated by IoT devices. Innovations in decentralized identity and verifiable credentials further contribute to the security of IoT ecosystems by providing tamper-resistant and privacy-enhancing solutions for identity management.

Challenges persist amidst these emerging innovations, ranging from the need for widespread adoption of quantum-resistant cryptography to addressing regulatory uncertainties surrounding privacy-focused blockchains. Scalability concerns persist as blockchain networks strive to accommodate increasing transaction volumes and user demands. Usability remains a critical factor, emphasizing the importance of user-friendly interfaces and educational efforts to enhance understanding and adoption of secure blockchain practices.

In conclusion, the landscape of blockchain security is undergoing a transformative phase marked by a constellation of innovations. Cryptographic advancements, consensus model diversification, privacy-enhancing technologies, and holistic security approaches collectively contribute to fortifying the foundations of decentralized systems. The trajectory of blockchain security reflects a dynamic interplay between technological breakthroughs, regulatory considerations, and the evolving threat landscape. As blockchain technology continues to mature and integrate with diverse industries, the ongoing quest for innovative security measures remains pivotal for realizing the full potential of decentralized, secure, and trust-enhancing digital ecosystems.